Contents

Guest Editor's Introduction

Lao-tse, an ancient Chinese sage, said "the hardest object may be penetrated by the most yielding and non-resisting object, water, through even the minutest cracks and openings." Likewise, among the peoples of different countries, there is at least one thing that can pass through and back and forth quite freely, namely, culture. And indeed its freedom of movement is of primary importance, for it stimulates and cultivates higher civilization among new peoples.

The free interchange of culture among the different peoples of the world does not only deepen a degree of better understanding among them, but functions as if it were a friendly handshake of mankind. As grease keeps the wheels of a machine from burning, so does cultural intercourse mitigate friction between the peoples, and leads them into "the country without boundary" where they live a communal life of world brotherhood, instead of a rigid nationalistic life, surrounded by antagonism and suspicion. . . .

But, when we look around us we find that a strong sentiment of nationalism is prevalent everywhere. And some of those who adhere to this school of idealism

positions 8:3 © 2000 by Duke University Press

look upon cultural interchange as "cultural invasion." They claim that culture is an expression of "nationalism" somewhat disguised, and its free interchange must be checked even by building walls against it. . . .

If the word "invasion" connotes the process of anything entering one country from another, well and good, the introduction of one culture to another would be an "invasion." But in that case we must not overlook at least one important difference from such [an] act as military invasion, because cultural invasion neither endangers the life or property of the people whose land is invaded, nor is their happiness threatened thereby. On the contrary the invaded will be so much enriched by coming into contact with the new. —Hasegawa Nyozekan, "You Must Know Me As I Know You"

When socialist-turned-nationalist Hasegawa Nyozekan wrote these words in 1936, Japan was already over fifty years into developing its imperialist project in Asia. Empire building became an integral component of Japanese nation building soon after the establishment of the nation-state in 1868. Government officials felt that in order to compete with the leading nations of the world and maintain sovereignty, Japan needed to be more modern, and this in part translated as being aggressively imperialistic on the Western model. As the scholar of Japanese colonialism Mark Peattie has bluntly stated, there was a "self-evident connection between power and territorial expansion."[1] In this sense, one can say that the Japanese modern imperialist enterprise was itself a reaction to imperialism. To borrow a phrase from John and Jean Comaroff, it was the result of a "colonization of consciousness," clearly manifested in the Japanese modernization project of "civilization and enlightenment" (expressed in the buzzword "*bunmei kaika*").[2] This project produced a skillful (and strategically selective) mimic representation of Japan's Western cultural colonizers inaugurating everything from a new constitution with attendant ceremonial pomp and circumstance to imperialist enterprises at home and abroad.

Japan's dual location as colonized and colonizer, and the extent to which the two identities interpenetrated, provides a unique opportunity to interrogate these persistent binaries. Moreover, while the colonial relationship traditionally has been seen as unidirectional and merely coercive, recent scholarship has shown that the identities of the metropole/empire and periphery/colony were mutually constitutive, leading Edward Said, among others, to call for a "contrapuntal reading" between the two.[3] The colonies by their very existence reformed Japan as much as Japan shaped colonial space.[4]

Japanese empire building began with domestic consolidation within the Japanese archipelago that involved colonizing formerly Ainu and Ryukyuan territories to the north and south, incorporating them into Japan proper in the 1870s. Japan's sphere of interest then soon expanded with the Sino-Japanese War in 1895 to incorporate Taiwan (Formosa), which remained a colony until the end of the Asia Pacific War. The formal empire further expanded to include Korea, first as a protectorate in 1905 and then annexed as a colony in 1910. Japanese formal colonial territories also included southern Sakhalin (Karafuto), portions of the Liaotung Peninsula (the Kwantung Leased Territory), and islands in Micronesia. Victory in the Russo-Japanese War in 1905 provided Japan with leaseholds in north China (southern Manchuria) that were later expanded and transformed into the Japanese puppet-state of Manchukuo after the Manchurian Incident in 1931. By the late 1930s the articulation of an informal Japanese empire in the pan-Asianism of the Greater East Asia Co-Prosperity Sphere brought a large portion of East Asia and its environs under the umbrella of the Japanese imperialist vision, which was then concretized by military conquest during the Asia Pacific War.[5]

As Homi Bhabha has clearly explicated, nations are narrations.[6] They have an overriding impulse for self-definition. The self-defined community of the Japanese nation was a means by which to transform individuals with disparate interests into self-conscious, unified Japanese imperial subjects. And within this shifting process of self-definition we must situate the cultural representations of Japanese empire at home and abroad. Studies of Japanese imperialism have extensively documented the construction of the empire in terms of the political, economic, and social components of colonial rule; but relatively less has been written about the cultural mechanisms that accompanied these policies, and practically nothing has addressed the visual instantiation of Japan's cultural relationship with its colonies, which of necessity must be triangulated with articulations of Japanese identity vis-à-vis the imperialist powers of the West.[7] Formations of Japanese national identity and subjectivity were unquestionably intertwined with representations of its others. In his prefatory essay "Two Exotic Currents in Japanese Civilization," penned in 1930, Nitobe Inazō, a member of the House of Peers and a well-respected thinker, inscribed Japan as the critical nexus in this triangle:

> Japan is more than herself. She is Asia and Europe in one. As two ocean currents, the one flowing from the north and the other from the south, wash and meet at her shores, and furnish her with [a] wealth of sea products, so do two cultural streams, the occidental and the oriental, run in her soul, now uniting and now separating but always enriching its contents with their several tributes. Her past shows that Japan is the place where exotic culture finds easy lodgement, and her present promises that in the future she will play still more the rôle of a mediator between the conflicting cultures of the East and the West. So to be is her mission in universal history and her contribution to mankind.[8]

The objective of this special issue is to explore the ways in which visual culture produced during the years of the Japanese empire both envisioned and sustained a diverse imperialist enterprise in East Asia that extended to representations in Euro-America. Martin Jay has reiterated the belief among many scholars that there was a distinctive privileging of the visual in modern Western culture, which one can surmise was effectively communicated to the non-Western world as part of the ideological underpinnings of the modernization project of imperialism. Jay writes of the "ubiquity of vision as the master sense of the modern era" but qualifies this with a careful consideration of competing scopic regimes.[9] Over a decade ago he argued that "the scopic regime of modernity may best be understood as a contested terrain, rather than a harmoniously integrated complex of visual theories and practices. It may, in fact, be characterized by a differentiation of visual subcultures, whose separation has allowed us to understand the multiple implications of sight in ways that are now only beginning to be appreciated."[10] Recent scholarship has brought together the burgeoning fields of postcolonial studies, culture studies, and visual culture studies to illuminate the integral role of vision and visuality in the formation of colonial modernity. As the authors in Tim Barringer and Tom Flynn's edited volume *Colonialism and the Object* well demonstrate, art and other cultural objects/artifacts mediated the power relations underlying the colonial project.[11] Through an examination of a wide range of cultural forms and practices such as exhibitions, photography, tourism, aesthetic appreciation and interpretation, collecting, consumption, personal adornment, and the built environment, the essays here continue to expand this line of inquiry, revealing how visual culture vividly imaged the often imperceptible aspects of the colonial relationship.

While this collection takes Japan as its principal focus, the widespread impact of Japanese imperialism on the development of continental and peninsular culture during the first half of the twentieth century and into the postcolonial era makes the issue of pressing concern for anyone interested in the study of modern East Asia.

Culture and Imperialism

As Hasegawa shrewdly notes in the epigraph to this essay, culture was a powerful tool for crafting international relations, a tool often so malleable, transportable, and imperceptible that it masked its own profound instrumentality. Yet there is no comprehensive definition of the term *culture* that suits every purpose. While Hasegawa's usage of the term accords with one definition proposed by Raymond Williams, where culture is broadly conceived of as "a general process of intellectual, spiritual and aesthetic development," the essays included here collectively articulate a slightly narrower interpretation akin to Williams's alternative reading of culture as "the works and practices of intellectual and especially artistic activity."[12] Within this framework, the authors analyze material production, systems of signification, and the production of meaning.

The cultural mechanisms formed under the rubric of imperialism are sometimes viewed as a form of "cultural colonization" to underscore their material as well as ideological aspects. It bears mentioning here that the terms *colonialism* and *imperialism* take on overlapping meanings when employed in regard to culture. While colonialism refers to the direct control of one power over a dependent area or people, it has been more loosely interpreted in the cultural sphere to include forms of ideological suasion or coercion that have comparable influence in geopolitical terms when based on unequal power relations or when used in conjunction with direct colonial control. Interpreted in this sense, it is analogous to imperialism, which refers to the extension of the power and dominion of a nation either directly or indirectly over the political, economic, and in this case, cultural life of other areas. Although none of the authors in this issue in any way means to equate the physical hardships of colonization with its often more indirect cultural ramifications, we still want to emphasize that the manipulation of culture to cement colonial policy and the effects of cultural policy on both the colonizer and the colonized were formidable, and that these forces should not be excluded from any consideration of Japan's colonial project.

Since the cultural projects discussed here took place during the tenure of the Japanese empire, there is a direct connection to formal and informal manifestations of colonialism. But the continuation of related cultural practices into the postwar period after the dissolution of the colonial empire, when cultural domination was predicated more on the global reach of capitalism than on the political or economic system of imperialism, calls into question this somewhat arbitrary division. Due to the limits of space and the pressing need to address the pre-1945 period in greater depth, however, we must leave discussions of the later period to another time.

The Project

The articles in this issue are organized largely chronologically, roughly spanning from the beginning of the Meiji period (1868–1912) through the Pacific War. In spite of the rapidity of change during this period, a number of concerns continue to recur throughout. Defining and differentiating Japaneseness vis-à-vis the West and within Asia was an ongoing project requiring constant renegotiation in relation to changing geopolitical conditions. Japan's drive for self-definition gave rise to a range of neotraditionalist and pan-Asianist cultural theories, as well as a curious form of exoticizing occidentalism. Japanese intellectuals struggled to create a usable past with correlate traditions, in the process essentially orientalizing themselves. Proponents of pan-Asianism couched their imperialist manifest destiny in terms of purveying enlightenment to revive the decaying cultures of Asia, thereby orientalizing Asian others.

The authors represented here show the multiplicity of theoretical axes upon which examination of culture under Japanese imperialism can proceed. Undoubtedly public presentation for consumption by others was a critical arena of visuality for all of these projects, whether through the costuming of the individual body, the reformulation of domestic space (public and private), the reordering of international or colonial space, or the creation of a virtual space through the mass media. In the end, all the projects hinge on the question of who among a wide array of competing interests will exercise the ultimate command over representations.

Christine Guth's contribution, "Charles Longfellow and Okakura Kakuzō: Cultural Cross-Dressing in the Colonial Context," reveals how the self-conscious act of clothing the body (including tattooing) was enlisted by Longfellow and Okakura, two culturally distinct yet surprisingly comparable individuals, "to fix identity and underscore otherness," which, as she forcefully argues, served both "to reinforce and subvert dominant colonial ideologies." Guth employs the term *cultural cross-dressing* to refer to the rhetorical use of clothing as a strategy of self-presentation where the individual is able to re-ethnicize through costuming. But, she notes, intention and reception often diverged as one could never have total control over self-fashioning.

In an age of mechanical reproduction, the critical function of photography as a means of framing self-representation is brought into sharp relief in a number of the essays. The photograph provided a manipulable but seemingly unmediated record of the staging of identity. In the context of Japan and East Asia the photograph was additionally imbricated with its contemporaneous touristic use for authenticating exotic experiences of the Orient. And this was not limited to the Western tourist. Whereas Longfellow cloaked himself in exoticized images of traditional Japaneseness by donning a tattooed collage of orientalist fantasies, Okakura also took on the role of tourist with alacrity while traveling in China and India (Japan's Asian others), his strange pan-Asian tunics an expression of the liberty of eccentricity taken by a tourist in a foreign land.

The question of photographic representation reemerges in Jordan Sand's article "Was Meiji Taste in Interiors 'Orientalist'?" this time in relation to the reordering of the domestic interiors of the Meiji elite in metropolitan

Japan. Sand argues that the highly selective eclecticism of Meiji home decoration photographically illustrated in the women's journal *Fujin gahō* (Ladies' graphic) was a kind of "colonization of the lived environment," because it reinscribed the colonial mentality through commodified representations of Japan's orientalizing and occidentalizing view of its others. The triangulated relationship in this case manifests itself in Western-style reception rooms.

Magazines like *Fujin gahō* and other pictorial journals also exemplified the profound connection between the colonial mentality and capitalist consumerism in the metropole. Capitalism and consumerism were integral to the colonial project on a number of levels. Most blatantly, the urge for territorial expansion was linked to the search for additional economic resources (agricultural and industrial). This search extended to aesthetic commodities as well. Kim Brandt demonstrates in her essay, "Objects of Desire: Japanese Collectors and Colonial Korea," that a group of Japanese art collectors generated a new domestic audience and market for Korean pottery in the 1920s and 1930s that extended beyond the circumscribed sphere of wealthy tea enthusiasts by producing exoticized knowledge of "Yi dynasty wares," which satisfied metropolitan tastes for authentic Asian artifacts but offered more affordable wares than those that had been imported from earlier periods. This knowledge, intentionally or not, contributed to the Japanese colonial project in Korea by buttressing notions of Korean culture as melancholic and stagnant, which naturalized and legitimized Japanese colonial paternalism. It also helped systematically strip Korean colonial subjects of their antiquities.

Yanagi Sōetsu, later the central proponent of the Japanese folk craft movement (*mingei undō*), was one of these professional aesthetes who served as an arbiter of taste among the Japanese urban elite. Like Hasegawa, Yanagi also saw art and culture as a means of resolving conflict between Japan and its others, writing, "Art transcends frontiers and the differences of men's minds." But as Brandt effectively argues, Yanagi's intentions cannot be construed in any simple sense as mere collaboration with a Japanese colonial agenda in light of his ardent championing of Korean cultural autonomy and his fervid opposition to the homogenizing processes of modernity. Yet preservation and maintenance of Korean cultural patrimony under Yanagi's plans continued to reside with the Japanese, who were deemed uniquely qualified to appreciate and safeguard Asian culture, once again reinscribing the legitimacy of colonial rule. Evidence of Yanagi's efficacy in marketing Asian folk crafts shows the extraordinary extent to which the *"mingei* myth" of authenticity, as opposed to the impure, hybrid products of modernity, has been assimilated by the Japanese general public and Western aficionados of Asia. This myth still supports a strong market for handcrafted goods from small trinkets to exorbitantly priced art objects, the artifacts produced by Yanagi's craftsmen colleagues now suitably installed in his folk craft museum, individual house museums, and prefectural collections—all enshrined as must-see tourist sights.

As mentioned above, the tourist industry was deeply implicated in the colonial relationships in the region from the very beginning as annexation of land provided a physically and ideologically extended destination for the visitor. Needing to produce an attractive visual representation of the empire in order to sell the destination, the tourist industry reinforced colonial identities. In my article, "Touring Japan-as-Museum: *NIPPON* and Other Japanese Imperialist Travelogues," I argue that the Japanese Western-language promotional magazine *NIPPON* served as both a propagandistic self-representation and an invitation to the Western tourist to authenticate the Japanese empire. By modifying "Japan" to suit the tourist's expectations, the magazine accommodated the colonizing gaze of the West. Sand finds a similar impulse in the spatial reformation of the Japanese home in the reception room, which was redesigned partly on a Western model to accommodate Western visitors or, more commonly, Japanese visitors in Westernized dress (such as the emperor in his new shoes), who required a suitable room for their costuming.

The centrality of representations of women and women as consumer subjects in Japanese cultural imperialism is also stressed in several of the essays. For Sand, elite Japanese women, readers of *Fujin gahō*, were consumers of the commodified exoticized Meiji interior. They were also the subordinated subjects of a colonial relationship that was displaced onto the home with male authorities validated as instructors of proper decoration and their wives subservient students of this civilizing enterprise. The home, then, became a crucial site for establishing and legitimating the power relations that sustained Japan's entire imperial order. In my essay, women of the metropole and the colonies are subjects of a multidirectional orientalist and colonialist gaze that reveals the constant slippage between colonizer and colonized as Japanese national political concerns were embodied in the autoethnologizing representations of the empire.[13]

The constant renegotiation of identity in Japanese architectural discourse is addressed in Cherie Wendelken's commentary, "Pan-Asianism and the Pure Japanese Thing: Japanese Identity and Architecture in the Late 1930s," which like Sand's essay does not focus on governmental monuments but, rather, on the equally exalted spaces of the Buddhist temple and the modern home. By reexamining areas of architectural production that historically have been seen as immune to the political tumult of the period, the author shows that the stylistic hybridity of the architectural programs designed by celebrated architect Itō Chūta for the True Pure Land Sect went hand-in-hand with the sect's aggressively expansionist missionary activities, which while couched in terms of universalist religious values, were in fact intimately connected to the Japanese war machine. At the same time, the Japanese-style "new *sukiya*" elite residences built by Yoshida Isoya provided nostalgic sanctuaries that reinforced notions of Japanese aesthetic purity. In this respect, she argues, nonofficial architecture supported the goals of empire as much as monuments to the loyal war dead. Wendelken's observations reveal the almost schizophrenic obsession of Japanese intellectuals with determining the unique nature of Japan's cultural contribution, whether it be pure or hybrid, original or appropriated.

The world theater of international expositions proved an effective forum for presenting constructed images of Japanese culture and for asserting Japan's emergence as a full-fledged, world-class imperial power. By exhibiting a "microcosm of the larger imperial domain" in the Euro-American arena, and by displaying "the malleability and transportability" of the "secondary or lesser cultures" of its colonies, the Japanese government hoped to demonstrate its superior position in Asia.[14] In Asia, Japanese exhibitions asserted metropolitan power in colonial space. Analysis of Japan's participation in world's fairs reveals the country's representatives as dynamic agents in self-presentation.

In "'The Sole Guardians of the Art Inheritance of Asia': Japan at the 1904 St. Louis World's Fair," Carol Ann Christ presents one of the earliest international expositions in which Japan promoted itself as an imperialist power, more precisely, as the *only* imperialist power in Asia. As an official spokesman of Japanese culture at the fair, Okakura declared that Japan was the "sole guardian of the art inheritance of Asia," with the exhibits at the fairgrounds as evidence of the country's capacity for cultural leadership. In its function as conservator of Asia's artistic legacy, Okakura envisioned Japan as a museum, an institutional type that was recognized by many at the time as legitimating culture and providing a privileged space of public presentation. Twenty-five years later, *NIPPON* would continue Okakura's vision by constructing a virtual tour of Japan-as-museum.

For the Japanese, Christ argues, fine arts, the highest category of artistic production in the Western canonical cultural hierarchy, was the preeminent domain for displaying national civilization. For this reason, the Japanese representatives at the St. Louis fair placed particular emphasis on Japan's display in the fine arts pavilion. Christ also reveals how the Japanese promoted their civilization at the expense of the Chinese, who were denied an equivalent voice on the fairgrounds because of geopolitical circumstances.

The articulation of a division between civilized and uncivilized races was used as a justification for colonial expansion throughout the imperialist world. In St. Louis, Japanese civilization was manifested in its contribution to the rarefied realm of fine arts and in its command over the representation of the empire's primitive colonial subjects, the Ainu and the Taiwanese aborigines, displayed in their native habitats. Guth's essay complicates the relationship between the civilized and uncivilized—colonizer and colonized—in her discussion of the carnivalesque association of tattoos worn by Longfellow to symbolize his entry into the uncivilized races, which segues into a related subject taken up by Leo Ching in his essay, "Savage Construction and Civility Making: The Musha Incident and Aboriginal Representations in Colonial Taiwan." Ching addresses the relationship between the Japanese colonial government and the head-hunting aborigines of colonial Taiwan (the same aborigines exhibited in St. Louis). After a wholly unexpected, shockingly brutal rebellion by the supposedly domesticated aborigines, the Japanese were forced to reconsider their colonial policy, gradually turning away from the direct use of force to the manipulation of culture as the "privileged sphere in which colonial power was exercised and consolidated," a

process referred to as "imperialization" (*kōminka*). Integral to this imperialization process was a civilizing mission akin to the *mission civilisatrice* of the
French colons, which in this case sought to transform aboriginal savagery
into patriotic civility. The civilizing mission justified Japan's colonial project
in Asia through moral elevation, as Japan purveyed enlightenment and the
benefits of modernity to the darkest, most primitive regions in Asia. Ching
shows how various forms of symbolism, most prominently popular myths
and their visual representation, were used to facilitate this process. However, with the incorporation of savages into Japan, aboriginal issues became
part of the Japanese metropolitan consciousness, and the colonizers began to
uncover the barbarity within themselves.

Mark Peattie has written that "colonialism was as much a state of mind—a
constellation of attitudes and assumptions—as it was a system of bureaucratic
mechanisms, legal institutions, and economic enterprises."[15] The essays in
this issue reveal how the Japanese colonial state of mind was constructed in a
triangulated relationship with its others, Asia and the West. Culturally, Japan
was simultaneously colonized and colonizer, two positions that mutually
resonated to form a unified, but still deeply conflicted, whole. In any analysis
of the cultural forms spawned during the period of Japanese imperialism,
the constantly shifting field of representations and the dynamic agents who
functioned within this field must never be forgotten, as they illuminate the
critical role of art and culture in the formation of empire.

Gennifer Weisenfeld, Guest Editor

Notes

1 Mark Peattie, introduction to *The Japanese Colonial Empire, 1895–1945*, ed. Ramon Myers
   and Mark Peattie (Princeton, N.J.: Princeton University Press, 1984), 7.

2 John Comaroff and Jean Comaroff, *Ethnography and the Historical Imagination* (Boulder,
   Colo.: Westview Press, 1992), 235–263.

3 Edward Said, *Culture and Imperialism* (New York: Vintage, 1993), 66. See also Frederick
   Cooper and Ann Laura Stoler, eds., *Tensions of Empire* (Berkeley and Los Angeles: University
   of California Press, 1997).

4 Two excellent recent examples of this kind of study on Japan are Louis Young, *Japan's
   Total Empire* (Berkeley and Los Angeles: University of California Press, 1998), and Jennifer

Robertson, *Takarazuka* (Berkeley and Los Angeles: University of California Press, 1998), chap. 3, "Performing Empire," 89–138.

5   For a detailed historical consideration of the Japanese colonial project see Myers and Peattie, *Japanese Colonial Empire*, and Peter Duus, Ramon Myers, and Mark Peattie, eds., *The Japanese Informal Empire in China, 1895–1937* (Princeton, N.J.: Princeton University Press, 1989). For more specific considerations of the colonization of Korea and the colonial project in Manchuria see Peter Duus, *The Abacus and the Sword* (Berkeley and Los Angeles: University of California Press, 1995), and Young, *Japan's Total Empire*.

6   Homi Bhabha, ed., *Nation and Narration* (London: Routledge, 1990).

7   For recent scholarship on colonialism and culture in East Asia see Tani Barlow, ed., *Formations of Colonial Modernity in East Asia* (Durham, N.C.: Duke University Press, 1997).

8   Nitobe Inazō and others, *Western Influences in Modern Japan* (Chicago: University of Chicago Press, 1931), 1.

9   Martin Jay, "Scopic Regimes of Modernity," in *Vision and Visuality*, ed. Hal Foster (Seattle: Bay Press, 1988), 3.

10 Ibid., 4.

11 Tim Barringer and Tom Flynn, eds., *Colonialism and the Object* (London: Routledge, 1998). For a survey of recent interdisciplinary developments in the study of visual culture/material culture in relation to colonialism see the introduction to this volume. For an example of some of the innovative work being done in this area related to Asian culture, specifically Buddhism, see Stanley Abe, "Inside the Wonder House: Buddhist Art and the West," in *Curators of the Buddha*, ed. Donald Lopez Jr. (Chicago: University of Chicago Press, 1995), 63–106.

12 Quoted in John Tomlinson, *Cultural Imperialism* (Baltimore, Md.: Johns Hopkins University Press, 1991), 5.

13 The term *autoethnologizing* is taken from Marilyn Ivy, *Discourses of the Vanishing* (Chicago: University of Chicago Press, 1995), 29.

14 Said, *Culture and Imperialism*, 112.

15 Peattie introduction, 5.

Charles Longfellow and Okakura Kakuzō:

Cultural Cross-Dressing in the Colonial Context

Christine M. E. Guth

In the nineteenth- and early-twentieth-century colonial world, where photography often functioned as a tool of visual surveillance and codification, body markings, physiognomy, and costume were key determinants in fixing identity and underscoring otherness. Photographers working under British colonial authorities in India compiled vast dossiers of the subcontinent's many ethnic groups, classifications based on their distinguishing physical traits and attires. European commercial photographs from the same period essentialized Japanese alterity in the form of samurai and geisha, showing that Japan, though never part of a European colonial empire, was not exempt from these cultural practices. Later, as Japan developed its own empire, its authorities also embraced photography as a potent new technology for documenting and classifying ethnic minorities both within its borders and on the Asian continent. By inscribing Ainus, aboriginal Taiwanese, and Koreans into what Timothy Mitchell has called an "Orientalist exhibitionary

positions 8:3 © 2000 by Duke University Press

order," Japan showed the Western world it had become a modern imperialist power.[1]

Clothing—or the lack thereof—was a primary means of articulating ethnic differences in colonial photography.[2] Photographers encouraged their subjects to don the various costumes and accessories that confirmed exotic expectations, even though these were not their customary attire. They further devised quaint and scenic settings that maximized the distance between Western viewers and the subjects they beheld. To achieve the visual effects they desired, photographers even hired artists to hand-paint their products, thus blurring the lines between the photograph as documentary fact and artistic fiction.

Although there is no denying the "disciplinary gaze" of photography, many photographs that appear to inscribe a colonial vision in fact disclose ambivalent meanings not intended by the power behind the camera. Photographic subjects sometimes subverted their assigned social roles through inventive poses, gestures, and facial expressions. Moreover, when this technology was available to the colonized, they often made use of it to try to alter the identities imposed on them by colonial norms. Though often ignored or unknown because they were produced in limited numbers for personal or family use, such photographs constitute valuable and revealing documents in the history of colonial relations. The photographs that I examine here fall into this category, underscoring the potential the camera offered both colonized and colonizer as a creative tool for subverting social and racial stereotypes and creating individual identity.

The focus of this essay is a corpus of photographic portraits of Charles Appleton Longfellow (1844–1893) and Okakura Kakuzō (1862–1913). Taken as a whole this work raises complex and challenging questions about the use of the body and its coverings to articulate social and ethnic differences. Charles Longfellow, the eldest son of the New England poet Henry Wadsworth Longfellow, was a bohemian who devoted his life to travel in exotic lands, most notably Japan, where he lived from 1871 to 1873 and more briefly in 1885 and 1891, and amassed a significant collection of Japanese art.[3] Unlike Longfellow, who is virtually unknown today, the international reputation Okakura Kakuzō enjoyed during his lifetime grew even greater following his death. His professional career included posts at the Tokyo Imperial

Museum and later the Boston Museum of Fine Arts, as well as the directorship of the Tokyo School of Fine Arts (Tokyo Bijutsu Gakkō). He also authored numerous influential essays, including *The Ideals of the East* (1903), *The Awakening of Japan* (1904), and *The Book of Tea* (1906), all originally written in English.

I was first drawn to the photographs of these two men because of their shared use of cultural cross-dressing as a strategy of self-presentation. Despite the differences in their nationality, age, professional aspirations, and personal fantasies, both Longfellow and Okakura believed clothing—and I include in this term tattoos that "clothe" the body—to be a powerful aesthetic language that allowed them to transcend time and space. By donning exotic, often provocative, clothing from cultures other than their own, they expressed ideas about themselves, about their society, and ultimately about ethnic identity, in ways that simultaneously reinforced and subverted dominant colonial ideologies.

Photographs spanning the late nineteenth and early twentieth centuries record many variations on the practice of cultural cross-dressing. In the 1860s Nagasaki prostitutes adopted Western fashions to better attract Western clientele. In 1872 the young Emperor Mutsuhito was photographed, decked out in European military dress, to comply with European diplomatic requests for his portrait. Conversely, many Western residents of Japan and China "went native," even as they asserted the superiority of their own culture. American tourists in Japan authenticated their exotic experiences by having themselves photographed in samurai costume, just as Japanese tourists in the Middle East posed for photographers in Bedouin robes.[4] While sharing some of the political, social, and personal motivations of these cultural cross-dressers, both Longfellow and Okakura also seem to have been exceptionally sensitive to the potential of photography as an instrument of self-fashioning.

Because of their unusually cosmopolitan childhoods, neither of these men had to travel abroad to become sensitized to the mythologies of otherness. As an internationally renowned poet, Henry Wadsworth Longfellow was visited by dignitaries from around the world.[5] The family also counted among their close friends men involved in the China trade as well as pioneering travelers to Japan. Richard Henry Dana, the author of the maritime saga

Two Years Before the Mast (1840) and one of the first Americans to visit Japan as a tourist, was a neighbor.

Young Charles Longfellow's love of sports and dangerous escapades made him the odd man out in a family that carefully cultivated an image of bourgeois respectability and literary refinement. As a child he shot off his thumb with a new shotgun and on another occasion narrowly escaped drowning. At age seventeen, romantic visions of military valor led him to run away and join the Union army. During a brief home leave, he was arrested and taken to court for bathing in the nude. A serious wound suffered at the Battle of New Hope Church in 1863 brought an end to his military career but did little to quell his enthusiasm for adventurous travel.[6] Much to his family's dismay, Charles never attended college, married, or established himself in a profession, choosing instead to lead the life of a peripatetic expatriate.

Importantly for my subject here, Longfellow also grew up in a family of photography enthusiasts. His father both shaped and reflected the growing culture of personal celebrity in which photography played such a vital role.[7] Tall and handsome, Charles was equally captivated with this new technology and had himself commemorated at every opportunity. Photographs he sent home from the front offer the first hints of his effort to fashion himself both within and against the constraining environment of New England society. In one taken shortly after he was promoted to the rank of lieutenant in the Massachusetts Cavalry, Charles's theatrically self-confident pose, with his hands in his pockets and cap perched rakishly on his head, leaves no doubt that he recognized the symbolic power of clothing (fig. 1).

Photography and sartorial styles also loomed large in Okakura Kakuzō's youth. He was born in 1862 in Yokohama, a port city opened to foreign residents four years earlier under the treaty with Western powers. The presence of enterprising merchants, missionaries, diplomats, and tourists from Europe and the United States, as well as China and Korea, made Yokohama one of Japan's most cosmopolitan cities. Because of this foreign presence, Yokohama also became an early center for the adoption and dissemination of both Western dress and photography in Japan. During Okakura's youth, both Shimooka Renjō (1823–1914), one of the first Japanese professional photographers, and Felice Beato (1825–1908?), a photographer of Venetian origin, were active there. Missionaries, including S. R. Brown, at

Figure 1 Lieutenants Longfellow and Gleason, Culpeper, Virginia, 21 September 1863. Photographer unknown. Courtesy National Park Service, Longfellow House Historical Site.

whose school Okakura studied, were instrumental in instructing and making available to Japanese photographers the materials needed for this new technology.[8] Although there is no evidence that Okakura had any direct contact with photographers in Yokohama, his early exposure to the power of the camera no doubt contributed to the energy and emotional involvement he later invested in creating a personal visual legacy.[9]

Okakura's father, a former samurai who had become a silk merchant, was in close contact with the foreign community. Hoping to provide his son with the tools necessary to function in Japan's rapidly expanding world, he sent him at the age of six or seven to study English under the American missionaries S. R. Brown and James Hepburn. Okakura continued his studies under Brown until 1873, when Okakura moved with his family to Tokyo, where he entered the Kaisei *gakkō*, the school that would later become Tokyo University. Okakura's early missionary education gave him a comparative

Figure 2 Okakura Kakuzō with (from left to right) Edward Morse, Ernest Fenollosa, and William Bigelow, Tokyo, ca. 1882. Photographer unknown. After *Chanoyu Quarterly* 40 (1984), 10.

perspective on his own culture that most of his peers achieved only much later in life, when they first traveled abroad.

A commemorative photograph taken around 1882 leaves little doubt of Okakura's early identification with the world of his Western teachers (fig. 2). He appears fastidiously dressed in a well-tailored suit closely matching those of the three Americans with whom he stands. Also like them, he has a fashionable handlebar mustache. His self-confident, theatrical pose is that of a man who believes himself to be dressed for success. The three men flanking Okakura are New Englanders with whom he would share a lifelong engagement with traditional Japanese art and culture. To his right is Edward Morse, formerly a professor of zoology at Tokyo Imperial University; to his left stands Ernest Fenollosa, also a professor at the university, and beyond him is William Bigelow, an affluent Bostonian who would later support Okakura's appointment to the Boston Museum of Fine Arts.

At the time of this photograph, Okakura was serving as interpreter, thus mediating all three Americans' experiences of Japan. He was also gaining a reputation as a Japanese spokesman for the preservation of traditional Japanese art and culture, values being promoted by Fenollosa. In 1882 the Western-style painter Koyama Shōtarō had written an essay denying calligraphy's status as an art form, since written characters are merely symbols like the Western alphabet. Taking the utilitarian stand shared by other early Meiji modernizers, he further asserted that calligraphy was of little value since it did not contribute to progress or to the national good.[10] Okakura published a response in which he extolled calligraphy's value as a traditional art.

In *The Awakening of Japan*, a book he later wrote to explain modern Japan to a Western public, Okakura offered clues to his early outlook on the significance of adopting Western attire. Commenting on the motivations of Sakuma Shōzan, whom he believed to be the first Japanese to dress in Western style, he wrote: "It was the expression of a desire on the part of the progressionist to cast off the shackles of the decadent East and identify himself with the advance of Western civilization. Our kimono meant leisure, while the European dress meant activity, and it became the uniform of the army of progress, like the chapeau rouge in revolutionary France."[11] This photograph suggests that at the time, Okakura believed that he too was suitably arming himself with modernity. Despite their participation in Japan's modernization, many Europeans and Americans wanted Japan to remain a timeless, exotic refuge from modernity. Even Edward Morse, the most progressive of Okakura's associates, complained that "the attempt that some Japanese make to appear in our costume is often most ludicrous."[12]

A pair of photographs from the von Stillfried studios that Bigelow purchased in Japan in the 1880s makes this point even more emphatically (figs. 3 and 4). In figure 3 a samurai magnificently attired in a *nagashimo*, the ceremonial garb of the warrior class, stands with his back to the viewer. In figure 4 the same man, now wearing an ill-fitting dress coat and top hat, is transformed into a vaudevillian figure.[13] As Homi Bhabha has written, "Mimicry emerges as one of the most elusive and effective strategies of

Figure 3 Transformation of a samurai, ca.
1860–1870. Photo: Stillfried and Anderson.
Courtesy Peabody Museum of Archaeology and
Ethnology, Harvard University.

colonial power and knowledge" because reproduction challenges and desta-
bilizes the authority of the original.[14] The profound anxiety produced by
what was perceived to be a monkeylike aping of Western dress throws light
on the wellsprings of the disturbingly racist yet pervasive view expressed in

Figure 4 Transformation of a samurai, ca.
1860–1870. Photo: Stillfried and Anderson.
Courtesy Peabody Museum of Archaeology and
Ethnology, Harvard University.

von Stillfried's photographs. This view is echoed in the biting caricatures of
Georges Bigot, who was also active in Japan in the 1880s.[15]

It is hard to imagine that Okakura was not aware of such imagery or
the attitudes underlying it. Certainly by 1886, when he made his first trip
abroad, he had come to understand that donning Western dress would not
gain him respect or equality.

The experience of international travel gave direction and focus to both Longfellow's and Okakura's rhetorical use of clothing. Alienation from their respective societies led both to seek authentic experience and individuality in a utopian space beyond the confines of a civilization that, by virtue of its modernity, was incompatible with these aims. While Longfellow would satisfy his need to travel across time and space in Japan, Okakura would satisfy his own desire in "Japan's Orient," that is, China and India.[16] Rejection of a world they believed to be contaminated by the modern West and adoption of clothing invested with mythic properties through its association with traditional art and literature are common threads running through both men's dramatic self-presentation.

Charles Longellow's exoticism had its origins in a rebellious quest for heroic individuality as a soldier and sailor—professions unacceptable to his family. Both these ideals remained touchstones that fed into the alter egos he fashioned for himself in Japan. During his first visit, when the Japanese government was ordering Japanese men to cut their top-knots (*chonmage*) and the emperor himself was being photographed in Western military uniform, Longfellow had himself photographed in guises including that of a rogue in a Kabuki play and a carpenter (fig. 5).[17] Being photographed in native costume was a common way for tourists to authenticate their experience in exotic locales throughout the Orient. Commercial photographers in Japan even kept a stock of costumes from which visitors could select the particular exotic identity they desired. Longfellow was unusual in wearing clothes made expressly for him. The blue short jacket (*happi*), personalized with his initials in red on the back, and matching trousers he wore to pose as a carpenter are still preserved in Longfellow National Historical Site.

Longfellow also dressed as a samurai, making visible his immersion in Japanese culture and his appropriation of the status and privileges of its elite (fig. 6). In so doing he was borrowing the authority of the samurai to reinforce his own masculinity, for behind the image of the samurai, of course, lies that of military and sexual prowess. He sent home a studio portrait in this guise, with the playful comment, "I send you the photo of a gentleman of Kioto, who I met several times in the streets, particularly in the evening."[18] By his reference to evening strolls, Longfellow alludes to his realization of the erotic fantasies about Japan prevalent among European and American men. The

Figure 5 Charles Longfellow as a Kabuki actor, Nagasaki, 1872. Photo attributed to Uyeno Hikoma. Courtesy National Park Service, Longfellow House Historical Site.

very active sexual life he led there is confirmed in his personal albums by the numerous, more casual snapshots of him in the company of kimono-clad women.[19] As an outsider in the self-invented role of an insider, Longfellow felt free to make a photographic record of activities publicly discouraged within both his own and Japanese society.

Figure 6 Charles Longfellow as a samurai, Kyoto, 1872. Photographer unknown. Courtesy National Park Service, Longfellow House Historical Site.

In his analysis of comparable photographs of Europeans in the guise of Turkish "pasha," David Bate has pointed out that such cultural cross-dressing involves far more than a simple two-way social repositioning:

> Historically the fundamental relation of the Occident to the East was one of occupation. In imitating the East, the European colonizes and disrupts the authenticity of indigenous clothing; but by incorporating the Orient into his or her self-image, the European also acknowledges that the East

has entered into the West, disturbing those polarized references on which the fixed image of the Occident/Orient depends: civilized/uncivilized, clean/dirty etc.[20]

This assessment may also be applied to Longfellow, and as will be discussed below to Okakura.

Longfellow's tattoos further underscore both his preoccupation with making visible his virility and his ambivalent relationship to modernity. Elaborate, multicolored full-body pictorial tattoos had been fashionable in Japan since the early nineteenth century, especially among members of professions that relied on physical strength for their livelihood, such as carpenters, palanquin bearers, firemen, and sailors. A form of subversive aesthetic expression by which members of the lower classes could create distinctive personae for themselves, they were a source of fear and fascination to the Japanese public as well as Western visitors. [21]

During his first and second trips to Japan, Longfellow himself underwent the time-consuming, painful, and costly process, ultimately transforming his back, chest, abdomen, and arms into a pictorial collage of his exotic fantasies (figs. 7 and 8). On his back he had tattooed a carp ascending a waterfall, a motif with connotations of stamina and virility common in woodblock prints. The unusual image of Kannon seated in the mouth of a dragon, tattooed on his chest, may be an iconographic variant of the figure of Kannon standing on the head of a dragon (Ryūtō Kannon), a popular motif in nineteenth-century painting. An avid sailor, Longfellow may also have been attracted to Kannon because of her status as a special protector of men at sea.[22]

While Longfellow recognized tattoos as a form of personal ornamentation and the men who created them as artists, this view was not widely shared in the New England social world to which he belonged. In the United States in the late nineteenth century, tattooing was deemed a form of disfiguration practiced chiefly by members of marginal social groups such as soldiers, sailors, and prisoners. Since physical appearances were thought to represent inner character, tattoos were assumed to make visible personal depravity.

Tattoos also implied an exhibitionistic cultivation of the body associated with the carnivalesque. It is no accident that the voyeuristic photograph of

Figure 7 Charles Longfellow's carp tattoo, Japan, 1872.
Photographer unknown. Courtesy National Park Service,
Longfellow House Historical Site.

the paunchy Longfellow, his face partially hidden by a mask and his chest
clothed in tattoos, resembles publicity photos of Captain Costentenus, the
self-styled "Tattooed Greek Prince," who made appearances at expositions

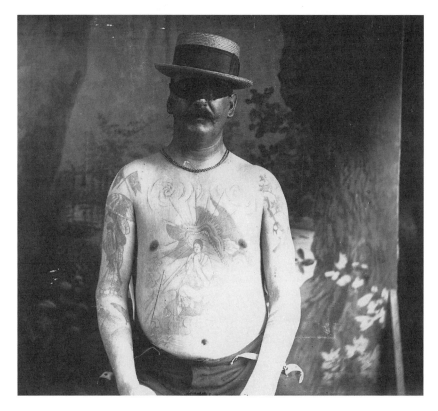

Figure 8 Charles Longfellow's Kannon tattoo, Japan, 1885. Photographer unknown. Courtesy National Park Service, Longfellow House Historical Site.

and circuses throughout the world in the 1870s and 1880s (fig. 9).[23] In his letters home, Longfellow boasted that his tattoos were "far ahead" of those of Costentenus because the designs were by "celebrated artists."[24]

Tattoos were most threatening, however, because of their association with the primitive, unbridled sexuality of barbaric peoples—a theme developed at some length in popular nineteenth-century maritime sagas such as Herman Melville's 1846 novel *Typee*.[25] Melville's novel is set in the South Seas, but illustrations in the U.S. popular press indicate that by the 1870s and 1880s, China and Japan were also commonly associated with tattooing (fig. 10).[26] It was partly to counter this image that the Japanese government

Figure 9 Captain Costentenus,
cover from 1881 autobiography.
Courtesy Ron Becker Collection,
Syracuse University Library,
Department of Special Collections.

sought, unsuccessfully, to ban tattooing in 1872.[27] By having himself tattooed, Charles symbolically joined the uncivilized races whose unruly lives
the colonial powers were striving to bring under their paternalistic oversight.
In so doing, he implied not only that he was aware of how the West saw the
Orient, but that he was willing, like its inhabitants, to live as an observed
specimen.

But even as Longfellow was inviting comparison to a circus freak or a
barbarian, tattoos, like exotic clothing, were taking on new meaning as
tourist souvenirs, commodities that made visible the dynamics of power and
influence. The future King Edward VII, while still the Prince of Wales, had
some tattoos done during a pilgrimage to the Holy Land in 1862 and later
urged his sons to do the same while on tour in Japan. When they were in
Yokohama in 1882, the Duke of Clarence and the Duke of York, later King
George V, visited Horichō, the tattoo artist who had decorated Longfellow.
Czar Nicholas II, who followed them, was another of a growing number of
royals to be tattooed.[28] It may be argued that by having themselves tattooed,

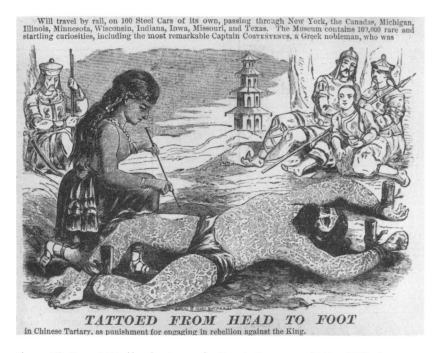

Will travel by rail, on 100 Steel Cars of its own, passing through New York, the Canadas, Michigan, Illinois, Minnesota, Wisconsin, Indiana, Iowa, Missouri, and Texas. The Museum contains 100,000 rare and startling curiosities, including the most remarkable Captain COSTENTENUS, a Greek nobleman, who was

TATTOED FROM HEAD TO FOOT
in Chinese Tartary, as punishment for engaging in rebellion against the King.

Figure 10 *Harper's Weekly* advertisement for Captain Costentenus, 26 May 1877. Courtesy Ron Becker Collection, Syracuse University Library, Department of Special Collections.

aristocrats were "asserting a class privilege that permits them to dress down by dressing up—to carnivalize their political or cultural power."[29]

Okakura's efforts to step outside modern Japanese society to reposition his identity were equally dramatic. As mentioned earlier, his contacts with Western missionaries and scholars exposed him early in life to disparities in ethnic and cultural norms, and to deep-rooted racial prejudices vis-à-vis Japan. They also gave him an outsider's perspective on the impact of his and his countrymen's appearance in Western garb. He initially displayed his sartorial response to this awareness in 1886, when he made his first trip abroad as a member of a government commission assigned the task of studying art education in Europe and the United States. By the 1880s, when most Japanese diplomats and other public officials wore Western clothing in public, Okakura chose to situate himself exceptionally vis-à-vis both his countrymen and the West by wearing a "traditional" garb consisting

Figure 11 Okakura Kakuzō in kimono, Boston, 1904.
Photographer unknown. Courtesy Isabella Stewart Gardner
Museum, Boston.

of a *haori* and *hakama*.[30] Kuki Ryūichi, the Japanese ambassador to the
United States, criticized Okakura on the grounds that such attire offended
Westerners, but the idealistic Okakura countered that it forced people to
deal with his ideas rather than his appearance.[31] Okakura made a point of
wearing Japanese clothing during subsequent journeys abroad, as seen in
the formal portrait photograph taken in 1904, when he became a consultant
to the Boston Museum of Fine Arts (fig. 11).

By donning such attire Okakura sought to assert some measure of symbolic resistance to the West's cultural colonization of Japan. Yet in so doing
he was placing himself at the very center of the Orientalist exhibitionary

order he was seeking to resist. Nonetheless, he believed that even as he confirmed Western expectations of Japan, he could transcend them because his exceptional knowledge of English language and culture set him apart from other Japanese, allowing him to dictate the terms of his interactions with the West. As he explained to his son, "From my first trip to Europe, I wore kimono most of the time. I suggest you travel abroad in kimono if you think that your English is good enough. But never wear Japanese costume if you talk in broken English."[32]

Okakura's attitude toward Western dress closely paralleled that of Ananda Coomaraswamy, an Anglo-Ceylonese art critic and philosopher who had been brought up in England. Like Okakura, he later spent considerable time in Boston, where he became an influential cultural figure. In a 1905 publication aptly titled *Borrowed Plumes*, Coomaraswamy criticized the adoption of European dress, describing it as part "of the continual destruction of national character and individuality and art."[33] He developed this theme in a speech before an audience in Jaffna: "I believe it is difficult for any of us who have not been brought up in England to realize the hopeless inadequacy of any attempts at imitation; to Englishmen the absurdity is obvious, but to us it is not revealed."[34] As Emma Tarlo has noted, Coomaraswamy's attitude was colored by the exoticist ideology of the British Romantics.[35] This was also an undercurrent in Okakura's thinking, as was his belief that by dressing in Japanese attire he was setting a moral and aesthetic example for his compatriots.

This ideologically motivated adoption of the kimono subsequently made Okakura a much admired agent in its revalorization as a signifier of Japaneseness. Self-fashioning, however, is a social and symbolic process over which individuals can never have complete control. If dressing in "native costume" endeared Okakura to many of the Bostonians he met, it no doubt was because it confirmed their expectations of Japan. By wearing a beautiful silk kimono that transformed his person into a work of art, Okakura made visible the widely held Western view that Japan was "a pure invention" and the Japanese people "simply a mode of style, an exquisite fancy of art."[36] Indeed, the Boston art collector Isabella Stewart Gardner, with whom he developed a particularly warm relationship, "liked Japanese to attend opera in her company dressed in a kimono," suggesting that they represented

Figure 12 Okakura Kakuzō with Isabella Stewart Gardner and friends, Gloucester, Mass., 6 October 1910. Photographer unknown. Courtesy Isabella Stewart Gardner Museum, Boston.

fashionable accessories (fig. 12).[37] Her attitude is reminiscent of that of the hostess in Oscar Wilde's *Picture of Dorian Gray*, who declares, "I can't afford orchids, but I spare no expense in foreigners. They make one's rooms look so picturesque."[38]

Okakura's trademark kimono also reinforced the stereotype of Japan as effeminate. In a letter to her friends Bernard and Mary Berenson, Gardner in fact characterized Okakura himself as a "very interesting, spiritual, and feminine person."[39] Although Okakura may not have wanted to convey this impression, there is little doubt that he capitalized on it to gain entrée into the circle of Gardner and other society matrons, who welcomed him and his artistic protégés. Like the High Anglican priests in their cassocks, who were also part of the Gardner entourage, Okakura in his robes attained the status and freedom of an individual who transcended gender divisions. The congruence between Okakura's self-constructed androgynous persona and that of other respected aesthetes, such as Bernard Berenson, who was Isabella Gardner's closest artistic adviser, no doubt also contributed to his success in Boston.

Okakura used clothing as a code of aesthetic discourse in Japan as well as abroad. In 1890 he was appointed director of the Tokyo School of Fine Arts. The school, which had opened the previous year under the authority of the Ministry of Education to train art teachers and professional painters, sculptors, and craftspeople, was a hotbed of conflicting ideas about the role of art and artists in modern Japanese society. Okakura looked to the ancient past for models of artistic dress and behavior. In his effort to mold both faculty and students in his romantic vision, he mandated a tuniclike costume, maroon for teachers and black for students, completed by a brimless cap like that worn by aristocrats during the Nara period.[40] Paintings, such as a famous eighth-century portrait of Prince Shōtoku and two attendants, were probably the source of inspiration for this costume.

His pride in his uniform is clear from a formal photograph showing him astride the pony he rode to and from the school every day. Okakura's antiquarian attire led those in his neighborhood to dub him the Prince on Horseback (fig. 13).[41] With this mocking epithet his neighbors implied that Okakura was not merely appropriating the visible trappings of the past but also the symbols and prerogatives of an elite to which he was not entitled. Even his closest associates in the art school were embarrassed by this effort to live history.[42] The overwhelmingly negative reaction to these idealistic efforts to control how Japanese artists presented themselves to the world would later be used by those seeking to oust Okakura as director of the Tokyo School of Fine Arts.

Following his forced resignation from the school in 1898, Okakura reiterated in other sartorial idioms both his growing disengagement from modernity and his conviction that the true artist lives an artistic life, becoming increasingly notorious for bizarre dress and behavior.[43] Already in Boston in 1886 Okakura had insisted on dressing outside the Japanese and American social conventions of his day as a way of making visible his status as as exceptional man. The persona of the transcendent Taoist sage, or *kijin*, on whom he now began to model himself, made this self-image more

Figure 13 Okakura in Tokyo School of Fine Arts
uniform riding his pony, ca. 1891. Photographer
unknown. Copyright *Okakura Tenshin zenshū*
(Tokyo: Heibonsha, 1981).

explicit. His image of the Taoist sage, however, was highly personal and
elastic and embraced elements of the Buddhist recluse as well as Romantic
ideals of artistic autonomy. The Taoist costumes in which he had himself
photographed were equally eclectic, ranging from formal Chinese robes to
a hooded tunic, and to a fishing outfit complete with sheepskin cape and
brimless cap (fig. 14).

Okakura held Taoism in particularly high esteem because of its contributions in the realm of aesthetics and its emphasis on individuality.[44] In
cloaking himself in the mantle of the *kijin*, he was embracing a paradigm
of exceptionalism, creativity, and sociopolitical resistance with deep roots in
Chinese and Japanese culture.[45] In the earlier Edo period, sinophilic artists
including Ike no Taiga and Itō Jakuchū had self-consciously constructed

Figure 14 Okakura in fisherman costume, Izura, ca. 1907. Photographer unknown. Copyright *Okakura Tenshin zenshū* (Tokyo: Heibonsha, 1981).

their public personae in this mold. The eighteenth-century eccentric Baisaō Kō Yūgai, the Japanese Zen monk regarded as the founder of the Chinese-style tea ceremony (*sencha*) was also noted for adopting Taoist garb.[46]

Okakura's infatuation with Chinese costume first surfaced in 1893, when he traveled to China at the behest of the Imperial Household Museum to study archaeological sites, museums, and private collections. Upon arrival both he and his nephew Hayasaki adopted Chinese-style dress, later claiming that this was intended to help them fulfill their mission.[47] Did Okakura, who spoke no Chinese, really believe that this would provide him with a protective camouflage at a time when relations between Japan and China were particularly tense? More likely he opted to dress in the local manner in the belief that the Chinese he encountered would be flattered. This gesture

Figure 15 Yokoyama Taikan, *Qu Yuan*, 1898. Color on paper, 132.7 × 289.7 cm. Itsukushima Shrine, Miyajima. Copyright Shodoko Company, Ltd.

of noblesse oblige foreshadowed the pan-Asianism that would become a dominant theme of his later writings.

A portrayal of the fourth-century Chinese Taoist poet-scholar Qu Yuan (Kutsugen in Japanese) painted in 1898 by his disciple Yokoyama Taikan (1868–1958), and widely thought to be a disguised portrait of Okakura, provides further visual evidence of Okakura's identification with this ideal (fig. 15). Although this conflation is not actually recorded until the Taishō era, it seems clear that after his forced resignation from the School of Fine Arts, Okakura, like Qu Yuan, came to see himself as an exile from his own culture because of his unwillingness to compromise his lofty ideals.[48] The tragicomic photographic reality of the Taoist costumes Okakura later devised for himself, however, was a far cry from the poetic melancholy of Yokoyama's painting.

Okakura's attraction to the Taoist sage was in essence a manifestation of an exoticist impulse directed toward a "China" detached from historical reality. Despite his many journeys there, Okakura persisted in proclaiming his vision of China as a coherent cultural entity. Like Western tourists who visited Japan only to have their expectations confirmed, Okakura saw China primarily through the distorting prism of traditional art and literature. A 1906 photograph of him dressed as a Taoist priest during a visit to the White Cloud Temple, headquarters of the Taoist Perfect Realization sect, located

Figure 16 Okakura at White Cloud Temple, Beijing, ca. 1906.
Photographer unknown. Copyright *Okakura Tenshin zenshū*
(Tokyo: Heibonsha, 1981).

outside Beijing, is in many ways analogous to that of Longfellow as a samurai (fig. 16). Okakura in China, like Longfellow in Japan, was a visitor with the means to purchase the costume of his chosen persona. Both men sought to cloak themselves in glorious, Romantic traditions, but today their portraits, with their carefully choreographed poses, costumes, and props, look like records of amateur theatricals. They leave the beholder with a disquieting awareness of the photograph's doubleness.

While traveling in both the United States and India, Okakura wore Taoist robes that he had had made in China (fig. 17). The cultural confusion he caused when he traveled in India dressed in this way has been recorded by the philosopher and poet Surendranath Tagore. When the two men went on a trip around India together in 1902, Tagore wrote, "Okakura had thought fit to adopt as travelling costume, a cloak and hood he had designed with the help of a Chinese print and a Calcutta tailor, to represent the garb of a Taoist monk, and weird is not the word for its effect in his present surroundings!" At every stop, when fellow travelers took Tagore aside to inquire why his friend was dressed in such a fashion, he was compelled to explain that Okakura was "a far-Easterner on pleasure bent."[49]

Tagore's explanation suggests that he understood Okakura's peculiar attire not simply as a sign of personal eccentricity but as a manifestation of unseemly touristic behavior akin to that of British colonialists. Okakura was traveling in India as the representative of an Asian nation seeking to challenge Western dominance by establishing itself as a power in the world and in Asia—in other words, a nation with its own colonialist ambitions. By 1902 Japan had initiated the effort to dominate Korea, Taiwan, and Manchuria that would be formalized following its victory in the Russo-Japanese War of 1904–1905. Even as he downplayed the differences between the various countries that constituted Asia, in his slogan "Asia is one," Okakura also insisted that Japan was "the real repository of the trust of Asiatic thought and culture."[50] By donning this outlandish costume in India, Okakura was laying claim, indeed embodying, the outward symbols and prerogatives of the imperialist nation to collect and display the experiences of different people and places.

Cross-dressing is a form of cultural appropriation that encodes complex assumptions about power relations in the colonial world. Longfellow's and Okakura's self-fashioning clearly discloses asymmetries in the relationship between colonizer and colonized. Longfellow's sartorial choices were possible because he was in Japan as a member of a powerful imperialist nation. Dressing down to dress up and revealing or concealing his tattoos were options for him. Okakura's various styles of dress were in large part a response to his sense of inferiority as a Japanese male within that sociopolitical order. As a tourist in India, however, this unequal power relationship was reversed,

Figure 17 Okakura Kakuzō in Taoist costume, Boston, 1904. Photographer unknown. Courtesy Isabella Stewart Gardner Museum, Boston.

as he presented himself as the representative of the dominant Asian colonial power.

By the same token, these men show how dress can be empowering, despite the fact that it is bound up in symbolic and social systems beyond any individual's control. Their sartorial choices had in common a retreat from modernity and a search for a utopian past, often mediated by art. For both, clothing was a vehicle for social critique, a metaphor for resistance to social regulation. Their photographic legacy, separating form from content and making visible their conviction that clothing was a matter of personal style rather than ethnicity, challenged the existing social, ethnic, and cultural codes characteristic of much colonial photography.

The symmetries between Charles Longfellow's and Okakura Kakuzō's cross-dressing further illustrate how even as colonial culture created a dialectic between "us" and "them," it also laid the foundations for a new sartorial pluralism. By creatively exploiting the mythologies of otherness, these men participated in a new transcultural traffic in personal style. One might reasonably characterize them as representatives of a kind of alternative consumerism, much like wearers of African beads or Indian clothing in the West today. Their manipulation of clothing and body treatment was in fact symbolic of the performance of modernity—and therefore of history.

By turning their bodies into works of art, both Longfellow and Okakura seem to have been trying to achieve a personal transformation in the form of a de-ethnicized, transnational identity. But their manipulation of sartorial stereotypes of the primitive and the exotic for spectacular ends instead made them into oddities. Even as they tried to fashion individualistic personae for themselves by turning their backs on the commodified culture of their day, their process of reinvention depended on the consumption practices of colonialism.

Notes

An earlier version of this article was presented in February 1998 at the annual meeting of the College Art Association. In revising and expanding it, I have benefited from conversations and criticism from many colleagues. Special thanks are owed to Allen Hockley, Jerome Silbergeld, Gennifer Weisenfeld, Lila Wice, and two anonymous readers.

1   See Timothy Mitchell, "Orientalism and the Exhibitionary Order," in *Colonialism and Culture*, ed. Nicholas B. Dirks (Ann Arbor: University of Michigan Press, 1995), 289–317.

2   See Melissa Banta and Susan Taylor, eds., *A Timely Encounter: Nineteenth-Century Photographs of Japan* (Cambridge, Mass.: Peabody Museum Press, 1988); Elizabeth Edwards, ed., *Anthropology and Photography, 1860–1920* (New Haven, Conn.: Yale University Press, 1992); Christopher Pinney, *Camera Indica: The Social Life of Indian Photographs* (Chicago: University of Chicago Press, 1998); and Emma Tarlo, *Clothing Matters: Dress and Identity in India* (London: Hurst, 1996).

3   For an account of his first trip see Christine Wallace Laidlaw, ed., *Charles Appleton Longfellow: Twenty Months in Japan, 1871–73* (Cambridge, Mass.: Friends of Longfellow House, 1998).

4   The painter Mitsutani Kunishirō, for instance, had himself photographed in this manner on his visit to the Middle East in the early Taishō era. See Deborah L. Clearwaters, "Occidentalism in Meiji Japan: The Hybrid Art of Mitsutani Kunishirō" (M.A. thesis, University of Maryland, 1996), 30.

5   Longfellow's epic narratives—among them *Evangeline* (1847), *Hiawatha* (1855), and *Tales of a Wayside Inn* (1863)—did much to consolidate and propagate American ideas about national identity. The nostalgic myth of an arcadian realm inhabited by the noble savage Hiawatha in many ways influenced the vision that young Charles would carry with him to Japan.

6   On Longfellow's youth and war experiences see Andrew Hilen, "Charley Longfellow Goes to War," *Harvard Library Bulletin*, spring 1960, 59–91, and winter 1960, 283–303.

7   The poet used photographs as sources of visual inspiration for some of his epics. Alexander Hesler's daguerreotypes, including depictions of Minnehaha Falls in the Minnesota Territory, were catalysts for *Hiawatha*. See Robert Taft, *Photography and the American Scene: A Social History, 1839–1889* (New York: Dover, 1964), 98. Longfellow himself was photographed by many of the leading photographers of the day, including Julia Cameron and Albert S. Southworth.

8   On the advent of photography in Japan see the excellent exhibition catalog *Shashin torai no koro* [The advent of photography in Japan] (Tokyo: Tōkyōtō shashin bijutsukan, 1997).

9   Okakura's keen interest in this technology also may have prompted him to press his nephew Hayasaki Kōkichi to become a professional photographer.

10 For a discussion of this essay in its broader cultural context see John M. Rosenfield, "Western-Style Painting in the Early Meiji Period and Its Critics," in *Tradition and Modernization in Japanese Culture*, ed. Donald H. Shively (Princeton, N.J.: Princeton University Press, 1971), 181–219. The essay is reproduced in *Okakura Tenshin zenshū* [Collected works of Okakura Tenshin], 9 vols. (Tokyo: Heibonsha, 1981), 3:5–12.

11 Okakura Kakuzō, *The Awakening of Japan* (New York: Century, 1904), 150.

12 Edward S. Morse, *Japan Day by Day* (New York: Houghton Mifflin, 1917), 1:275.

13 For background on this and other forms of Western dress in the early Meiji era see Julia Meech-Pekarik, *The World of the Meiji Print: Impressions of a New Civilization* (New York: Weatherhill, 1986), 64–74.

14 Homi Bhabha, "Of Mimicry and Man: The Ambivalence of Colonial Discourse," in *Tensions of Empire: Colonial Cultures in a Bourgeois World*, ed. Frederick Cooper and Ann Laura Stoler (Berkeley and Los Angeles: University of California Press, 1997), 153.

15 See Meech-Pekarik, *World of the Meiji Print*, 188.

16 Stefan Tanaka coined this term to refer to the way Japan constructed its own Orient, following the European imperialistic model. See his *Japan's Orient: Rendering Pasts into History* (Berkeley and Los Angeles: University of California Press, 1993).

17 A photograph of him as a carpenter appears in Laidlaw, *Charles Appleton Longfellow*, 163.

18 Ibid., 141.

19 Two personal albums from his 1871–1873 trip to Japan are preserved at Longfellow National Historical Site, Cambridge, Mass.

20 David Bate, "The Occidental Tourist: Photography and the Colonizing Vision," *Afterimage* 20, no.1 (summer 1992): 12.

21 On the history of Japanese tattoos see W. R. Van Gulik, *Irezumi: The Pattern of Dermatography in Japan* (Leiden: Brill, 1982). On cultural meanings of tattoos in nineteenth-century Europe and America see Alfred Gell, *Wrapping in Images: Tattooing in Polynesia* (Oxford: Clarendon, 1993), 8–18. For a revisionist history of tattoos in the West see Jane Caplan, ed., *Written on the Body: The Tattoo in European and American History* (London: Reaktion Books, 2000).

22 For more details see Christine Guth, "Longfellow's Tattoos: Marks of a Cross-Cultural Encounter," *Orientations* 29, no.11 (December 1998): 36–42.

23 On Costentenus's career see Robert Bogdan, *Freak Show* (Chicago: University of Chicago Press, 1988), 243–249. He was exhibited at the Vienna World Exposition in 1873, according to George Burchett, *Memoirs of a Tattooist* (London: Oldbourne, 1958), 104.

24 In a letter from Japan to his sister in 1855 Longfellow wrote, "Now we are getting ready to come home. Weld has curioes to pack and he and I have finishing touches to be added to some beautiful tatoe [*sic*] work we have been ornamenting ourselves with. I will give you a private exhibition when I get home. We think ourselves far ahead of Capt. Constantinus [*sic*] and we certainly are as far as art goes, our designs being from celebrated artists" (unpublished manuscript in National Park Service, Longfellow National Historical Site; transcribed by Christine Wallace Laidlaw).

25 See Herman Melville, *Typee* (Oxford: Oxford University Press, 1996), esp. 257–266.

26 An illustration in the *Illustrated London News*, 2 December 1882, for instance, shows a Western man being tattooed in Nagasaki while women entertain him with music and offer him tea. My thanks to Allen Hockley for bringing this picture to my attention.

27 Donald McCallum, "Historical and Cultural Dimensions of the Tattoo in Japan," in *Marks of Civilization: Artistic Transformations of the Human Body*, ed. Arnold Rubin (Los Angeles: Museum of Cultural History, 1988), 124 n. 27.

28 Burchett, *Memoirs of a Tattooist*, 100–103.

29 Marjorie Garber, *Vested Interests: Cross Dressing and Cultural Anxiety* (New York: Routledge, 1992), 66.

30 Sartorial practices among Japanese diplomats and officials underwent changes between the time of the first diplomatic mission in 1860 and the early twentieth century. Initially, emissaries dressed in formal Japanese attire; in the 1880s Western dress was the norm. The surge of cultural nationalism in the 1890s fostered a return to the kimono. Throughout there were individual variations, however.

31 F. G. Notehelfer, "On Idealism and Realism in the Thought of Okakura Tenshin," *Journal of Japanese Studies* 16, no. 2 (summer 1990): 327; Saitō Ryuzo, *Okakura Tenshin* (Tokyo: Yoshikawa kobunkan, 1960), 54.

32 Okakura Kazuo, *Chichi Okakura Tenshin* [My father Okakura Tenshin] (Tokyo: Chuo koronsha, 1971), 42, as cited in Horioka Yasuko, *The Life of Kakuzō* (Tokyo: Hokuseido Press, 1963), 24.

33 Cited in Tarlo, *Clothing Matters*, 10–11.

34 *Ibid.*, 11.

35 *Ibid.*

36 Oscar Wilde, *The Decay of Living*, as quoted in Camille Paglia, *Sexual Personae: Art and Decadence from Nefertiti to Emily Dickinson* (New York: Vintage, 1991), 516.

37 Morris Carter, *Isabella Stewart Gardner and Fenway Court* (Boston: Houghton Mifflin, 1925), 81.

38 Cited in Paglia, *Sexual Personae*, 516.

39 Cited in Horioka Yasuko, *Okakura Tenshin: Ajia bunka senyō no senkusha* [Okakura Tenshin: Pioneer advocate of Asian culture] (Tokyo: Yoshikawa kobunkan, 1974), 187. The letter, dated 24 October 1904, is not included in Rollin Van N. Hardley, ed., *The Letters of Bernard Berenson and Isabella Stewart Gardner, 1887–1924* (Boston: Northeastern University Press, 1987).

40 Saitō, *Okakura Tenshin*, 60–61.

41 Horioka, *Life of Kakuzō*, 31.

42 Years later the Nihonga painter Yokoyama Taikan, who was a student at the school during Okakura's tenure, recalled, "I wore it because it was a school rule; I didn't think about it looking strange. If you were shy, you'd never be able to wear it on the street for all the stares." Cited in Gloria Weston, *East Meets West: Isabella Stewart Gardner and Okakura Kakuzō* (Boston: Isabella Stewart Gardner Museum, 1992), 13.

43 Okakura, *Chichi Okakura Tenshin*, 126.

44 Fukunaga Terukazu's close reading of Okakura's writing underscores the degree to which he was influenced by various Taoist writings. However, Fukunaga does not identify the Ming and late Edo period heterodox influences that no doubt mediated Okakura's understanding of Taoism. See "Okakura Tenshin to Dōkyō" [Okakura Tenshin and Taoism], in *Okakura Tenshin zenshū*, 8:479–494.

45 On *kijin* in the Edo period see Tsuji Nobuo, *Kisō no zufu* [Figures of eccentrics] (Tokyo: Heibonsha, 1989), and Tsuji Nobuo, *Kisō no keifu* [Lineages of eccentrics] (Tokyo: Bijutsu shuppansha, 1970).

46 Money L. Hickman and Yasuhiro Sato, *The Paintings of Jakuchū* (New York: Asia Society, 1989), 138–139.

47 Horioka, *Okakura Tenshin*, 9. The son of Okakura's stepsister, Hayasaki, was a painting student at the Tokyo School of Fine Arts when he accompanied Okakura to China in 1893. There Hayasaki made an extensive photographic record of works of art, monuments, and sites (for a list see *Okakura Tenshin zenshū*, 5:117–119). Hayasaki later developed a keen interest in Taoism and, during the years he lived in China, maintained a close relationship with the Temple of the Eight Immortals in Xian. An undated photograph of him in the robes of a Taoist priest, suggesting that he shared Okakura's esteem for Taoism, is reproduced in *Selected Masterpieces of Asian Art* (Boston: Museum of Fine Arts; Tokyo: Japan Broadcasting Pub. Co., 1992), 10.

48 The conflation is first recorded in Taikan's autobiography, published in 1951. My thanks to Victoria Weston for providing me with this information.

49 Nakamura Sunao, ed., *Okakura Kakuzō: Collected English Writings* (Tokyo: Heibonsha, 1984), 3:238.

50 Okakura Kakuzō, *Ideals of the East* (London: John Murray, 1903), 1, 5.

Was Meiji Taste in Interiors "Orientalist"?

Jordan Sand

The Meiji elite adopted many of the styles and tastes of the Victorian West. In domestic architecture, this is seen particularly in the interiors of "Western-style" pavilions and reception rooms (*yōkan* or *yōma*). This style, however, cannot be construed in any simple sense as Western. Most of these houses were built by Japanese carpenters and reveal the construction techniques to which native craftsmen were accustomed. Rooms were often appointed with furnishings both domestic and foreign in manufacture, along with Japanese, Chinese, and other Asian antiquities, arranged and designed in accordance with contemporary Japanese conceptions of Western taste (or of the elements of that taste conceived to harmonize with Japanese taste). Both of these terms—*Western taste* and *Japanese*—must themselves be recognized as unstable, receiving definition in the process of their complementary deployment.

positions 8:3 © 2000 by Duke University Press

This essay is exploratory. My exploration draws primarily from an issue of the magazine *Fujin gahō*, or the *Ladies' Graphic*, published in 1906. The *Ladies' Graphic* began publication in 1905, at the height of the Russo-Japanese War. A special issue on interior decorating appeared the following year. The images in this issue invite a number of questions about the aesthetic choices of the Meiji elite and about the relations between objects, interiors, and photographic representations in Japan's domestic market during the age of global imperialism. The intent of this essay is to bring these questions to the fore and propose some schemas for ordering our observations.

The theoretical frame for these questions is the problem of orientalism. At the risk of radically reducing the subtleties of Edward Said's formulation, I will treat orientalism as a colonial way of seeing the world that situates or interprets culture so as to legitimate existing relations of political power.[1] Japan's ambiguous international position clearly complicates the application of Said's term. The interest of our common theme, colonizer and colonized, derives from precisely this complication.

Since the end of the Meiji period, the Meiji elite have often been characterized as superficial imitators of the West. Western houses, along with the bustle and the frock coat, are icons of an era conceived as politically bold but culturally derivative. As the business of recovering and preserving the national heritage in Japan has progressed, a number of Meiji buildings have now been included in the Japanese architectural canon. Ex post facto recognition of the originality of certain exceptional Japanese designers does not, however, alter the standard view of Meiji modernizers as "mimic men" trying in vain to be Western but doomed merely to be Westernized. We could call this interpretation of Meiji a discourse of Japan the colonized. The West is the cultural imperialist and Japan the colonized subject. This view of Japanese modernity continues to flourish today.[2]

At the opposite pole, the Japanese might instead be seen as uniquely well-situated to adapt the cultural knowledge and goods of both East and West, drawing freely from the West, from China and Korea, and from native traditions. If these appropriations work somehow to reaffirm the project of Japanese imperial expansion and Japan's role as colonizer in Asia, then we might call the result orientalist in a manner true to Said.

The opposition of these two aesthetic assessments seems ultimately reducible to a question of command over representations. We view Japan or Japanese people (note that the two often get conflated in this context[3]) as either in control of representations of Japaneseness or in the thrall of representations emanating from the dominant West. The question of command over national representations, however, imagines individual agents as mere shadows of nation-states, dominant and appropriating or dominated and derivative. In an era when the Japanese state was unquestionably struggling for a position in the global imperial order, the problem of nation inevitably loomed large in every domain of culture. Yet actual individual tastes always depend on a complex set of variables, including region, gender, generation, class, and status. To talk about the cultural effects of the Meiji state's ambiguous global position, we need therefore to analyze how that position insinuated itself into cultural strategies within domestic society, the mechanisms of displacement through which the global political order was reiterated, reflected, or inverted within domestic social and cultural hierarchies.

The *Ladies' Graphic* in 1906 offers a representational node in which such mechanisms operated, a point of intersection for several cultural vectors in the imperial field. Its images encourage us beyond the binarism of colonizer and colonized. Before turning to the specific problem of orientalism and Meiji taste, I will first consider the graphic magazine itself, as a medium for cultural and aesthetic displacement of political structures. Two ordering principles emerge from this displacement, one that might be described as fetishistic, and the other as colonizing or orientalist. The first ordering principle supplants persons and social relations with fetish objects. Fetishism is a form of displacement, whether one means the misperception of relations between people as relations between things in Marx's sense of the word, or the substitution of one object of desire for another in the Freudian sense. Orientalism relates to another sort of displacement, in which the international political order is misperceived as natural. The second ordering principle reflects this misperception, which permits the transference of global hegemonic structures onto the domestic political and cultural order. But explication of these principles alone will not answer my initial question, for which we must attempt a closer reading of the actual language of Meiji interiors as well as their photographic representations.

Medium: *The Ladies' Graphic*

In February 1906 the *Ladies' Graphic*, then in its second year, published a special issue on interior decorating, the first two dozen pages of which reproduced photographs of richly appointed interiors, mostly showing guest rooms in the houses of titled Japanese aristocrats.[4] The magazine's name tells us the two essential things to know about it: it targeted a market primarily of women, and it sold them graphic reproductions. Japanese print capitalism, rapidly expanding since the 1880s, found a large potential market in bourgeois female readers educated at the new higher schools for women (*kōtō jogakkō*). Ōya Sōichi would later describe the revelation to journalists in this period that educated women would buy their product as "like the discovery of a vast new colonial territory."[5] Nor was the interest of publishers in colonization limited to this domestic market. In 1907 the name *Ladies' Graphic* was briefly changed to *Oriental Ladies' Graphic* (*Tōyō fujin gahō*), and photo captions ordinarily in Japanese and English were augmented with Chinese.

Following the formula already proven successful in U.S. periodicals such as *Godey's Ladies' Book* and a handful of Japanese predecessors, the *Ladies' Graphic* mixed entertainment and instruction. Along with fiction, reports on activities at the women's higher schools, and fashion, the first three issues included articles by a male doctor on women's hygiene, by Marchioness Ōyama on the responsibilities of Japanese women in wartime, and by several male authors on the traits of a good wife.

Photographs of high-society families were the special appeal of the *Ladies' Graphic*, which was neither the first nor the best selling of the women's magazines. Two illustrated monthlies like the *Ladies' Graphic*, *Jogaku sekai* [Women's school world], which began publication in 1901, and *Fujin sekai* [Ladies' world], which began in 1906, are said to have had the highest circulation among women's magazines at the time. A 1911 survey of sales of women's magazines at Tokyo bookshops placed *Ladies' Graphic* third after these two.[6] What set the *Ladies' Graphic* apart from these rivals in style of presentation was its generous use of high-quality photo reproductions, which still had the appeal of novelty. Collotype and halftone printing, the key technologies that made possible the mass marketing of photographic images, came into use in Japan in the late 1880s. The first periodical marketed explicitly for its photo reproductions was the monthly *War Graphic*, which relayed images from the front during the Sino-Japanese War of 1894–1895. Less dramatic images were also beginning to circulate in other popular periodicals.

When the camera turned toward domestic subjects, photographic reproduction transformed social position into celebrity. Prefiguring the portraits of elite families that would fill the *Ladies' Graphic*, the first issue of the *Sun* [*Taiyō*], in 1895, featured a photograph of Count Ōkuma Shigenobu with his wife and mother.[7] Readers of the *Sun* would have known Ōkuma as a statesman. The portrait presented him in private, making his comportment, the details of his personal appearance, and those of his family part of his public persona. The *Ladies' Graphic* made this formula its specialty, fashioning aristocrats into popular figures and social exemplars while exploiting the images of their wealth to sell magazines.

The figures photographed, it should be noted, were not only manufactured celebrities (all celebrity is manufactured, after all) but members of a newly coined aristocracy as well, since in 1884 the Meiji government had consolidated the families of both military and court elites into a single aristocracy on a European model, then had begun the practice of granting instant rank to statesmen, soldiers, and eventually businessmen for service to the nation.[8] Graphic publications displaying the wealth and status of this composite modern elite were as integral to constituting a new representational and social order as the police photography and slum reportage that enhanced official surveillance and exposed society's lower margins to the public gaze.[9] By adopting the system of aristocratic titles created by the Meiji oligarchs and transforming it into a fantasy realm of celebrities, the graphic magazine fetishized it, supplanting the political reality of a structure of relations created by the new regime with images of attractive individuals and families.

Ordering Principle 1: The Emperor's Cupboard

The first layer of meaning within the magazine lies in the order and presentation of photographs. The overall layout of the photo section in the *Ladies' Graphic* mirrored the emperor-centered Meiji social hierarchy. Issues typically began with individual portraits of imperial princesses and princes, followed by family and individual portraits of aristocrats according to rank and, finally, by the families of commoners. The interior decorating issue was structured in the same manner. This pattern is found in other contemporary publications as well—for example, in the introductions to popular domestic manuals. But in the interiors feature, the magazine replicated this social order in a particular way, conveying meanings beyond merely the existence of a vertically stratified society. Photographic depictions of the private apartments within aristocratic mansions offered models to readers for decorating their own homes. Yet perhaps more significantly, just as Jacob Riis's famous pictures of New York slums exposed bourgeois readers in the United States to a hidden world, the *Ladies' Graphic* showed a nonaristocratic reading public the hidden domestic world of the country's elite—how the *other* other half lived. Replacing the usual photo portraits of aristocrats and their families with images of the unoccupied interiors of their homes, the magazine performed a further fetishization in which glimpses of houses and possessions substituted for intimate contact with the unattainable targets of social-climbing desire. The popular Count Ōkuma, for example, was represented here not by his person but by his furnished parlor, which revealed such intimate particulars as the special arrangement of stacked cushions he used as a seat (Ōkuma had lost a leg in an assassination attempt) and his wife's embroidery table, left in plain view and explicitly mentioned in the caption.

Three pages of photographs showing a piece of furniture from the imperial palace crown the graphic series. The magazine does not depict the palace itself, perhaps due to Imperial Household Ministry restrictions. Described as a "Parlour Cupboard belonging to the Imperial Household," the cabinet was designed, according to its caption, by the Faculty of the Government Fine Arts Academy and constructed over a period of ten years at a cost of thirty thousand yen. A clinical, documentary style distinguishes the presentation of this ornamental cabinet, which stands alone, filling the photographic frame, a screen behind it preventing any reading of the space in which it has been placed. In contrast, other photographs in the issue reveal broad interior expanses. Shots of the cabinet taken from three angles provide the most detail of any images in the magazine. Following two photographs of the exterior, a third shows the front with the doors thrown open to reveal the decorated walls of an empty interior (fig. 1). Like the innermost chamber of a Shinto shrine that conceals no sacred image, the cabinet is made more rather than less numinous by the fact that it contains nothing, for the imperial mystery remains uncompromised by any tangible object of veneration. In its isolation and through its lack of everyday context, the emperor's empty "cupboard" speaks of august distance, while its detailed presentation and the photographic medium itself offer the illusion of an immanent and completely knowable object for the penetration of the reader's gaze. The caption announces imperial authority, sustained by the Government Fine Arts Academy, and the capacity to command the labor of craftsmen for ten years at extravagant expense. This staging of an imperial object (significantly, a receptacle for personal effects) suggests an extension to architecture and furnishings of the careful management of representations that Taki Kōji and Takashi Fujitani have discussed with regard to the emperor's person. By permitting us to view only the cabinet, the imperial household and the *Ladies' Graphic* are not so much hiding the emperor as exhibiting the imperial absence.[10]

Imperial house image-management continues in the four pictures that follow, showing the personal quarters of Prince and Princess Higashi-Fushimi, members of an imperial collateral house (fig. 2). Built in the *shoin* construction usual for Tokugawa and Meiji residences, with no signs of Western furnishings, the rooms are given more page space but less explanatory information than the nonimperial interiors that fill the rest of the issue. They are followed by the houses of two princes not of the blood (*kōshaku*)—Iwakura and Nijō—each with one interior and one exterior shot (the only exterior shots to appear on glossy paper[11]), then by the houses of other aristocrats in order of rank and by the house and museum of business magnate Ōkura Kihachirō (the only nonaristocratic house reproduced on glossy paper). Exterior views of imperial prince Higashi-Fushimi's palace are not provided. The first exterior views show the Iwakura palace. No comments are offered on the aesthetic characteristics of rooms until the captions for the house of a marquis (one rank below nonimperial prince).

Set apart from the other images in style of presentation, the austere Higashi-Fushimi interiors (which are rooms for daily use rather than reception) serve as metonyms for their noble occupants more than as models

帝室の御道具

Parlour Cupboard belonging to the Imperial Household.   The same cupboard.   Upper picture: front vi w with the doors left open.   Lower picture: flank view.

Figure 1 "Parlour Cupboard belonging to the Imperial Household," *Fujin gahō,* 15 February 1906.

for home decorating. One step yet more abstract and removed from the everyday, the emperor's cupboard grounds a set of ordering principles that carries through subsequent images; if the collections of objects in each image stand in for their owners, this cabinet is densest with signification, and the images thereafter progressively approach the ordinary, where the disparity between what is seen and what can be known is slightest. The images thus not only articulate the official hierarchy of the emperor-state by adhering to

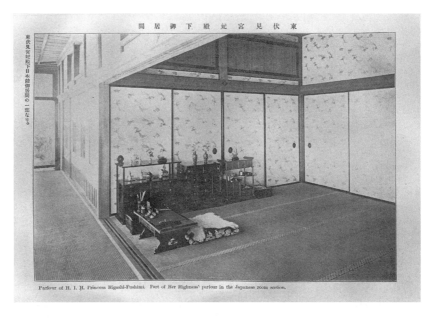

東伏見宮妃殿下御居間

東伏見宮妃殿下日本館御居間の一部なり。

Parlour of H. I. H. Princess Higashi-Fushimi. Part of Her Highness' parlour in the Japanese room section.

Figure 2 "Parlour of H. I. H. Princess Higashi-Fushimi. Part of Her Highness' parlour in the Japanese room section," *Fujin gahō*, 15 February 1906.

rank in their order but elaborate it with a distinct representational vocabulary. With decreasing rank, the tendency is toward inferior quality in certain aspects of presentation (for example, paper stock, image size, and generosity of space allotted), while in the content of the images and captions the trend is in the opposite direction, from isolation to increased spatial context (including exterior photographs), increased variety of what is shown, and increased written comment relating the objects in the image to their possessors (implying personal judgments of taste). Metaphorically, the imperial cabinet might be read as the master fetish, the empty signifier from which all other signifiers emerge.[12] This displacement of the system of political hegemony constructed by the Meiji oligarchs onto the representation of material objects must be seen as the creative work of the *Ladies' Graphic* and its photographers, neither imposed by imperial fiat nor willed by "nationalistic" editors but emerging from strategies of celebrity-making and -marketing within the imperial state.

Ordering Principle 2: The Emperor's Shoes

From 1872, when he was first presented to the Japanese populace in Western military dress, the Meiji emperor never removed his shoes in public view. The initiation of this policy (still maintained today) offers a symbolic point of departure for the second ordering principle, which concerns the cultural determinants of the interiors themselves. The emperor's shoes, treading indiscriminately inside and outside, embody succinctly the self-colonizing process of civilization (*bunmei*), a material and spatial ordering principle which operated in Meiji society at the level of everyday practice as well as representation.

Shoes in the Japanese case have had a very direct influence on the shape of domestic architecture. Why did the first generation of Meiji aristocrats build Western-style pavilions? The answer cannot be reduced simply to a vogue for everything Western. The requirements of formal reception, so important in business and diplomacy, dictated the need for these rooms. Here, fashion and necessity were inseparable. Japan remained exotic, ori-entalized, and therefore unequal in the eyes of the Western powers as long as Japanese imposed unfamiliar customs upon Westerners. The issues of tariff autonomy and extraterritoriality lay latent in every encounter be-tween Japanese host and Western guest until the end of the century (and in some cases beyond). In this encounter manners, comportment, cuisine, dress, and interiors formed an integral, articulate whole. The shogunate had taken a different approach to diplomatic theater, holding to as much of its own protocol as possible, but the Meiji government made an about-face, embodied in the Westernized appearance of the emperor. Thereafter, Japanese would participate in the international imperial order by displacing its dictates and its structure into domestic society. This is what was at the heart of the regime's so-called emulation of the West. This displacement, more than the direct pressure of foreigners on Japanese soil, was responsi-ble for the first generation of aristocratic Western pavilions. Most of these pavilions were in fact built to accommodate the emperor on his provincial tours.[13] Wherever he visited, the emperor's new shoes created the need for Western-style rooms, with wooden floors and carpeting in place of tatami mats (where custom rooted at the deepest level of native habitus forbade

the wearing of shoes). Built for the emperor, these rooms served a recon-
ception of the public (both the public as embodied in the monarch and the
nascent bourgeois public). As Fujitani has observed, the emperor's provincial tours marked national territory. In much the same way, visits from the
Western-dressed emperor to elite residences imprinted civilization on their
interiors.

The Meiji monarchy artfully combined elements of native tradition (often partially invented but presented as timeless) with the modern Western
repertoire of royal pomp. The rhetoric of synthesizing the native and the
Western predates the Meiji Restoration (Sakuma Shōzan coined the famous
phrase "Eastern spirit Western technology" in the 1850s) and is not peculiar
to the Japanese context.[14] This rhetoric was commonly governed by a single
principle, namely, the privileging (or, better, imagining and privileging) of
an essential native spirit to be preserved against the onslaught of the modern
West. As Partha Chatterjee has shown for nineteenth-century India, this is
a discourse fundamental to the colonized intellectual situation.[15] In Japan
it served the needs of the state by cloaking hegemony in the vestments of
sacralized imperial tradition. But the discourse of native spirit (and the sacred
manifestation of the emperor) also served the broader need of modernizing
elites (including the publishers of women's magazines) for self-legitimation
through hallowed national symbols.

The *Ladies' Graphic* interiors issue reveals imperial nobility functioning as
a privileged preserve of cultural essence while it shows modern aristocrats,
their houses in effect colonized by the imperatives of the emperor-led civilizing process, projecting their own status within domestic society through a
Western material vocabulary. The photographs of the emperor's ornamental
cabinet and the Japanese portion of the Higashi-Fushimi palace reflect this
overlapping of the political order and its cultural inverse. The cabinet is a
native craft product, and the palace interiors are distinguished from others photographed in the issue by the absence of chairs, carpeting, and other
marks of Western style. These images of native design receive pride of place
but are distanced from the discourses of fashion and taste in which other images are situated, where Westernness is the language of dominance. Brack-
eted as tradition and protected by its sanctified place as the imperial heritage,
a native aesthetic is thus allowed to triumph over Western civilization in a

supposedly timeless sphere removed from both political necessity and the vicissitudes of fashion.

Displacing the material rhetoric of the relationship between the West and Japan onto the relationship between monarch and nation shifted the terms of other relationships. The rhetoric of class domination was altered by the fact that Western-style clothing, furniture, and architecture were generally more expensive to produce, acquire, and maintain, so that the state elite who displayed the cosmopolitanism of the new government simultaneously displayed a new conjunction of power and wealth.[16] Gender was similarly affected; Westernness became the rhetoric of a masculine public and Japaneseness that of a private sphere reconstituted as feminine. Since the reception rooms that made up the majority of the photographs in the *Ladies' Graphic* were semipublic spaces within the house, they were configured primarily as Western (*yōma*), and masculine signifiers predominated.

Western writings on interior decorating complicated the gendering of the *yōma*, since they tended to assume that women decorated the whole house. The problem was exacerbated by the fact that *zashiki kazari*, the closest native equivalent to the Western art of interior decorating, was customarily the practice of leisured males.[17] Drawing on the Western women's magazine and domestic advice genres, the *Ladies' Graphic* portrayed decorating as a woman's task but did so through written advice provided by men, thus reproducing the colonial relationship displaced onto gender relations: male authorities instructing women on the proper constitution of a Western, male domain within the female preserve of the native home.

The April 1906 issue of the *Ladies' Graphic* opens with the words of Baron Ōtori Keisuke on interior decorating. Ōtori urges Japanese women to include interior decorating among their daily tasks, as Western women do. He warns his readers that a room's decoration tells guests of the host's character and disposition. He then relates that he himself does all the decorating in his household. Accompanying photographs show the Japanese and Western drawing rooms in Ōtori's house and Ōtori himself in informal kimono seated with his granddaughter on a sofa in the Western room. The Western room contains no less than five animal skins spread on the floor and draped over chairs. Evocative of wildness and the hunt, this bestial environment conveys the baron's masculinity, while the representation of Ōtori with his

granddaughter seems calculated to soften his image for the female readership. Hairiness as the body language of masculine identity also associates
these skins with their owner, whose full beard would have seemed barbaric
to Japanese a generation earlier. Tiger and leopard, animals not native to
Japan, further impress with their suggestion of exotic conquests, whether or
not Ōtori himself was actually the hunter.[18] A leopard skin sprawls across the
center of the carpet in Baron Kaneko Kentarō's parlor, where the masculinity of the occupant is further underscored by a dramatic door-panel painting
of a hawk, a side table piled with heavy leatherbound volumes, and a Roman
bust on the desk. The parlors of Prince and Princess Higashi-Fushimi feature
"his-and-hers" bearskins, the prince's large and dark and the princess's small
and white. These imperial interiors remain subtle in their expression of gender, however, when contrasted to the nonimperial Ōtori and Kaneko rooms,
where the copious furs belong clearly to a Victorian Western vocabulary of
maleness expressed through the subjugation of wild nature.

Several women's parlors also appear, in both Western and Japanese style.
The women's Western rooms tend to have smaller, lighter furniture and
armless chairs. They also draw more on native aesthetic motifs. The parlor of Countess Ogasawara has curtains, tablecloth, and upholstery in the
Genroku pattern that had been revived for kimono fabric during the Russo-
Japanese War. This historical appropriation defines the gender of the room
as female because the adoption of Western business dress by men had placed
the decorative patterns of traditional dress in the feminine sphere. Similarly, the parlor of Mrs. Ōkura contains a standing silk screen (kichō) of the
kind common in Heian palace architecture, thus reaching back to classical antiquity for a decorative object associated with both native tradition
and femininity. The colonization of the living environment begun by the
emperor's Western shoes thus modulates through discourses of interior aesthetics to emerge with a reordered language of gender built of both exotic
and native, contemporary and antique objects and motifs.

Orientalisms

How does the language of ornament spoken in these rooms—the selection
and placement of objects and the treatment of surfaces—express nation and

empire? Here we return to the question of an orientalist relationship to cultural artifacts, which situates objects in a way reaffirming political dominance. A Meiji Japanese orientalist gaze might move along three possible axes of cultural-political relation: vis-à-vis continental Asia (manifested as social science in the *Shinagaku* analyzed by Stefan Tanaka in *Japan's Orient*), vis-à-vis the West (the inverted exoticizing of occidentalism), and in an involuted way, vis-à-vis the past of Japan itself.[19]

These photographs were published when Japan was still in the flush of newly acquired imperial glory. We should not assume an immediate and confident orientalization of the rest of Asia simultaneous with military victory and the acquisition of new territory.[20] Japan's position in Asia was still uncertain. In the arts the debt to China was large and recognized. Chinese paintings, at least, seem to have occupied a common space with Japanese works in the sphere of collecting and connoisseurship, and were often more prized. A page in the interiors issue reproduces photographs of two Chinese paintings in the possession of Viscountess Akimoto. Captions name the Sung painters to whom the works were attributed and label the paintings *meiga*, or famous pictures. These are the only paintings given a page of their own.[21]

Elsewhere in the issue, however, Western interiors display Chinese objects with Japanese in a profusion that suggests trophy collecting. Photographs of the remarkable interior of a private museum built by commercial magnate Ōkura Kihachirō show items of Japanese, Chinese, and uncertain origin set in exotic architectural surroundings redolent of pan-Asian fantasy. Three images of the museum interior in the magazine show a portion of a Tokugawa mausoleum flanked by two Buddhist icons from elsewhere; a corridor revealing the architect's unusual decoration of posts, brackets, and cabinetry (with Chinese, Mongol, or perhaps ancient Japanese overtones); and a large silver sculpture of a flower basket with crystal balls in place of blossoms, set in front of two chairs possibly of Chinese manufacture and painted screens reported to come from Hideyoshi's Jūrakudai palace.[22] Elsewhere in the issue a photograph of the Ōkura dining room reveals a combination of native architectural elements and ostensibly Chinese objets d'art in a room arranged for Western dining. The pièce de résistance, however, is a contrived display of entwined nature and modern technology: a creeping plant rises from the center of the table, hung with artificial clusters of grapes containing

Figure 3 "Dining-room in the Residence of Mr. Okura. Interior of the Room, the creeping-plant is Lycopodium to which artificial grape vine is fastened, nine grapes of which are fitted with electric light contrivance to illuminate the room," *Fujin gahō*, 15 February 1906.

electric lights (fig. 3). The peculiar combination of technical ostentation and pan-Asian aesthetic panoply recalls the orientalism of Okakura Kakuzō's idealized East, in which Japan occupies a unique position simultaneously as missionary bearing the gospel of civilization and enlightenment to Asia and as the "museum of Asiatic civilization."[23]

Public discourse in Japan has commonly occidentalized Western people and things by rendering them as parts of a monolithic totality defined by its antithesis to the East, or to Japan. In Meiji period descriptions and prescriptions of Western-style interiors, Westernness was stereotyped with adjectives such as "heavy and opulent" (*nōkō kabi*), in contrast to the "light and refined" (*seiga tanpaku*) character of Japanese rooms.[24] This occidentalism made it possible to assert a victory in the cultural sideshow to military and diplomatic competitions for imperial power.

Reification of Westernness in Meiji occidentalism manifested itself not only in the language of description but in the treatment of Western goods, as can be seen in the fully appointed Western interiors of the wealthiest and highest-ranked houses in the *Ladies' Graphic*, where finances permitted and formality required a *yōma* unvitiated by compromise with native living habits or craft techniques. The Western furniture is, for the most part, heavy indeed, and it seems to have been chosen for its contrast to Japanese interior features, uninfluenced by the contemporary vogue in much of Europe for less ponderous and elaborate furniture (for example, the Kuroda house, fig. 4). As furniture not only decorates but molds the human occupation of space, this rigid contrast translates the East-West polarity into comportment and practice (what Pierre Bourdieu calls bodily hexis), dictating the manner of the encounter between host and guest. The irregularly dispersed arrays of chairs and sofas in the Western reception rooms seem to demand of the visitor a mode of behavior different from the planar simplicity and rectilinear clarity of the Japanese *zashiki* (tatami-matted reception room), where a tokonoma, proximity to which corresponds to social status, provides instant orientation, and where the lack of large fixed furniture makes the subtleties of social interaction contingent on the bodily definition of space through position in relation to the walls, thresholds, tokonoma, and other people in the room. Perhaps the most striking anomaly in these rooms from the standpoint of Japanese reception practices is the round sofa found in three of the houses photographed. A *zashiki* (regardless of whether it is eighty mats in size or two) is foremost the place where host and guest face each other. Bodily orientation is paramount. In contrast, it is difficult to imagine the proper use of this seat, which has no orientation. If its function, however, is merely to be appropriate to the ensemble needed to fill the space, making the Western room replete, then it is curiously fitting in its unfittingness to Japanese social situations, contributing to the exoticism of the *yōma* not only in appearance but in the physical encounter with and negotiation of unfamiliar spatial contours that it requires.

I have so far avoided addressing a crucial question preliminary to any matters of taste. How had the objects displayed in these photographs been acquired? To speak of imperialism and art is to speak of loot. Are there no direct links to be drawn between Japanese imperialism and what is found

敷座表邸爵男子金

金子早太郎氏邸表座敷の光景なり。

Baron Kaneko's Residence. Interior of the Reception-room in the Residence of Baron Kaneko.

Figure 4 "Residence of the Marquis Kuroda. Part of the reception room of the Marquis, famous for its walls hung with old pictures by master painters," *Fujin gahō*, 15 February 1906.

in the domestic interiors of imperial Japan? To answer this question, we need more information not only about the objects in these houses but about the provenance of furniture and art objects in Japanese private collections generally, including that of the imperial house.

While information on other collections displayed in the magazine is wanting, the Ōkura case suggests that Japan's achievement of imperial power status had a direct material impact on domestic interiors. At the time that the photographer from the *Ladies' Graphic* visited, Ōkura's collection of Chinese art had been very recently acquired. Ōkura had begun his career as an arms dealer and in 1900 had turned to expanding his business empire on the continent.[25] Political disorder in China provided the opportunity for his large acquisitions. A pamphlet published by the museum in 1932 reports that he bought most of it at the time of the Boxer Rebellion in order to prevent it from being taken to the West.[26] Suppression of the Boxers by the imperial powers was followed by one of the most extravagant incidents of looting in modern history. Western reports on this orgy of pillage described the Japanese soldiers as particularly interested in Chinese art and antiquities. When Japanese forces entered Tientsin, the commander even issued guidelines ranking the loot according to how it should be disposed of, placing first priority on things to be offered to the imperial house; second, to items for commemorative display in museums and schools; third, to items to be kept as officers' trophies; and so forth. That looting actually proceeded in such an orderly fashion, however, is dubious.[27] The Ōkura museum pamphlet does not describe the route by which the magnate's Chinese antiques came into his hands, but Ōkura himself did not visit the continent until two years after the rebellion. His memoirs describe him purchasing most of the collection from Western ships in Nagasaki.[28] Ōkura's personal complicity in the theft of Chinese treasure is clearly less the issue, however, than the fact that Japan's role in the suppression of the Boxers and the collapse of the Qing affected not only Japanese perceptions of China but the Japanese market in Chinese antiquities and, by extension, Japanese bourgeois interiors. The Sumitomo family amassed one of the world's largest collections of Chinese bronzes in the same period, and doubtless other examples among late Meiji industrialists could be found. On the other hand, in view of the long history of trade with China and Korea, there is no reason to expect that the collections of continental antiquities displayed by aristocratic families with longer pedigrees (Viscountess Akimoto's paintings, for example) all comprised products of Meiji imperialism.[29]

Nothing we see was looted from the West, of course. On the contrary, the imported Western furniture and few artworks visible would have been acquired with far greater difficulty than Japanese art objects were by Westerners, at least in the early Meiji period. It bears noting that there are no miniature models of Western buildings (by contrast, miniature pagodas were popular items in the West, sold particularly at the Japanese concessions of world expositions), no pieces of Western religious art (Buddhist icons were exported to Western collections), and few oil paintings. Such disparities mark these as the rooms of a struggling second-class power in the world cultural order defined in Europe.[30]

The Japanese past was more available for looting, in a metaphoric and perhaps in a literal sense as well. Figurative looting may be seen in the exploitation of Japanese objects to give a native touch to Western-style rooms, where they are displayed much as orientalia were in the West. Japanese objects displayed in these rooms thus abandon their former meanings to function in the representational system established by Western interior decorating as objets d'art or antiques. The actual economy of native loot is less clear. The nouveaux riches (among whom we may include the imperial house itself) would have found precious Japanese artworks more available than Western ones but, by this time, perhaps less available than Chinese or Korean items. As Christine Guth has pointed out, most daimyo continued to hold their enormous assets into the twentieth century, so that when Charles Freer visited Japan in 1907, he found the major daimyo collections (including those of Akimoto and Kuroda, whose possessions are represented in the *Ladies' Graphic*) still intact.[31] Nevertheless, there can be little doubt that the social reordering of the Restoration resulted in an increased flow of goods previously out of circulation. Some Meiji dealers and collectors were able to "loot" old wealth within Japan as things came onto the market from formerly wealthy temples, tea schools, and samurai households after 1868.[32]

Susan Stewart speaks of two motives of antiquarianism: the "nostalgic desire of romanticism" and the "political desire of authentication."[33] It is in some sense to authenticate a native culture in opposition to the West that objects and elements of native aesthetic traditions are appropriated, transformed, and redeployed in these interiors. The political desire manifested in this appropriation self-orientalizes by essentializing the native object toward the political end of defining a Japanese style. In the *Ladies' Graphic* representation of interiors, it seems possible to read three interrelated aesthetic moves in the self-orientalizing composition of this Japanese style. These are exaggeration of size, material transposition of media, and recontextualization.

Gigantism was a characteristic of many objects exhibited at world expositions.[34] In this context, where the cultural competition among nations was at its most explicit, the function of oversized products is plain enough. On a subtler level, the *Ladies' Graphic* photographs suggest similar efforts to communicate authority through exaggerated size. Although none of the domestic interiors photographed displays the large bronzes or bizarrely oversized ceramics that commonly went to expositions, several show a clear

金子爵邸客室の光景。　　金子爵邸客室

Baron Kaneko's Residence.   Interior of the parlour in the Residence of Baron Kaneko, Privy Councillor.

Figure 5a "Interior of the parlour in the Residence of Baron Kaneko, Privy Councillor," *Fujin gahō*, 15 February 1906.

preference for large-format paintings (Ōkuma and Ōkura houses) with bold motifs (Kaneko house; see figs. 5a and 5b), large pieces of framed calligraphy (Shimoda and Akimoto houses), and objects such as folding screens and tea shelves of unusually large size. It will require closer study of Tokugawa interiors to ascertain whether each of these objects and styles of display represented a clear break with the past. The cumulative effect, though, particularly when contrasted with the diminutive objects and motifs associated with tea taste, is of grand scale.

One immediate source for a trend toward oversized works in traditional media was the new imperial palace, constructed in 1888. The new palace provided a key model for upper-class eclectic interiors. Its construction was also a boon for contemporary artists in the traditional school. The imperial house began purchasing pieces from domestic expositions shortly before this time, showing a preference for Kyoto artists and highly naturalistic depictions.[35] The size of the new palace and its quasi-Western design called

Figure 5b "Interior of the Reception-room in the Residence of Baron Kaneko," *Fujin gahō*, 15 February 1906.

for unusually large works. An art magazine reported in 1889 that the imperial house had ordered mountings of the unprecedented width of two *ken* (approximately twelve feet) and was having "a noted artist" paint "trees, flowers, birds and Japanese figures" (*Nihon jinbutsu*) to be put in these mountings for decoration of walls in the palace. The magazine explained that these new paintings were needed because old paintings would look unsuitable in the newly constructed interior, particularly "in the eyes of Westerners."[36]

By transposition of media I mean removal of aesthetic forms or motifs from the settings in which they customarily appear. In these rooms it is seen particularly in efforts to decorate surfaces in a way that "Japanizes" them. The parlor of Countess Ogasawara mentioned above displays one such transposition, in the use of kimono fabric for upholstery and drapes. Transposition is seen particularly in the treatment of walls. A photograph of the Kuroda house shows a wall decorated with round, square, and fan-shaped paintings (fig. 4).[37] The tradition existed of resetting small paintings, particularly fan paintings, on folding screens. Here the use of this device has been expanded to two large walls.[38] The wall planes above the lintel (*nageshi*) in this room have also been papered with a decorative pattern. This transposition of medium is found in several of the rooms, where the patterned silk or paper commonly used for *fusuma* sliding panels is put into service to decorate wall surfaces, particularly above the lintel, an area that was seldom papered in *shoin* interiors of the Tokugawa period (Kuroda dining room and Hosokawa Cherry Room). The same choice of patterned wallpaper covering all surfaces is exhibited in the ostensibly "pure Japanese" *shoin* rooms of Prince and Princess Higashi-Fushimi, where a single phoenix pattern blankets the entire interior, covering sliding panels, tokonoma walls, and wall surfaces above the lintel.[39]

Recontextualization, the third self-orientalizing aesthetic move, can be related to the long tradition of tea aesthetics prior to modern imperialism. Since the sixteenth century, teahouse design had taken elements from the farmhouse and the hermit's cottage and made them parts of a consciously rustic ritual-aesthetic environment. Masters of rustic tea transformed flax buckets and other humble "found objects" into tea utensils.[40] The Meiji tea masters liberally expanded on this inherent tendency in tea, as Christine Guth has shown. They displayed Buddhist icons, fragments of buildings, and even maps in their tokonoma, transforming them into art objects.[41]

The eclectic interiors of the imperial palace also reveal the Meiji predilection for recontextualizing native objects, in a manner less radically innovative but equally significant to contemporary taste. Examining the condition of hanging scrolls surviving in the imperial house collection, art historian Ōkuma Toshiyuki has found that many show signs of having been exposed for long periods of time. This is probably due to their having been treated like framed Western paintings, hung on the walls in large numbers and kept on semipermanent display, rather than being taken out one or two at a time and displayed for short periods in a tokonoma alcove in the manner originally intended. Traditionally mounted scrolls can be seen displayed on the papered walls of several eclectic-style rooms in the *Ladies' Graphic* as well. With a lot of new wall space to cover and the richly decorated Victorian parlor as a standard for the display of Western wealth, aristocratic collectors had considerable incentive to follow the imperial example and treat their scroll paintings as part of a permanent decorative scheme.[42]

Practically anything belonging to native tradition was available for recontextualization, yet the choices and redefinitions were never arbitrary. In contrast with the aesthetic appropriations common in pre-Meiji tea, the context in which the objects in the *Ladies' Graphic* interiors have been framed is a generalized Japaneseness, or Japanesque style, informed by Western orientalism and collecting practices. An article in the interiors issue mentions that the practice of placing bonsai indoors, unheard-of before the Meiji Restoration, had now become widespread.[43] Several of the rooms photographed confirm this. Another article endorses the practice of displaying collections of objects, citing arrangements of ancient ceramics, sword guards, toys, stuffed birds, and other items.[44] Although there were many antiquarian collectors before the Meiji period, the notion of displaying collections to decorate domestic interiors was imported from the West. Mounted on walls or exhibited in cabinets, collections of sword guards, ceramics, and other objects from Japan's past departed from their original functions and became visual diversions, like photo albums (also recommended by the writer), means to fill a visitor's time and the space of the Western room.

Historicism in the period room recontextualizes much as the collection does, turning systems of objects and architectural techniques into a style, a signifier for an imagined past. The idea of the period room also came to Japan from the West, and the Japanese period room also appeared first at the expositions. The *Ladies' Graphic* interiors issue does not include any period rooms explicitly described as such, although it does display the revivals already mentioned of furniture and motifs from the Heian and Genroku periods, and several photographs show coffered ceilings and richly decorated door panels whose use in domestic architecture suggests a return to Momoyama architecture. Chōrakukan, the Kyoto house of tobacco millionaire Murai Kichibei, completed in 1909, featured European and Chinese theme rooms designed by American James McDonald Gardiner on the first two stories, and rooms in Momoyama and Tokugawa style on the third.[45]

In a broad sense the exaggerations of size, transpositions of media, and recontextualization of objects that work together in these interiors to compose a Japanese style are all moves in the same direction, that of generalization and aggrandizement, expanding the material presence of Japanese things and motifs and extending the conceptual range of Japaneseness. There is a political substrate to these moves, which suggests the orientalist appropriation of native cultural objects to legitimate power relations, even if the power being legitimated is not explicitly power over colonial subjects. The aggrandizing character of the Meiji aesthetic construction of Japaneseness seems to parallel and reiterate the state political program of forming a universal national culture and the imperialist project of aggrandizing physical territory in the name of the Japanese nation. The correspondence here between moves in the aesthetic and political fields is homological, that is, a functional/positional relation, like the bird's wing and the human arm. The taste for oversized Japanese art and for applying Japanese decorative motifs to more and larger surfaces does not *express* Japanese imperialism; rather, it stands in the field of aesthetics as territorial expansion stands in the political field.

Filling the Frame: Commodity Ensembles Commodified

The photograph tempts us with an illusion of transparency. Interiors are the matter at hand, and here they seem to lie before us, unmediated, awaiting our entry. Yet we cannot ignore the significance of the frame. In fact, at the time that the interiors issue was published, the meanings of the bourgeois parlor and its reproduction in the graphic magazine overlapped. Both the Western-style parlor (*yōma*) and the photograph were frames for display of commodities. There are actually two points here: first, that both the parlor and the photograph were frames, and second, that these frames, in different ways, dictated forms of commodification.

The *yōma* was an assemblage of new goods arranged for display. Although this is part of the character of reception rooms generally, it was particularly evident in the Meiji *yōma*, since the mode of display was new and depended on new goods. Western-style rooms were boxes to be filled with things— walls to be decorated, floors to be covered, and empty spaces to be furnished. The *yōma* had thus to be composed, and its composition was fraught with awareness of signification. If space in *shoin* architecture was fluid, lacking fixed walls or furniture and defined by temporarily placed decoration and partitions, as well as by human incumbency itself, the Western room was, in contrast, static and bounded, a three-dimensional frame. Unlike the bourgeois parlor in Europe, which was likely to contain the sediment of more than one generation's tastes and acquisitions, these rooms were constituted *in entera*, from furniture that had been imported or custom-made following Western patterns. They also constituted an environment completely different from the houses their owners had inhabited in childhood and were, in most cases, still inhabiting for the majority of each day. Clearly, all interiors photographed for publication are to a greater or lesser extent staged. We can be fairly sure, however, that the rooms represented in the *Ladies' Graphic* are closer in kind to exposition displays and further from everyday life than their counterparts in the West. These were not and could not be places of accumulation and sedimented family history because the order of the physical environment in Meiji Japan had been altered so radically.

By photographing these interiors the *Ladies' Graphic* reframed the frame, and by selling the images to a mass public (readers who might otherwise never see the guest rooms of aristocratic mansions), the magazine created a kind of metacommodity, commodifying the ensemble of commodities selected originally for display to a narrower public of household guests. The photograph fixes the interior space, compelling the viewer to read the room from one position. This reinforces the perception of the room as a frame to be filled with display objects rather than a place defined by human incumbency. Much architectural photography, with its preference for removing human occupants and their mess and with its avoidance of movement, seeks to deny the social polysemy of inhabited space. The result is particularly transformative when the camera is turned toward *shoin* interiors, where privileging the visual works a stronger reading, as the photograph transforms the arbitrarily cropped portion of a fluid interior space into a literally empty frame. In the effort both to represent the whole space and to capture as much as possible of its contents for display, the *Ladies' Graphic* photographer chose oblique camera angles that stress depth. These interior perspectives stand in contrast to the architectural and interior renderings common among craftsmen, etiquette masters, and practitioners of tea before this time, which showed the room and its ornament in plan and elevation, thus interpreting an interior as an interlocking assemblage of articulated planes rather than as a hollow volume.[46]

Interior decorating did not exist as an independent profession in Japan at the time.[47] The *Ladies' Graphic* interiors issue represents work by men identified as "decorators" (*sōshokushi*) at what were in all likelihood the only two institutions where anyone went by such a title at the time. These were the Mitsukoshi department store (still referred to here as Mitsukoshi Drapery Store) and the imperial house. Two photographs on the last page of the graphic section show a "Reception-room in Hybrid Style" [*Wayō setchū no ōsetsushitsu*] designed by Yoshida Kōgorō, "House-Furnisher to the Imperial Household," and a reception room on Mitsukoshi's second story. The former combines elements of Japanese folk craft and a screen of ostensibly Chinese design with Western chairs and table. The Mitsukoshi reception room is high Victorian, with floral trim around the ceiling and heavy curtains with valances, but there is also a suit of Japanese armor set in front of a bright (probably gold leaf) folding screen. Imperial decorator Yoshida's eclectic style room appears humbler in both proportion and lavishness of decoration. In contrast to Mitsukoshi's thoroughly Western setting and reduction of the indigenous component to an objet d'art, Yoshida's design blends Japanese and Western motifs and objects, conspicuously employing Japanese, or Japanesque, elements to envelop and shape the entire room. The imperial household decorator is thus positioned aptly as a master of synthesis. The location of the room is unnamed, making it more a model than a specific site, and preserving the distance of the imperial house from the ordinary (fig. 6).

Despite the differences between these two model interiors, their presentation on the same page with the same treatment implies comparability. This final pair of images, one associated with the sacred precincts of the imperial house and the other with a commercial establishment lacking any claim to aristocratic status, thus seems to contradict the hierarchical ordering principle operating in the layout of the magazine as a whole. But, of course, this leveling impulse has been in operation all along. The images are presented, after all, to appeal to the readers, a task in which the drapery store can enjoy parity with the imperial household. The editors have given preeminent position to artifacts associated with the imperial house, then to

間接應店吳服三越と應接の直折洋和

Reception-room in HybridStyle and Reception-room at the Mitsukoshi Drapery Store. Upper picture: Reception-room in Japanese-European hybrid style designed by Mr. Yoshida, House-furnisher to the Imperial Household. Lower picture: Decoration in the Reception-room on the second storey of the Mitsukoshi Drapery store.

Figure 6 "Reception-room in Hybrid Style and Reception-room at the Mitsukoshi Drapery Store," *Fujin gahō*, 15 February 1906.

the possessions of imperial kin and aristocracy ranked according to title, yet this does not mean that the emperor-centered social order defined or guaranteed, de facto, an immutable hierarchy of legitimate taste. We might imagine a simple colonized order of taste, according superior status to all things Western, or a simple reactionary order, which did the reverse in order to promote "national essence." Yet the dictates of marketing will not always obey distinctions of status or national ideologies. In the end, consumer desire orders the *Ladies' Graphic*. The magazine's catchall of images for mass consumption, whether as an edifying portrait of the new social order or as a compendium of decorating ideas, implied the exchangeability of East and West as styles—representational modes rather than essences—revealing that the aesthetic dichotomy was in reality just a mask for a single regime of commodities, in which differentiation served the single purpose of enhancing potential market value.[48]

Conclusion: Japanese Interiors in the Global Exhibitionary Complex

In *Orientalism* Said focuses on a discursive relationship between colonizer and colonized in which the authority of the former is presumed to be total. Said's imperialists seem to have uncompromised control of the language of representation, allowing them to "write" everyone else into a politically determined narrative frame. Influenced by Said, studies of orientalism since have tended to focus on manifestations of the imperial order directly replicating the lines of political power between nations.

Within this paradigm of political-cultural domination, in which the cultural producers on the dominant side alone appropriate and define their object freely, the *Ladies' Graphic* interiors, as products of the non-Western periphery, are striking for their boldness. The authors of these eclectic settings redefine Japaneseness and a broadly conceived East, then juxtapose these "orientalisms" with pieces of occidental furniture and ornament in a surprising and sophisticated fusion. We need not decide whether these rooms are aesthetically successful or kitsch to recognize this. They are not products of mimicry, not subsumable in any simple sense to an aesthetic order established in Europe. There is a paradox in this: Japan entered the global cultural competition at a time when eclecticism was itself a European fashion, and bourgeois Japanese, compelled by the logic of the international order to display national distinctiveness, reinvented the native as an eclectic motif. We should not be surprised to find that they proved unusually adept at it, the self-orientalizing oriental having a certain advantage over the foreign orientalist.

Yet on the other hand, the eclectic combinations of Western, native, and Chinese objects in these rooms do not represent choices made freely. Practically all of the rooms shown have chairs and tables, which generically categorizes them as Western rooms (*yōma*) and reminds us that in practice, preemptive self-colonization underlies the aesthetic expression in Meiji "interior decorating" (the Japanese term for which was itself a translation from English). Imperialist representations of the oriental subject are not the only cultural modality in which imperialism manifests itself. In the peculiar position of the Meiji elite and in these photographs—representations of themselves to themselves—we see other levels of resonance with the global cultural condition created by imperialism, some harmonizing and some in dissonance.

As Bourdieu has stressed, the powerful do not simply generate taste while the weak submit to their choices.[49] There is a struggle over symbolic goods that corresponds to the political struggle, with the difference that claims to authority are made not only through political dominance but through the opposite—distance from politics. This is the logic by which dominant and dominated positions in the political sphere reemerge in the aesthetic. It can be seen in international politics as well in the internal struggle between social classes over the production of meaning, and it provides one explanation for the privileging of native spirit over foreign imperial might that is common to all anticolonial nationalisms. Japaneseness enjoys a special place in a domestic hierarchy of values, even though the display of wealth on the part of the most politically powerful members of the Japanese bourgeoisie occurs always at least partially through Western forms.

In an essay titled "Orientalism and the Exhibitionary Order," Timothy Mitchell proposes that the visual order of international expositions, department stores, museums, and the modern city itself had a fundamental correlation with colonial worldviews.[50] These sites constructed an "object-world," a "system of commodities, values, meanings and representations." They used verisimilitude, separation of objects from the viewing subject, and replication in plans and explanatory guides to produce an illusion of certainty, representing realities generated by imperialism "in 'objective' form." The photographic magazine had comparable capacities. Like the exhibitions Mitchell analyzes, the photographic magazine creates an object-world, implying immanence and authenticity at the same time that it establishes an unbridgeable separation from the viewing subject. It invites the gaze

with the illusion of penetrability. Photographs of interiors offer a particularly voyeuristic experience. Arranged for the camera, framed, exposed, and
reproduced, the interior passes from lived space to commodity.

But this is only to speak of the nature of a technology, without regard to the
specific social context of its exploitation. Through a coincidence of technological development (halftone printing), domestic market change (Japanese
and Chinese antiquities on the market, as well as the growth of private wealth
needed to purchase Western furniture), and military expansion (which facilitated a reimagining of Japaneseness vis-à-vis Western and Asian others,
swelled the ranks of the aristocracy, and introduced more wealth and foreign
goods into the domestic market), upper-class Japanese entered the imperial
exhibitionary order. This exhibitionary order transformed the objects it appropriated (of course, individuals were doing the actual appropriating, and
we must not allow ourselves to lose sight of them for long). Some things
were created for it (eclectic furniture and interior designs, for instance), others were physically transformed (paintings remounted to paper walls, tatami
rooms carpeted), and still others were redefined by context (hanging scrolls
removed from tokonoma alcoves, a tokonoma decorated with a miniature
replica of the Venus de Milo). In the graphic magazine the exhibitionary order fetishized new political constructions such as the imperial state and the
system of aristocratic titles through visual evocations of mystery, celebrity,
native essence, and cosmopolitan taste.

I titled this essay with a question. What if I now conclude that all of this
was *not* orientalist? Then I have taken my readers for an intellectual ride to
nowhere. Or perhaps not, because by testing the useful limits of Said's term,
we have arrived somewhere outside his paradigm for understanding cultural
production in an imperialist world. As Mitchell points out, orientalism was
part of something larger, a whole system of "new machinery for rendering
up and laying out the meaning of the world." Like a labyrinth without exits,
imperialism formed a space in which every move encountered an object
already configured within its own bounds. Once inside, Japanese found
their aesthetic choices circumscribed by their political place in the world
as Europe defined it and by politically preordered oppositions of native
and Western, traditional and modern. Clearly these aesthetic moves, in the
configuration of interiors and in their representation in print, were not all

orientalist in the sense of validating colonial conquests, but each of them may be seen performing a displacement, creating microcosms that replicated or mirrored the imperial order within domestic space.

Notes

This essay has benefited from the suggestions of Christine Guth, Gen Weisenfeld, and others who shared a lively discussion at the College Art Association in 1997, as well as Alan Tansman, Ōkuma Toshiyuki, and two anonymous readers. My thanks also to Lalitha Gopalan for asking the question that started me thinking on the subject.

1 Edward Said, *Orientalism* (New York: Pantheon, 1978).

2 For a rereading of the cultural relation between colonizer and colonized that suggests the threat of subversion lurking in the colonial subject's mimicry see Homi Bhabha, "Of Mimicry and Man: The Ambivalence of Colonial Discourse," in *Tensions of Empire: Colonial Culture in a Bourgeois World*, ed. Frederick Cooper and Ann Laura Stoler (Berkeley and Los Angeles: University of California Press, 1997), 152–160.

3 That is, within critiques of orientalism that seek to recover an autonomous subjecthood for the colonized, the danger is always present of assuming race or ethnicity as a common defining attribute, just as colonialist discourse did.

4 *Fujin gahō teiki zōkan: Shitsunai sōshoku* [Ladies's graphic periodic expanded issue: Interior decorating], 15 February 1906.

5 Ōya Sōichi, "Bundan girudo no kaitaiki" [Era of the literary establishment guild's dismantling] (1926), quoted in Maeda Ai, *Kindai dokusha no seiritsu* [Birth of the modern reader] (Tokyo: Iwanami shoten dōjidai raiburarii, 1993), 212.

6 Kawamura Kunimitsu, *Otome no inori: kindai josei imeeji no tanjō* [The prayers of virgins: Birth of the modern woman's image] (Tokyo: Kiinokuniya shoten, 1993), 25–27. Circulation figures for this period are uncertain but probably ranged between 10,000 and 100,000 per issue.

7 Tsubotani Zenshirō, *Hakubunkan gojūnenshi* [Fifty-year history of Hakubunkan publishing company] (Tokyo: Hakubunkan, 1937); John Clark, "Changes in Popular Reprographic Representation as Indices of Modernity," in *Modernism, Modernity, and the Modern: Japan in the 1920's and '30's*, ed. John Clark and Elise Tipton (Sydney and Honolulu: Australian Humanities Research Foundation and University of Hawai'i Press, 2000). The newspaper *Hōchi shinbun* provided another precedent by running pictures of aristocratic ladies (along with actresses) in its New Year's Day issue for 1904 to demonstrate the new technology that made it possible to combine print and photographs on a single page. See James L. Huffman, *Creating a Public: People and Press in Meiji Japan* (Honolulu: University of Hawai'i Press, 1997), 283.

8 Asami Masao, *Kazoku tanjō: meiyo to taimen no Meiji* [Birth of the aristocracy: Honor and face in Meiji] (Tokyo: Riburopōto, 1994), is a recent work in Japanese on the invention of Japan's modern aristocracy. For an English account, see Takie Sugiyama Lebra, *Above the Clouds: Status Culture of the Modern Japanese Nobility* (Berkeley and Los Angeles: University of California Press, 1993).

9 On the use of photography in the maintenance of social order see John Tagg, *The Burden of Representation: Essays on Photographies and Histories* (London: Macmillan, 1988), esp. chaps. 2 and 3. Jacob Riis's famous photographic exposé of New York tenement life, *How the Other Half Lives*, was first published in 1890. The camera would enter Japanese slums two decades later.

10 Taki Kōji, *Tennō no shōzō* [Portrait of the Emperor] (Tokyo: Iwanami shinsho, 1988); Takashi Fujitani, *Splendid Monarchy: Power and Pageantry in Modern Japan* (Berkeley and Los Angeles: University of California Press, 1996).

11 Referred to in the table of contents as "art paper" (*aato peepa*).

12 Slavoj Žižek proposes viewing the premodern veneration of kings as a "fetishism of interpersonal relations," in contrast to the commodity fetishism of modern capitalist society. See Žižek, *The Plague of Fantasies* (London: Verso, 1997), 100–102. In this light the charismatic cupboard might be read as a pithy expression of the hybrid nature of the Meiji imperial state. Inasmuch as the modern emperor cult sought to fetishize the relationship between Japanese subjects and their sovereign by elaborating the mystery around the imperial person, there may be some merit to reviving the view of the emperor system as evidence of an incomplete modernity. The issue of commodification is discussed further below.

13 Uchida Seizō, *Nihon no kindai jūtakū* [The modern Japanese house] (Tokyo: Kajima shuppankai, 1992), 14–19.

14 Taki argues that Shōzan was able to see the West in relativist terms because spirit and technology did not yet represent a strict dichotomy for intellectuals of his generation. See Taki, *Tennō no shōzō*, 60–61. In addition, the idea of synthesizing the imported and the native has a long cultural history in Japan. Isoda Kōichi, among others, treats the encounter with and absorption of foreign cultures as a fundamental historical pattern that has defined Japanese culture since the founding of the Nara state. See Isoda, *Rokumeikan no keifu: kindai Nihon bungei shishi* [A genealogy of the Deer-Cry Pavilion: Historical notes on modern Japanese arts and letters] (Tokyo: Bungei shunju, 1983), particularly chap. 11, "Sannin no rokumeikan enshutsusha: Shōtoku Taishi, Itō Hirobumi, Yoshida Shigeru" [Three Deer-Cry Pavilion dramaturgists: Shōtoku Taishi, Itō Hirobumi, Yoshida Shigeru].

15 Partha Chatterjee, *The Nation and Its Fragments: Colonial and Post-colonial Histories* (Princeton, N.J.: Princeton University Press, 1993).

16 This would not remain the case long for clothing, as a new white-collar class of "paupers in Western clothes" grew up in the 1910s, and traditional dress for men became a mark of leisure and wealth rather than backwardness.

17 Native decorating practice centered around the display of art objects in the *tokonoma* alcove. The schools of tea, whose influence was great in this domain, were a male preserve until they began to seek new markets through female education in the Meiji period. See Kumakura Isao, "Kindai no chanoyu" [Tea ceremony in the modern era], in *Sadō shūkin 6: Kindai no chanoyu* [Treasury of the way of tea 6: Tea ceremony in the modern era], ed. Chiga Shirō (Tokyo: Shōgakkan, 1985), 84–85.

18 Animal skins were not unheard-of before Meiji. Military men prior to Tokugawa had used exotic furs. Portuguese missionaries described Nobunaga wearing them, and Ashikaga Yoshimitsu is reported to have decorated his finest rooms with imported rugs and tiger skins. See J. Edward Kidder, *Japanese Temples: Sculpture, Paintings, Gardens, and Architecture* (Tokyo: Bijutsu shuppansha; Amsterdam: Abrams, 1964), 476. One late Meiji author describes the use of fur on tatami disapprovingly as a Westernizing fashion. See Sugimoto Buntarō, *Nihon jūtaku shitsunai sōshoku hō* [Methods for decoration of Japanese domestic interiors] (Tokyo: Kenchiku shoin, 1910), 174.

19 Stefan Tanaka, *Japan's Orient: Rendering Pasts into History* (Berkeley and Los Angeles: University of California Press, 1993).

20 Donald Keene's classic article "The Sino-Japanese War of 1894–1895 and Japanese Culture" shows how quickly popular respect for the Chinese people fell with their defeat by Japanese forces. See Keene, *Landscape and Portraits: Appreciations of Japanese Culture* (Tokyo: Kodansha, 1971), 259–299. Others have shown a decline in the position of China within the Japanese worldview in the Tokugawa period. The issue, however, is not simply respect. Tanaka's study shows the gradual and contentious development of a scholarly vision of Chinese history and culture that would serve Japanese imperialism. A mature field of *Shinagaku* emerged only with institutionalization in the 1920s. Study is still needed to explicate the museological ties linking this academically constituted orient to the collector's orient. A start has been made in this direction by critical studies of Japanese colonial archaeology and architectural history. See Hyung Il Pai, "The Search for Korea's Past: Japanese Colonial Archeology in the Korean Peninsula,"*East Asian History* 7 (June 1994): 25–48; Muramatsu Shin, "Jūgun kenchikuka no yume" [Dreams of the home-front architect], *Gendai Shisō*, July 1993.

21 Christine Guth notes that Sung paintings commanded higher prices among Meiji connoisseurs than any Japanese paintings. See Guth, *Art, Tea, and Industry: Masuda Takashi and the Mitsui Circle* (Princeton, N.J.: Princeton University Press, 1993), 133.

22 The original building was destroyed, along with much of the collection, in the Kantō earthquake. Surviving pieces were placed in a new museum on the same site built by architecture historian Itō Chūta, whose design featured explicitly Chinese- and Korean-style pavilions.

23 Okakura Kakuzō, *Ideals of the East* (1904), quoted in Tanaka, *Japan's Orient*, 13. On Okakura's vision of Japan as a museum see also Karatani Kōjin, "Japan As Museum: Okakura Tenshin and Ernest Fenollosa," in *Japanese Art after 1945: Scream against the Sky*, ed. Alexandra Munroe (New York: Abrams, 1994), 33–39. Ōkura's possession of screens associated with Hideyoshi

brings to mind this earlier era of Japanese expansionism. Momoyama interiors are also known for their scale and opulence.

24 Shimoda Utako, *Katei bunko dai 7 hen: Kaji yōketsu* [Home library volume 7: Essentials of domestic management] (Tokyo: Hakubunkan, 1899), 263, 269. In this issue of the *Ladies' Graphic*, a writer on flowers presents a similar opposition between "alluring" (*yōya naru*) Western flowers and "reserved" (*suiga naru*) bonsai. See Maeda Shozan, "Nihon shitsu no kaki" [Flowers and plants for Japanese rooms], *Fujin gahō*, 15 February 1906, 13.

25 Watanabe Wataru and Mori Hisao, "Shoki Ōkura no taigai katsudō" [Ōkura's early overseas activities], in Ōkura zaibatsu kenkyūkai hen, *Ōkura zaibatsu no kenkyū: Ōkura to tairiku* [Studies of the Ōkura conglomerate: Ōkura and the continent] (Tokyo: Kondō shuppansha, 1982), 111.

26 *Ōkura shūkokan* [The Ōkura museum of antiquities] (Tokyo 1932), 3.

27 Kobayashi Kazumi, *Giwadan sensō to Meiji kokka* [The Boxer War and the Meiji state] (Tokyo: Kyūko shoin, 1986), 356, 364, 370.

28 Tanaka Hisao, *Bijutsuhin idōshi: kindai Nihon no korekutaa tachi* [History of the movement of art pieces: Collectors in modern Japan] (Tokyo: Nihon keizai shinbunsha, 1981), 104. Meanwhile, the career of architect Itō Chūta, who designed the second Ōkura museum, was profoundly affected by the Boxer Rebellion. Itō visited China for the first time immediately following the rebellion in order to survey the interior of the Forbidden City, which had been occupied by Japan along with the European powers. This was the first time it had ever been photographed and documented.

29 A guide to antique collecting published in 1922 notes that interest in antique Chinese bronzes had grown with the publication of several studies in the late Tokugawa period but that few examples existed in Japan until the Sino-Japanese War and the Boxer Rebellion, when large numbers of bronzes and other antiquities of the Three Dynasties period came to Japan. The guide makes special reference to the collection of Sumitomo Kichizaemon. See Imaizumi Yūsaku, *Shoga kottō sōsho dai 8 kan: kottō no chishiki oyobi kantei hō* [Painting, calligraphy, and antiques library, volume 8: Knowing and appraising antiques] (Tokyo: Shoga kottō sōsho kankōkai, 1922), 135–138. Sen'oku hakkokan, a private museum in Kyoto, today houses the Sumitomo Collection. On the sources of other art collections see Satō Dōshin, "Rekishi shiryō to shite no korekushon" [Collections as historical sources], in *Kindai gasetsu* 2 (Tokyo: Meiji bijutsu gakkai, 1993), 39–51.

30 Although imperial loot formed the basis of European collections, orientalism in interior design included subtler appropriations as well. According to Susan Buck-Morss, the European orientalist interior was shifting at the turn of the century from the display of exotic objects themselves to the adoption of design motifs. Buck-Morss also points out the critical role that photographic magazines played in the global circulation of images and motifs freed from their original cultural contexts, "allowing for broad imitation by every nationality of creative

Save over 20% off the newsstand price!

☐ Please enter my one-year subscription (three issues) to *positions: east asia cultures critique* at the low subscription rate of $29.*

Subscribers outside the U.S.: Please add $11 for postage. Canadian subscribers: Please add 7% GST to the subscription rate, in addition to the outside-U.S. postage.

☐ Enclosed is my check, made payable to Duke University Press.

☐ Please bill me (no issues will be sent until payment is received).

Please charge my ☐ VISA ☐ MasterCard ☐ American Express

_____   _____
Account Number   **Expiration Date**

_____
Signature

_____
Name

_____
Address

_____
City/State/Zip   **PS011**

* Individual subscriptions only. Annual institutional rates: U.S.: $85 Non-U.S.: $96
Send your order to the Journals Fulfillment Department, Duke University Press, Box 90660,
Durham, NC 27708-0660. To place your journal order using a credit card, call toll-free 1-888-DUP-JRNL
(1-888-387-5765). http://www.duke.edu/web/dupress/

Library request for a subscription/examination copy

Please enter my one-year subscription (three issues) to *positions: east asia cultures critique*.
Libraries and institutions: $85 (Add $11 for postage outside the U.S.; Canadian libraries: Please add
7% GST to the subscription rate, in addition to the outside-U.S. postage.)

_____
Institution

_____
Address

_____
                                                                PS011

☐ Purchase order enclosed.
☐ Please bill our agent:

_____

☐ Please send a free examination copy (libraries only).

positions is printed on acid-free paper, as are all journals published by Duke University Press.

Volume 8, 2000 (3 issues); ISSN 1067-9847
Send your order to the Journals Fulfillment Department, Duke University Press, Box 90660,
Durham, NC 27708-0660. To place your journal order using a credit card, call toll-free 1-888-DUP-JRNL
(1-888-387-5765). http://www.duke.edu/web/dupress/

BUSINESS REPLY MAIL

FIRST CLASS MAIL   PERMIT NO. 1000   DURHAM, NC

POSTAGE WILL BE PAID BY ADDRESSEE

Duke University Press
Journals Fulfillment
Box 90660
Durham, NC 27706-9942

NO POSTAGE
NECESSARY
IF MAILED
IN THE
UNITED STATES

BUSINESS REPLY MAIL

FIRST CLASS MAIL   PERMIT NO. 1000   DURHAM, NC

POSTAGE WILL BE PAID BY ADDRESSEE

Duke University Press
Journals Fulfillment
Box 90660
Durham, NC 27706-9942

artists." The point is of obvious pertinence here. I would add the caveat, however, that representations dislodged from their original settings are never in fact contextless, as new meanings are applied to them in the process of circulation and appropriation. See Buck-Morss, "The City As Dreamworld and Catastrophe," *October* 73 (summer 1995): 11.

31 Guth, *Art, Tea, and Industry*, 89–90, 138.

32 A Tokyo antique dealer describes the "revolution" in the antique business brought about by "festival style" daimyo and hatamoto estate sales following the Restoration, in "Bijutsushō no kaiko" [Recollections of the art business] (1936), reprinted in *Tōkyō bijutsu shijōshi rekishi hen* [History of the Tokyo art market], ed. Segi Shin'ichi (Tōkyō bijutsu kurabu, 1979), 166–167. The impact of the Restoration specifically on the trade in tea utensils is described in detail in Takahashi Yoshio, *Kinsei dōgu idōshi* [A history of recent movements of tea utensils] (1929; facsimile ed., Tokyo: Ariake shobō, 1990), 22–105.

33 Susan Stewart, *On Longing: Narratives of the Miniature, the Gigantic, the Souvenir, the Collection* (Durham, N.C.: Duke University Press, 1993), 140.

34 Peter Trippi, "Industrial Arts and the Exhibition Ideal," in *A Grand Design: The Art of the Victoria and Albert Museum*, ed. Malcolm Baker and Brenda Richardson (New York: Harry N. Abrams with the Baltimore Museum of Art, 1997), 80.

35 Ōkuma Toshiyuki, "Meijiki Nihonga to kōshitsu oyobi kunaishō: Meiji 10 nendai–20 nendai" [Meiji period *nihonga*, the imperial house and the imperial household ministry: Meiji 10's to Meiji 20's], *Kunaichō sannomaru shōzōkan kiyō: Meiji bijutsu saiken II* [Bulletin of the Sannomaru Shōzōkan Museum of the imperial collections: Reconsidering Meiji art II], September–December 1995, 5–6. On the competing schools of painting in this period and the state's role as patron see Ellen Conant, *Nihonga: Transcending the Past* (St. Louis, Mo.: St. Louis Art Museum, 1995), 15–43.

36 Quoted in Ōkuma, "Meijiki Nihonga to kōshitsu oyobi kunaishō," 8. It is interesting to see this reference to Japanese human figures as a subject for painting, clearly reflecting the Western gaze that appears to have been of special concern in the commissioning of works for the palace.

37 The caption describes this decorated wall as "particularly renowned." It should be noted that this transposition of decorative motifs from screens and sliding panels is partly a product of larger wall areas. In an ordinary *shoin* interior there would be few fixed walls to decorate.

38 I am aware of one precedent for decorating an entire architectural plane with fan paintings. This is the famous "fan room" in the Kyoto brothel Sumiya, where decorative fans covered the ceiling. Although there may be no genealogical link between the two, it is interesting that the interior of one of the highest-ranked brothels of the Tokugawa period should show an affinity of taste with the interior of one of the highest-ranked aristocratic residences of Meiji.

39 Hayashi Kōhei, the first interior decorator at the Mitsukoshi department store, would experiment with more daring transpositions of this kind a few years later in public and residential interiors. Hayashi took motifs from decorative arts, such as lacquerware, and transferred them to walls, ceilings, carpeting, and furniture.

40 On the origins of self-consciously fabricated rustic environments in urban Kyoto and Sakai see Takahashi Yasuo, *Rakuchū rakugai: kankyō bunka no chūseishi* [In and around the capital: a history of environmental culture in the medieval period] (Tokyo: Heibonsha imeeji riidingu sōsho, 1988), 47–76; Tani Naoki, "Shoki chajin no jū kankyō: Sakai o chūshin ni" [The living environment of the early tea masters, focusing on Sakai], in *Sadō shūkin* 7 [Treasury of the way of tea, volume 7], 104–115. On "found objects," see Louise Allison Cort, *Shigaraki, Potters' Valley* (Tokyo: Kodansha International, 1979).

41 Guth, *Art, Tea, and Industry*, 100–128, 146.

42 Ōkuma, "Meijiki Nihonga to kōshitsu oyobi kunaishō," 8.

43 Maeda, "Nihon shitsu no kaki," 13. Mitsukoshi designer Hayashi Kōhei used bronze lanterns from outdoors inside a Western room.

44 Tenpōsei, "Shitsunai sōshoku yonjissoku" [Forty rules for interior decorating], 19.

45 Dallas Finn, *Meiji Revisited: The Sites of Victorian Japan* (New York: Weatherhill, 1995), 212–213.

46 Since the Western-style interior as commodity ensemble and the metacommodity of the photographed interior both have roots in a representational order first manifested in the expositions, it seems fitting to find Baron Ōtori Keisuke appearing in the *Ladies' Graphic* as an expert on interior decorating. In addition to being a politician, diplomat, and one-time principal of the Peers School for Women (the likely connection to the magazine), Ōtori had had a career-long involvement in the domestic industrial expositions. In 1901 he was chief judge for the Fifth Domestic Industrial Exposition. Addressing *Ladies' Graphic* readers, Ōtori urged displaying as great a variety of objects as possible, frequently changing the items on display, and maintaining visual harmony among them so that guests do not encounter things they have seen on earlier visits.

47 *Dōbōshū*, attendants to the Muromachi shoguns who specialized particularly in aesthetic matters, represent an earlier tradition of what might be considered professional decorators. Like Meiji decorators, they demonstrated their expertise in substantial measure by their ability to combine native with imported objects (in this case, art pieces imported from the Asian continent, known as *karamono*). See Murai Yasuhiko, "The Development of *Chanoyu*," in *Tea in Japan: Essay on the History of Chanoyu*, ed. Paul Varley and Kumakura Isao (Honolulu: University of Hawai'i Press, 1989), 17.

48 Nakatani Norihito, *Kokugaku, Meiji, kenchikuka: Kindai "Nihonkoku" kenchiku no keifu o megutte* [National studies, Meiji, architects: Concerning the genealogy of the architecture of the modern "State of Japan"] (Tokyo: Ranteisha, 1993), 38. Nakatani discusses the idea of exoticism premised on exchangeability of East and West in a uniform space.

49 See, for example, Pierre Bourdieu, "The Field of Cultural Production, or: The Economic World Reversed," in *The Field of Cultural Production*, ed. and intro. Randal Johnson (New York: Columbia University Press, 1993), 29–73.

50 Timothy Mitchell, "Orientalism and the Exhibitionary Order," in *Colonialism and Culture*, ed. Nicholas B. Dirks (Ann Arbor: University of Michigan Press, 1992), 289–318. See also Mitchell, *Colonising Egypt* (Cambridge: Cambridge University Press, 1988).

"The Sole Guardians of the Art Inheritance of Asia":
Japan and China at the 1904 St. Louis World's Fair

Carol Ann Christ

On a frigid winter night in St. Louis in 1903, a man named Blackmer sat in a deep, brocade-covered chair sipping brandy and puffing on a thick cigar in front of a crackling fire. He was an experienced exposition planner who had gained his reputation at the 1893 Chicago World's Fair, and his hosts were entrepreneurs interested in the operation of lucrative concessions at the upcoming St. Louis World's Fair. A "Chinese Concession [would be] a failure," Blackmer asserted. "People won't go. [It would be] the most *un*interesting thing I've ever seen." A Japanese concession, he explained, "would be a winner . . . because the interest of the world is centered on Japan."[1]

Blackmer was right. The Japanese had the attention of the world and earned bemused respect both on and off the St. Louis fairgrounds. They transformed their country into a military industrial power complete with an expansionist agenda and mastered the Western mode of exhibitionary

positions 8:3 © 2000 by Duke University Press

practice in the grandiose world's fairs of the imperial era. From Blackmer's point of view, compared with the Japanese the Chinese embodied what Timothy Mitchell (after Edward Said) has called the "Orientalist reality," a Western construction that continued, in 1904, to depict the Chinese as an unchanging Other defined by inadequacies. The Japanese, according to Blackmer, were "winners" because they, along with Western nations in the St. Louis Exposition in 1904, applied what Mitchell has called the "modern representational order" and effectively assigned the Chinese subordinate status in the game of colonial competition.[2]

This was an era of international arm-wrestling in which losing countries were eclipsed, and China had been losing for some time. After the Opium Wars, it endured unequal treaties with Great Britain, France, and Russia, followed by the United States. China then went on to lose first the Sino-French War and then the Sino-Japanese War. Japan emerged from this same aggressively imperialist period much stronger than China but justifiably continued a defensive posture against Western encroachment. Although Japan took possession of Formosa and other Chinese territory after the Sino-Japanese War, its victory was mitigated by the Triple Intervention, and the Japanese were threatened by the U.S. seizure of the Philippines during the Spanish-American War. In 1900, when Japanese troops entered Peking with the Western powers in response to the Boxer Rebellion, it was apparent that the Japanese sought to measure up on the Western scale. And as Blackmer gave the St. Louis fair planners a piece of his mind, Japan prepared for both the fair and a war with Russia that would be fought on Chinese soil.[3]

Beginning with an overview of the 1904 St. Louis fair, followed by a consideration of related Japanese publications produced for an English-reading audience from the same era, I will investigate the ways in which the Japanese, for self-promotion purposes, used Western methods of display, journalism, and literature to take advantage of China's vulnerability. They did this to raise their international status from defamed Oriental to respected colonial power. As the exposition forum was designed by Western imperial powers to communicate their hegemony, the Japanese saw the St. Louis fair as a way to consolidate a dominant position in the Far East. They did this by participating in a system of signification in which objects and people were arranged in exhibits to suggest a world cultural hierarchy, rendering the world readable and manageable from the colonizers' point of view.[4] I will demonstrate that the Japanese enacted this exhibitionary ordering at the St. Louis fair to promote a new, alternative reading of Japan's political position, one that assigned it the titles of imperial nation and colonial power: the protector of Chinese territory and the inheritor of Chinese culture.[5] Another powerful Western mode of establishing hegemony was what David Spurr has called the "commanding view" of "colonial discourse." In his compelling analysis Spurr has asserted that this discourse offered the "non-Western world as an object of study, an area for development, a field of action."[6] In the survey of Japanese publications I will show how the Japanese used this colonial discourse to render China a potential Japanese colony. In the second half of this essay I will focus on the St. Louis fair's fine arts exhibit to suggest that Okakura Kakuzō's description of the Japanese as the "sole guardians of the art inheritance of Asia" worked to empower Japan and foster an image of China as the definitive Oriental Other.[7]

The World's Fair as Stage

Between 1855 and 1914 a world's fair was held nearly every two years. They were grand arenas in which nations established or bolstered their status by demonstrating a strong, centralized government, industrial and economic might, military potency, and a capacity for cultural leadership—all the requisite characteristics of a colonial power of the era.[8] In size alone, the St. Louis Louisiana Purchase Exposition, usually referred to as the St. Louis World's Fair, surpassed all previous expositions. It encompassed more than twelve hundred acres, almost double the area of the 1893 Chicago fair. It was an oversized *tableau vivant* that shored up national egos with reenactments of recent triumphs, and as much as any other colonial institution, it was a product of imperialism. Powerful and combative nations commemorated their victories by elevating the act of conquering to the level of ritual on the fairgrounds. Less triumphant governments often avoided costly and embarrassing participation; neither Spain nor Russia participated.[9]

Foreign policy of this era, according to George Kennan, was conducted "histrionically, as if on a stage," and the St. Louis fair was such a stage.[10] Celebrations of the Sino-Japanese War, the Russo-Japanese War, the Boer War, the Spanish-American War and its subsequent Philippine insurrection, and the U.S. colonization of Native American lands took place on the St. Louis fairgrounds. Daily, the fair's schedule was replete with demonstrations of how easily colonial properties and people could change hands. As Mitchell has argued, these spectacles arranged people and commandeered objects "to be investigated and experienced by the dominating gaze" of the Euro-American fair visitor. As Tony Bennett has asserted, they "marked out the distinction between the subjects and the objects of power . . . as organized by the many rhetorics of imperialism." The U.S. government's Philippine exhibit, for example, sprawled over forty-seven acres of fairgrounds and included almost a hundred buildings in which seventy-five thousand arti-facts and war trophies were displayed. During the opening ceremony, the secretary of war officially transferred ownership of the exhibit to the presi-dent of the St. Louis Exposition Company while eleven hundred Filipinos were compelled to pass in review. The Philippines and the Filipinos were, as Mitchell has asserted, "reduced to a system of objects" that evoked a "larger meaning." That larger meaning was Progress, as defined by industrialized civilization, and was made apparent across the fairgrounds.[11]

Education was the official theme of the fair, and as John Willinsky has shown, colonialism had, as essential parts of its process, educational and expositional goals. Acquired territories and peoples were categorized and exhibited for study. The president of the St. Louis fair put it this way: "The exhibit of every country and of every people, classified in a manner unequaled for clear and competitive comparison, . . . testified to the advance-ment of civilization."[12] A map of the fairgrounds illustrates the certainty with which the world was ordered for the edification of visitors (fig. 1). As an excellent example of what Bennett has called a "controlling vision," the map divides diagonally into two nearly equal triangles. In the northeast quadrant (lower left of the map), the section nearest the city of St. Louis, the displays demonstrated the superiority of advanced Western civilization; it held the main entrance, nine immense exhibition palaces, state and federal buildings, and European pavilions. The southwest quadrant (upper right in the map) held livestock arenas and undeveloped sections of forest, the U.S. government's Philippine and American Indian exhibits, Japan's exhibit of the Ainu, and horticulture displays.[13]

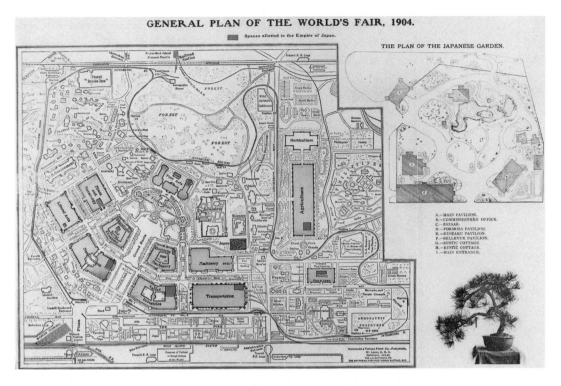

Figure 1 General plan of the St. Louis World's Fair, with plan of the Japanese garden. From Hoshi, *Handbook of Japan and Japanese Exhibits at the World's Fair, St. Louis.* Photo courtesy of the Missouri Historical Society.

In the southwest quadrant, hundreds of Native Americans lived on exhibit in traditional shelters they had constructed with their own materials. They learned "civilized" behavior in the government's Indian School while long lines of fairgoers passed through the classrooms. Their encampment was, symbolically, on the western edge of the fairgrounds, where railcars, passing through at three-minute intervals, eventually carried more than six million fairgoers through their "villages," reenacting a miniaturized version of the colonization of Native American lands. Close by, the U.S. government showed off its war trophies in its Philippine exhibit, where fairgoers enjoyed what Bennett has called "specular dominance." From the top of replicated Spanish fortifications, they purchased refreshments, rested, and looked out over "typical villages" inhabited by Filipinos brought to St. Louis for the fair.

Following Bennett's analysis, both the Native Americans and the Filipinos were used as exhibits that "historicized" the U.S. recent past and effectively turned nonwhites into "object lessons of evolutionary theory."[14] As we will see, these exhibits set the standard according to which the Japanese modeled their exhibits of Formosans and Ainu.

The ideology of imperial conquest pervaded much of the activity within the St. Louis fairgrounds, but it was especially apparent in the war concessions, where recent victories were ritualized through twice daily reenactments. In one of the largest concessions on the carnivalesque section of the grounds called the Pike, hundreds of thousands of fairgoers watched reenactments of battles from the Spanish-American and Russo-Japanese Wars. The South African Boer War Exhibit ennobled both the British and the Boers in a concession that employed six hundred veterans from the recent war. The real losers were represented by "specimens of Zulus . . . and Sambesis" who worked as laborers on the set and lent an air of authenticity to the show by inhabiting a "savage South African kraal" next to the battlefield. Although these exhibits represented complex, international political and economic issues, most fairgoers understood the message. Government-sponsored exhibits and popular entertainments reduced the issues to digestible tidbits of ideology; tens of thousands of fairgoers took their ice cream cones and hot dogs with big dollops of imperial propaganda.[15]

Publishing in English

Seeking to avoid the fate of Native Americans, Filipinos, and Africans, the Japanese positioned their country, vis-à-vis China, as the dominant colonial power in the Far East. By 1904 the Japanese were accomplished exposition participants and promoters of their state and culture, intercepting aggressive Western policies with the production of their own press and exposition propaganda. In the decade before the fair, Japanese writers published many books, journals, and articles in English for Western consumption. Nitobe Inazō published his *Bushido: The Soul of Japan* in 1901 and promoted it in the United States. By paralleling Japanese and Western traditions, he effectively portrayed Japan as the moral equivalent of the Western powers. His stated goal was the familiarization of foreign readers with Japan, and he was gratified to hear that President Theodore Roosevelt read *Bushido*. That same year, Hoshi Hajime started a monthly, bilingual journal titled *Japan and America*, in which he promoted Japan's political and economic interests to the international community. The April 1903 issue included an essay by Takahira Kogorō, Japan's minister to Washington, who diplomatically positioned Japan in the same category as the Western powers. Japan had, Takahira asserted, "the same cause to uphold in China and the same interests to protect as other civilized nations." The following year Takahira expressed Japan's determination to stop Russia from "acquiring any part of China's territory."[16]

Okakura Kakuzō published *The Ideals of the East* in 1903, the year that Japanese representatives were in St. Louis choosing the site for their pavilion. In it he proclaimed that Japan was well aware of the "portentous danger" of "Western encroachments on Asiatic soil" and delineated many measures Japan took to maintain its "national independence." The following year— the year of the fair—Okakura published *The Awakening of Japan* in English, sending a strong message with the title alone. Writing in English, Okakura proclaimed Japan's ability to participate in Western modes of communication. The publisher's preface underscored that message by pointing out that Okakura's text did not require translation.[17]

Ota Hajime, the Japanese commissioner general in St. Louis, personally handed out copies of *Japan by the Japanese* on the fairgrounds. In it, Baron Suyematsu employed a rhetorical style similar to that of European colonial administrators, who, Spurr argues, "saw the natural resources of colonized lands as belonging rightfully to 'civilization' and 'mankind.' " Suyematsu asserted that Japan's goals in the Russo-Japanese War were "in the interests of the whole civilized world."[18] The target audience for these publications was mainly American and British readers who were, Hoshi assumed, interested in "trade and political relations" with Japan, the sort that took place between equal colonial powers, not between an imperial power and a subjugated colony. One year prior to the opening of the fair, Hoshi predicted that Japan and the United States would share "the commercial and political domination of the Pacific."[19] These books, journals, and articles also promoted a politically expansionist style, called ethical imperialism by some, with which the Japanese dramatized their position and justified their military actions.

Hoshi once metaphorically threw his hands in the air: "What is [Japan] to do; what part is she to play; what role is to be hers in the great world drama that continues, unendingly, like a Chinese play, in the Far East?"[20]

Japanese publications during the era of the St. Louis fair advanced Japan's political and economic status in many ways, but for this essay two Japanese-produced images of China are most pertinent: (1) Chinese territory and people in need of Japan's protection against encroaching Western colonialism and (2) Chinese cultural traditions in need of Japanese conservation. Both of these assertions shored up Japan's claim to modern nation status, as the first necessitated a strong Japanese military, and the second advanced Japan as the conservator of China's (and by extension Asia's) ancient cultural heritage.

Nation-State and Colonizer

Modern nation status was a crucial first step to solid footing as a colonial power and the only course that Japan saw to political independence from the Western powers. E. J. Hobsbawm has persuasively argued that there were essentially five prerequisites for nation status. By 1904 Japan had achieved three: a centralized government, industrialization, and a shared economy. It still needed to demonstrate the depth and strength of its cultural heritage as well as its ability to conquer. Using China, Japan attained these final requirements for nationhood; it positioned itself as the inheritor of Chinese as well as Indian culture and proved its capacity for conquest on Chinese soil in the Sino-Japanese and Russo-Japanese Wars.[21]

Fred Notehelfer has noted that for the Japanese, "westernization was a deadly serious business." It was indeed crucial for Japan at this time to attain an autonomous position. A striking 1904 article from the U.S. journal *The Nation* illustrates the situation well; it satirized Japan's position by calling the Japanese "upstarts" who played "a game only white nations could play." The seizure of Japanese ports, this article scoffed, "was scheduled to occur without more serious resistance than the banging of gongs." Standing up against this sort of derision, Imperial Japanese Commissioner Tejima Seiichi spoke at the dedication ceremonies in St. Louis and forcefully asserted Japan's position. He proclaimed that with its participation in the fair, Japan demonstrated its place among the "powers of the world."[22]

From the group of Japanese authors mentioned above, at least three were present on the St. Louis fairgrounds: Takahira Kogorō, Okakura Kakuzō, and Hoshi Hajime (fig. 2). All of them pictured China in ways that supported Japan's claim to modern nation status. Okakura gave a lecture in the St. Louis fair's Congress of Arts and Sciences, and Hoshi published a bilingual newspaper on the fairgrounds and wrote the *Handbook of Japan and Japanese Exhibits at the World's Fair*.[23] Their views exemplified those of other Japanese writers publishing in English during the era; they championed Japanese nationalism as they depicted a broken and dependent China. In *Awakening of Japan* Okakura proclaimed that Japan stood "alone against the world" without "the benefit of a living art in China." In *Ideals of the East* he called Japan a "museum of Asiatic civilization" where "Chinese and Indian ideals" were preserved because "they were long since cast away by the hands that created them." In *Book of Tea*, published the year following the St. Louis fair, Okakura described the Chinese as "old and disenchanted." Hoshi had put the West on notice several years earlier by depicting Japan in a paternalistic stance, a common posture for colonial powers: "The nations of the West shall not be allowed to transform the soul of [the Chinese] people, no matter how much they may hack and cut at their flesh."[24]

Japanese actions during the St. Louis fair confirm that statements such as Okakura's and Hoshi's, which portrayed China as needing Japanese protection and cultural conservation, were skillful political rationalizations intended to help capture the titles of modern nation and colonial power while the time was right. The Western press was abasing China as a vulnerable, unwieldy conglomerate ripe for exploitation and heroizing Japan for its ability to engage in modern warfare. At the fair, then, the Japanese joined the West in denigrating China as they enjoyed the prestige it had won at China's expense. Okakura acknowledged Japanese awareness of the situation. He wrote that a greater admiration for Japanese "customs and art has been manifested since our victory over China ten years ago. We hope that our success over a stronger adversary than China [Russia] will give us a still deeper self-confidence."[25]

Figure 2 Professor Okakura Kakuzō of the Fine
Arts Museum, Boston, with Professor Hugo
Munsterberg of Harvard University at the St. Louis
World's Fair. From Bennitt, *History of the Louisiana
Purchase Exposition*. Photo courtesy of the Missouri
Historical Society.

Japanese exhibits and representatives in St. Louis disregarded China's
culture and focused on the conquest of Formosa and the ongoing conflict
with Russia on Chinese territory. When Prince Fushimi arrived on the fairgrounds, it was obvious that he had been sent as the embodiment of Japanese
military prowess. He was welcomed as a victorious warrior and was escorted
by a "platoon of U.S. cavalry." The *World's Fair Bulletin* pronounced him the
hero of one of the "bloodiest battles" of the Russo-Japanese War and ran a
photograph of him in his uniform covered with medals (fig. 3). Fushimi embodied what one official history of the fair called the "energetic little Yankees
of the Orient."[26] He was treated to a special performance of the Boer War, an
event meant to glorify Japanese military prowess. As the Boer War exhibit
paid homage to both the British and the Boers while denigrating Africans,

Figure 3 Prince Fushimi at a reception held by the Board of Lady Managers at the St. Louis World's Fair. Photo: Jessie Tarbox Beals. Courtesy of the Missouri Historical Society, Department of Photographs and Prints.

it operated on the fairgrounds as a metaphor for the Russo-Japanese War. Inviting Fushimi for a special performance acknowledged that he, like the Americans, British, Boers, and Russians, was a fellow colonizing warrior, unlike the weaker Native Americans, Filipinos, Africans, and Chinese.[27]

In some ways the Russo-Japanese War was fought on the fairgrounds. In the months leading up to the fair and the war, fair representatives working in St. Petersburg were frustrated because the Russians refused to commit to

JAPAN ASKS FOR
RUSSiAN SPACE
GO   2-17-1904

WORLD'S FAIR PROPOSAL

Czar's Abandonment of Official
Display Gives the Mikado
an Opportunity.

COMMISSIONER OTA'S REQUEST.

WOULD TAKE OVER EVERY FOOT
OF SPACE SURRENDERED BY
COMMISSIONER GENERAL
ALEXANDROVSKY.

Figure 4 Article headline from the *St. Louis Globe-Democrat*, 17 February 1904. Photo courtesy of the Missouri Historical Society.

participation. When the Russians decided, belatedly, not to send an official delegation, the Japanese took advantage of the situation by commandeering over forty-four thousand square feet of exhibition space previously assigned to Russia. Local newspapers congratulated Japan and explained Russia's late withdrawal as a reaction to U.S. support of Japan (fig. 4). As the Japanese fought Russians with modern weapons in Manchuria, they used the St. Louis fair as a platform from which to convince the international community of the righteousness of their position. As the first rising colonial power in the East, they claimed the right to challenge Russia on Chinese territory. On the St. Louis fairgrounds, they passed out buttons inviting fairgoers to the Japanese restaurant to celebrate their latest victory in the Russo-Japanese War (fig. 5).[28]

In many of their exhibits the Japanese aligned themselves with imperialist Americans, and the Formosans with colonized Filipinos. One exhibit labeled "The Japanese Empire" included a "walk around" map almost

Figure 5 Button passed out at the fair, reading, "Celebrate Japanese Victory at the Fair Japan Restaurant on the Pike. Victory to the Japanese Army and Navy." Photo: David Schultz. Courtesy of the Missouri Historical Society.

identical to one in the U.S. government's Philippine exhibit. Fairgoers held on to velvet-covered ropes on an elevated walkway while looking down on a very large topographical map (fig. 6), enacting Spurr's commanding view and Bennett's specular dominance. This kind of view, Spurr argues, is "an originating gesture of colonization itself" because it makes exploration possible, "which serves as the preliminary to a colonial order."[29] In this Japanese exhibit a distinct comparison was made between Japanese and Chinese use of resources. Exhibit labels asserted that the Japanese were "intelligently" exploiting Formosan resources that the Chinese had failed to recognize. In his journal Hoshi asserted that "like the Americans in the Philippines, the Japanese in Formosa" were "developing" their colony. The labeling of Formosans as "savages" and of Formosa as "unsurveyed land" suggested that the Chinese were irresponsible and uncivilized because they did not educate their people or inventory their territory. This exhibit also asserted that unlike China, Japan educated its Formosans, as the United States educated its Indians. These exhibits illustrated what Hoshi had declared in a recent book: Japan, like the United States, was engaged in the "civilization and uplifting of inferior races." Hoshi's journal and the Japanese exhibits in St. Louis utilized a fundamental principle of colonialism identified by Spurr in

Figure 6 Relief map of the Empire of Japan in Japan's transportation exhibit at the St. Louis World's Fair. Photo: Official Photographic Company, 1904. Courtesy of the Missouri Historical Society, Department of Photographs and Prints.

which "a colonized people is morally improved and edified by virtue of its participation in the colonial system." Next to Japan's map of Formosa another relief map depicted the Korean and Chinese coasts. When a reporter asked a Japanese attendant why Manchuria was not represented, he was told to "wait a little, the war is not over."[30]

In another exhibit close to the U.S. Philippine and Native American displays, the Japanese emulated the United States by collaborating with a U.S. anthropologist to exhibit Ainu people at the fair. "Eight good specimens" were chosen from the Isle of Ezo, modern Hokkaido. Fair propaganda set the modern Japanese in high relief against an Ainu backdrop of primitivity. A typically racist fair publication distinguished the Japanese from the Ainu, who were considered "simple barbarians . . . listed with the races" incapable of "civilization" (fig. 7). A frontispiece from an official fair publication illustrated that the Japanese were considered three levels above the Chinese and seven above the Ainu on the evolutionary ladder (fig. 8).[31] This illustration, touted to be as accurate as "the science of ethnology" allowed, delineated the types of mankind "in a progressive order of development from primitive or prehistoric man to the highest example of civilization." Classification of this sort, Spurr argues, was inherent to the colonial rationale, as the categorization of peoples legitimized the colonial venture. Although the Japanese held the third highest place in this illustration, after the Russians and the "Americo-Europeans" they were represented as a woman, in direct contrast to the male features of all the other "types." The feminization of Japan was a feature of Orientalism. One commentator had recently written that the Japanese seemed "ill fitted for the competition" they had entered, because "an army of Japanese" was to "an army of Europeans . . . what an army of females in the Occident would be to an army of males." In the St. Louis illustration, however, the feminization of the Japanese may have worked to sanction their position in the Far East. Although the illustration shows a woman in traditional Japanese clothing and hairstyle, her facial features are very similar to those of the allegorical figure who holds the "torch of Enlightenment" and the "book of Wisdom."[32]

Japan and China at World Expositions

Japan and China had widely differing levels of experience in international expositions. But as Blackmer and almost every interested and literate world citizen knew, the St. Louis World's Fair was a new experience for both countries. Japan, for the first time, would be acknowledged as a colonial military power, and for the first time there would be official Chinese dignitaries present on the fairgrounds.

By 1904 the Japanese Exhibit Association, chartered by the imperial government, was well organized and effective. The first truly international fair was the Crystal Palace Exhibition in London in 1851. Paris reciprocated in 1855, and London staged another in 1862. There were no government-sanctioned Japanese exhibits at these fairs because Tokugawa rulers did not want to expose their art to "foreign influences and interests." In 1867,

Figure 7 Ainu house and people in the anthropology exhibit at the St. Louis World's Fair. Photo: Jessie Tarbox Beals. Courtesy of the Missouri Historical Society, Department of Photographs and Prints.

however, Japan sent "a fine collection" of decorative arts to the Paris fair. This was due, according to Rutherford Alcock, to "political changes" giving "a new turn" to Japanese foreign policy—changes that surely led to the 1868 Meiji Restoration. The Vienna Exposition of 1873 marked the beginning of a more aggressive style of participation with which the Japanese announced their capabilities. The Meiji government spent three years planning the exhibit and another year choosing materials. From 1873 forward, Japanese governmental agencies staged exhibits in most international fairs.[33]

The competition was stiff, especially for those countries with something to prove in the international political arena. Japan, in the process of renegotiating unequal treaties, shipped more freight into Philadelphia in 1876 than any other country, with the exception of Great Britain, and prominently represented itself in Paris in 1878. In New Orleans in 1885 Hattori Ichizo,

Figure 8 "Types and Development of Man," chromolithography by World's Progress Publishing Co., 1904. Frontispiece illustration from vol. 5 of Buel, *Louisiana and the Fair*. Photo courtesy of the Missouri Historical Society.

Figure 9 Japanese grounds and buildings on the fairgrounds. Including all Japanese space in the fair's exhibition palaces, Japan's exhibits covered almost seven acres in St. Louis. From *The Greatest of Expositions* (St. Louis, Mo.: Official Photographic Company of the Louisiana Purchase Exposition, 1904). Photo courtesy of the Missouri Historical Society.

head of Japan's education exhibit, told a local reporter that the Japanese would soon be acknowledged "as equals."[34] Japan shipped five times more freight to Chicago in 1893 than it had to Philadelphia, repeatedly requested more exhibition space at the Paris Exposition of 1900, and was the first country to send a delegation to choose a pavilion site in St. Louis. Japan's exhibits in St. Louis covered three times the area of those in Paris in 1900 and five times those in Chicago eleven years earlier (fig. 9).[35]

Chinese objects considered valuable or collectible found their way to twenty-seven international expositions beginning with Vienna in 1873. The Chinese, however, had little to do with the exhibits. Sir Robert Hart, the inspector general of Chinese Maritime Customs for almost fifty years, organized the exhibits with the help of his staff. He had considerable power; China surrendered control of its customs system to Great Britain after it lost the Opium Wars, and it did not have the powerful, centralized government needed for self-representation in St. Louis. China did however send a member of its royal family to St. Louis in 1904, along with Chinese government dignitaries, making that fair the first attended by a Chinese royal. Hart probably encouraged their attendance; he had worked for modernization in China from the beginning of his tenure, supporting the formation of the Chinese navy in the 1880s and developing the national postal service in 1896. The empress dowager herself, always a staunch opponent of modernization, began to authorize many reforms beginning in 1902, the year of her return to Beijing after fleeing the city during the allied response to the Boxer Rebellion, which she had supported. Seeking to preserve the dynasty while mollifying both the international community and reform-minded Chinese, it is most likely that she handpicked the Chinese delegation sent to St. Louis.[36]

Although they were not part of the exhibit planning and had virtually no control over exhibits, Prince Pu Lun and his impressive group of Chinese dignitaries made it difficult for anyone to denigrate the Chinese on the fairgrounds (fig. 10).[37] Wong Kai Kah, the Chinese imperial vice-commissioner in St. Louis, spoke at the dedication ceremony of the Chinese pavilion and proclaimed, akin to Japan's Tejima, that China would "march in company with other powers" to honor the United States. A graduate of Yale, Wong Kai Kah moved to St. Louis with his wife and children for the run of the fair. He hosted many receptions and gave well-attended lectures on Chinese culture (fig. 11). There is evidence that the Japanese were unsettled by China's participation. As the fair's official agent to the Far East, John Barrett had spent a significant amount of time in China. He was welcomed by the emperor and empress dowager, who agreed to send a delegation to the fair. Not much later, Barrett was described in Hoshi's journal as lacking "dignity," "courtesy," and "tact" and was refused by Japanese officials when he was nominated to the post of U.S. minister to Japan.[38]

The Fine Arts Exhibit

There is evidence from almost every corner of the fairgrounds that the Japanese took a colonizer's stance toward China at the St. Louis World's

Figure 10 Prince Pu Lun and other Chinese dignitaries with David R. Francis, president of the fair, 4 May 1904. Photo: Jessie Tarbox Beals. Courtesy of the Missouri Historical Society, Department of Photographs and Prints.

Fair. The fine arts exhibit, however, offers a good case study. Japanese authors had been claiming for years that Japan was the most likely conservator of Chinese art. As several Japanese representatives had a considerable degree of influence with the chief of fine arts in St. Louis, they were in a position to support rhetoric with action and to intervene, on the highly visible stage of a world's fair, on behalf of Chinese art.

What, "other than armies," Hobsbawm has argued, "could express that elusive concept of the nation better than the symbols of art?" China had never been represented in the fine arts palace of a world's fair, and Japan had been invited into only one, the 1893 Chicago World's Columbian Exposition. In the ongoing delineation of exhibit categories in world expositions, art had become increasingly important, so much so that David R. Francis, president of the St. Louis fair, considered the buildings on top of St. Louis's "Art Hill"

Figure 11 Chinese Imperial Vice-Commissioner Wong Kai Kah with his wife and exposition dignitaries at a reception held in St. Louis for the empress dowager's seventieth birthday. Photo courtesy of the Missouri Historical Society, Department of Photographs and Prints.

the "apex, physically and ethically, of the Exposition." Indeed, without the arts the expositions would have been nothing, according to Paul Greenhalgh, but mere "trade fairs."[39]

Halsey C. Ives was the chief of the Department of Art for the St. Louis fair. His fine arts palace, now the St. Louis Art Museum, was one of the few permanent structures erected on the fairgrounds (figs. 12 and 13). His exhibit was both a product and a producer of nationalist ideology. To raise its prestige, he worked to allocate every square foot of space to an industrial military nation. If a fine art tradition was without the protection of such a nation, he disregarded it.[40] Ives made significant changes to the exhibit classifications, allowing the display of "applied art." Previously, applied art had been assigned to industrial or liberal arts buildings. In fine art palaces,

Figure 12 Portrait of Professor Halsey C. Ives, Chief of the Fine Arts Department, Louisiana Purchase Exposition. From Bennitt, *History of the Louisiana Purchase Exposition*. Photo courtesy of the Missouri Historical Society.

objects took on symbolic meaning, representing cultural refinement and national uniqueness. In industrial or liberal art buildings, displayed objects were approached by fairgoers as merchandise. Shugio Hiromichi (fig. 14), the Japanese commissioner of fine arts, had been a personal friend of Ives for a long time; they had probably met at the Chicago fair in 1893, for which Ives had also been art chief. In his letters to Shugio, Ives intimated that he made the changes to accommodate the Japanese. "You will find," he wrote, "that I have had in mind the work of the Japanese artists in forming the classification . . . [and] in designing the building."[41]

Figure 13 The Fine Arts Palace at the St. Louis World's Fair. From *The Greatest of Expositions* (St. Louis, Mo.: Official Photographic Company of the Louisiana Purchase Exposition, 1904). Photo courtesy of the Missouri Historical Society.

Japan's newly earned status as imperialist nation ensured its entry into St. Louis's fine arts palace. The bureaucrats and businessmen who made up the Japanese Commission corresponded with Ives for more than two years prior to the fair. They constantly requested more gallery space and held a juried event in Tokyo to choose the works to be sent to St. Louis. Shugio sent Ives a proposed gallery plan many months in advance and ended up with seven spacious galleries on which he spent an unusually large amount of money and attention, sending Japanese artists to St. Louis to paint friezes directly on the walls (fig. 15). The representative value of fine art was so high that Japan included an artist's studio in its pavilion, a feature that no other nation offered. In addition to many other publications about their exhibits,

Figure 14 Portrait of Shugio Hiromichi, Japanese
Resident Commissioner at the St. Louis World's Fair.
From Bennitt, *History of the Louisiana Purchase
Exposition.* Photo courtesy of the Missouri Historical
Society.

the Japanese produced an elaborate fine arts catalog complete with artists'
names and a full array of photographs.[42]

Ives considered himself a strong admirer of Japanese art. In letters to
Shugio before the fair, he was adamant that Japan send art "uncontam-
inated by Western influences." He would have been open to a Japanese
exhibit that illustrated the forwarding of Chinese traditions by Japanese
artists, and he almost certainly would have approved had Shugio suggested it. Shugio's influence was so strong that when an art jury awarded
medals to five Japanese artists, he arranged, through Ives, to have the awards
changed. The inclusion of a Japanese section that looked back to Chinese
origins would have been especially appropriate in 1904, when the U.S. art
exhibit itself bore witness to its roots: Old World traditions. In fact, an
official publication noted that the art of the United States had a "European
transfusion."[43]

JAPANESE SECTION—PALACE OF FINE ARTS.

Figure 15 A gallery in the Japanese section, Department of Fine Arts, St. Louis World's Fair. From *The Exhibition of the Empire of Japan Official Catalogue* (St. Louis, Mo.: International Exposition Co., 1904). Photo courtesy of the Missouri Historical Society.

The Japanese, however, could not risk illustrating their deep aesthetic connections to China in their St. Louis fine arts exhibit. In that arena at that time it was more prudent to appear, in the colonial sense, the conservators of Chinese art, not the beneficiaries. "Exhibitions," Bennett has argued "made the order of things dynamic, mobilizing it strategically in relation to the more immediate ideological and political exigencies of the particular moment." With Chinese representatives on the fairgrounds and Japanese troops fighting Russian soldiers in Manchuria, it was imperative that the Japanese maintain an imperial superiority over the Chinese in St. Louis. They were successful. One authoritative catalog proclaimed that the "Japanese may have imitated Chinese art in the beginning, but in skill, taste and technique they have left the Chinese far behind."[44]

To the disappointment of Ives and the critics, the Japanese included, in addition to their six galleries of traditional art, an entire gallery of works done in Western style.[45] In the politically charged context of the fine arts palace the Japanese chose to demonstrate their mastery of Western styles as they were demonstrating their ability to master Western technology, warfare, and colonial practices in other sections of the fair. Exhibiting Western-style paintings served the Japanese in two ways. It overturned the West's commanding view of Japanese art by enacting a temporary reversal of the colonial norm; Western art became an object of study by the Japanese. It also worked to discourage the Orientalist assumptions of Ives and the critics. In order "to represent something as Oriental," Mitchell wrote, "one sought to excise the European presence altogether." By including that presence the Japanese circumvented the Orientalizing tactics of the exposition organizers.[46]

There is no evidence that Robert Hart sought space in the fine arts palace for a Chinese exhibit. In fact, it appears that China, as represented by Hart's bureaucracy, disregarded the exhibitionary order as it had evolved by 1904. As we have seen, much of the activity at the fair falls into line with Mitchell's assessment of that order. The Chinese exhibits, however, do not. They were not arranged by the official fair categories of media and technique but, rather, by their place of origin, usually a large city, treaty port, or province in China. Chinese fine arts, then, were scattered throughout the fairgrounds. The Chinese catalog, without illustrations, was also arranged in this manner. The subcategories after location were manufacturers, dealers, or collectors. While this arrangement did not merge with the fair's order, it promoted the lucrative Chinese trade by making it easy for fairgoing businessmen to place orders.[47]

Mitchell's analysis calls for a "plan or program that supplies reality with its historical and cultural order." Since the Chinese exhibits did not do this, they left many visitors, like Edward Schneiderhahan, bewildered. He recorded that he "cared little for the China section" because "somehow it always impressed you as topsy-turvydom." Schneiderhahan's description sounds much like the effect of the "external reality" described by Mitchell, which was created by expositions and resembled "the Orientalist portrayal of the Orient," a place of "meaninglessness and disorder." The Chinese exhibits in St. Louis did not, like other exhibits, create this effect, an order against which China itself appeared disorderly. Instead they created an entrepreneurial framework to bring sorely needed capital into Chinese coffers seriously depleted by the Boxer Protocol.[48] It appears, then, that the Chinese, like the Japanese, found ways to benefit from the St. Louis exposition.

Figure 16 China's pavilion at the St. Louis World's Fair. Photo courtesy of the Missouri Historical Society, Department of Photographs and Prints.

While the Chinese most certainly profited financially from connections made in St. Louis, they appeared less than proficient at fine art conservation and display. This was apparent when China's pavilion was awarded a gold medal and Hart's representatives were either unable or unwilling to produce the architect's name; he remained anonymous. The pavilion contained exhibits of carvings, hangings, screens, paintings, and porcelains (fig. 16). In the last hours before the opening of the fine arts palace, Ives decided that there was no room for Chinese works. All art gleaned from the collections of Chinese viceroys, including paintings and ancient bronzes, was reclassified as applied art, moved to the liberal arts building, and temporarily excluded from the official fine arts catalog (figs. 17 and 18).[49] Francis Carl, a cousin of Robert Hart, headed the Chinese Commission in St. Louis. Carl did not protest the exclusion of Chinese art from the Fine Arts Palace. When space was later found, Ives had to request the reinstallation several times, which

Figure 17 Chinese art as part of exhibit in the Liberal Arts Palace at the St. Louis World's Fair. From Bennitt, *History of the Louisiana Purchase Exposition*. Photo courtesy of the Missouri Historical Society.

was done so poorly that he issued a reprimand asking that the works be placed "fully exposed" in their cases. Although the Chinese almost certainly sent a spectacular array of ancient as well as contemporary works, the only representative piece that remained in the fine arts exhibit was produced by an American. It was a portrait of the empress dowager painted by Kate Carl, another of Robert Hart's cousins. The portrait, like the atypical exhibit arrangement, may have worked to the benefit of the Chinese because it portrayed the empress, who just four years earlier had declared war on the Allied powers during the Boxer Rebellion, as accessible and perhaps a bit less imperious.[50]

Figure 18 Chinese art as part of exhibit in the Liberal Arts Palace at the St. Louis World's Fair. From Bennitt, *History of the Louisiana Purchase Exposition.* Photo courtesy of the Missouri Historical Society.

Conclusion

At the St. Louis fair, Okakura, Hoshi, other Japanese authors, and government representatives were struggling with the uncertainties of Meiji politics and the fear of Western domination. With colonial and exhibitionary language, they used Chinese art and territory to achieve the last two prerequisites for nation status: conservation of an ancient cultural heritage and a capacity for conquest. The colonizer, Spurr writes, "speaks as an inheritor," and his calculated proprietary stance hides his appropriative conduct; he claims that the colonized land and people cry out for help. Okakura used just this sort of colonialist rhetoric to promote Japanese nationalism at the St. Louis fair. Speaking in the Congress of Arts and Sciences, he proclaimed that the Japanese were making "heroic sacrifices" in the Russo-Japanese War. "A grim pride," he asserted, helped the Japanese face the "enormous odds" raised against them. The Japanese, he proclaimed, saw themselves as "the sole guardians of the art inheritance of Asia," and he phrased the role in military terms: "The battle must be one fought out to the last." Okakura's strong rhetoric was necessary. Henri

Cordier, a professor of Asian languages and history, also spoke, and he brought forward a fourth-century Chinese painting by Ku K'ai-che (Gu Kaishi). Cordier made it clear that he and Okakura could agree about Chinese art needing a guardian, but they could not agree that it would be Japan. He announced that the painting had been "happily discovered and rescued at Peking during the events of 1900, and now kept safely in the British Museum, forever we hope."[51] The St. Louis World's Fair, a forum replete with exhibits and entertainments celebrating imperialism and colonialism, was a made-to-order arena for Okakura and his fellow Japanese to counter the prevailing Orientalist attitude championed, in this case, by Cordier. Okakura's aggressive colonialist speech was delivered in the language of the fairgrounds, and the Japanese had learned to speak it fluently.[52] In St. Louis they used it to claim a dominant position in the Far East.

Notes

My sincere thanks to Julie Yuan, Robert Thorp, Karen Brock, Elizabeth Childs, Angela Miller, Christine Guth, and Gennifer Weisenfeld for their support and helpful criticisms.

1   Based on the economic and social status of the planners of the St. Louis fair, I have imaginatively reconstructed the context of Blackmer's interview where concession rights were discussed. Only concessions with an excellent chance of making a large profit were granted licenses. The Japanese Village for example, grossed almost $206,000 and paid the St. Louis Exposition Company a $27,000 fee. The transcript of this 10 December 1903 conversation is in box 13, folder 2, Louisiana Purchase Exposition Papers, Missouri Historical Society Archives, St. Louis.

2   Edward Said, *Orientalism* (New York: Pantheon, 1978); Timothy Mitchell, "Orientalism and the Exhibitionary Order," in *Colonialism and Culture*, ed. Nicholas B. Dirks (Ann Arbor: University of Michigan Press, 1992), 289, 290.

3   A good source for the contemporary Japanese view of these events is in Baron Suyematsu, "The Problem of the Far East," in *Japan by the Japanese, a Survey by Its Highest Authorities*, ed. Alfred Stead (New York: Dodd, Mead, 1904), 573–580. Takahira Kōgorō, the Japanese minister to the United States, politely explained why Japan was threatened by the U.S. takeover of the Philippines. See Takahira Kōgorō, "The Position of Japan in the Far East," *Japan and America* 3, no. 4 (April 1903): 21–26.

4   Mitchell, "Orientalism and the Exhibitionary Order," 295.

5   The Japanese began to acquire Western exhibitionary skills in the late 1860s. For a study of the Japanese participation in international fairs in the United States see Neil Harris, "All the World a Melting Pot? Japan at American Fairs, 1876–1904," in *Mutual Images: Essays in American-Japanese Relations*, ed. Akira Iriye (Cambridge, Mass.: Harvard University Press, 1975), 24–54. For Japan's participation in international expositions see Ellen P. Conant, "Refractions of the Rising Sun: Japan's Participation in International Exhibitions, 1862–1910," in *Japan and Britain: An Aesthetic Dialogue, 1850–1930*, ed. Tomoko Sato and Toshio Watanabe (London: Lund Humphries, 1991).

6   David Spurr, *The Rhetoric of Empire: Colonial Discourse in Journalism, Travel Writing, and Imperial Administration* (Durham, N.C.: Duke University Press, 1996), 26.

7   A transcript of Okakura's speech can be found in Howard J. Rogers, ed., *Congress of Arts and Science: Universal Exposition, St. Louis, 1904*, 8 vols. (Boston: Houghton, Mifflin, 1906), 4:663–676.

8   For excellent coverage of the development of world's fairs see Paul Greenhalgh, *Ephemeral Vistas: The Expositions Universelles, Great Exhibitions, and World's Fairs, 1851–1939* (Manchester: Manchester University Press, 1988).

9   Spain had lost the Spanish-American War in 1898, and Russia was well on its way to losing the Russo-Japanese War.

10   George F. Kennan, "Arbitration and Conciliation in American Diplomacy," *Arbitration Journal* 26 (1971): 29.

11   Mitchell, "Orientalism and the Exhibitionary Order," 293–295; Tony Bennett, "The Exhibitionary Complex," *New Formations* 4 (spring 1988): 80. For an excellent study of the U.S. government's Philippine exhibit in St. Louis see Robert Rydell, "The Louisiana Purchase Exposition, St. Louis, 1904: The Coronation of Civilization," in *All the World's a Fair: Visions of Empire at American International Expositions, 1876–1916* (Chicago: University of Chicago Press, 1984).

12   See John Willinsky, *Learning to Divide the World: Education at Empire's End* (Minneapolis: University of Minnesota Press, 1988); David R. Francis, *The Universal Exposition of 1904* (St. Louis, Mo.: Louisiana Purchase Exposition Co., 1913), vi.

13   Bennett, "Exhibitionary Complex," 79. This fairgrounds map was distributed by the Japanese. It highlights the locations of all Japanese exhibits. The United States, Germany, and Great Britain also "personalized" their maps.

14   Ibid., 79, 89, 96. For an analysis of how the U.S. government used its Philippine exhibition to rationalize its imperialist/militarist behavior in the Philippines see Sharra L. Vostral, "Imperialism on Display: The Philippine Exhibition at the 1904 World's Fair," *Gateway Heritage*, spring 1993, 18–31.

15   T. R. MacMechen, "Battleships in Action: A World's Fair Feature," *Syracuse Herald*, 20 March 1904. Out of gross receipts of $631,776, the Boer War concession paid St. Louis organizers $112,943. See J. W. Buel, ed., *Louisiana and the Fair: An Exposition of the World, Its People,*

and Their Achievements, 10 vols. (St. Louis, Mo.: World's Progress Pub. Co., 1904), 10:3830–3834. Not all of the propaganda was for popular consumption; international conferences on the fairgrounds provided prestigious platforms from which scholars and officials analyzed contemporary issues and rationalized aggressive imperialist behavior. See Rogers, *Congress of Arts and Science*. It is not true that ice cream cones and hot dogs were sold for the first time at the St. Louis World's Fair.

16 Nitobe Inazō, *Bushido: The Soul of Japan*, rev. and enl. ed. (New York: G. P. Putnam's Sons, 1905), v–xi; Takahira Kōgorō, "The Position of Japan in The Far East," *Japan and America* 3, no. 7 (April 1903): 21–26; Takahira, "What Japan Is Fighting For," *World's Work*, April 1904, 4620–4627.

17 Okakura Kakuzō, *The Ideals of the East with Special Reference to the Art of Japan* (London: John Murray, 1903), reprinted in *Okakura Kakuzō: Collected English Writings*, ed. Sunao Nakamura (Tokyo: Heibonsha, 1984), 117; Okakura Kakuzō, *The Awakening of Japan* (New York: Century, 1904).

18 Alfred Stead, ed., *Japan by the Japanese: A Survey by Its Highest Authorities* (New York: Dodd, Mead, 1904), 580; Spurr, *Rhetoric of Empire*, 28. Okakura Yoshisabura, Kakuzō's brother, published *The Japanese Spirit* (London: Constable, 1905) the year after the fair, and the following year Kakuzō's *The Book of Tea* (New York: Fox Duffield, 1906) appeared. Also in 1906 K. Asakawa revised and edited a book that had been presented at the 1893 fair: *Japan from the Japanese Government History*. His revisions justified the Sino-Japanese and the Russo-Japanese Wars. The first "was the only possible way to preserve [Japan] and save the East." The second established "once and for all the integrity of China in Manchuria." See Henry Cabot Lodge, ed., *The History of Nations*, vol. 7, *Japan from the Japanese Government History*, ed. K. Asakawa, (Philadelphia: John D. Morris, 1906), 297.

19 Hoshi Hajime, ed., *Japan and America* 2, no. 8 (August 1902): 9, and 3, no. 3 (March 1903): 26.

20 Akira Iriye, *Pacific Estrangement: Japanese and American Expansion, 1897–1911* (Cambridge, Mass.: Harvard University Press, 1972), 63–91; Hoshi Hajime, "Japan's Role in the World Drama," *Japan and America* 2, no. 12 (December 1902): 20.

21 See E. J. Hobsbawm, *Nations and Nationalism since 1780: Programme, Myth, Reality* (New York: Cambridge University Press, 1990), 10, 37–38. See also Hobsbawm, *The Age of Empire* (New York: Pantheon, 1987); Delmer M. Brown, *Nationalism in Japan: An Introductory Historical Analysis* (Berkeley and Los Angeles: University of California Press, 1955). For the way in which Japanese nationalism was manifested in art and architecture see Christine M. E. Guth, "Japan, 1868–1945: Art, Architecture, and National Identity," *Art Journal* 55 (fall 1996): 15–19.

22 F. G. Notehelfer, "On Idealism and Realism in the Thought of Okakura Tenshin," *Journal of Japanese Studies* 16, no. 2 (summer 1990): 310. See also Carol Gluck, *Japan's Modern Myths: Ideology in the Late Meiji Period* (Princeton, N.J.: Princeton University Press, 1985); "Japan and the Jingoes," *Nation*, 29 September 1904, 254–255. See also "A 'Christian' Nation against

a 'Heathen,'" *World's Work*, April 1904, 4608–4611. Tejima's speech was published in the *World's Fair Bulletin*, December 1903.

23 In March 1903 Hoshi was in St. Louis as a volunteer aide to the Japanese fair commissioners. He traveled to Japan to encourage the Japanese government to participate in the St. Louis fair. Okakura's presentation was published in Rogers, *Congress of Arts and Science*, 4:663–676. See also Hoshi Hajime, *Handbook of Japan and Japanese Exhibits at the World's Fair, St. Louis, 1904* (New York: Hajime Hoshi, 1904). It appears that there are no extant copies of Hoshi's newspaper published on the fairgrounds.

24 Nakamura, *Okakura Kakuzō*, 16, 121, 254; Hoshi Hajime, "Japan's Role in the World Drama," *Japan and America* 2, no. 12 (December 1902): 20.

25 In a speech delivered in the Congress of Arts and Sciences on the fairgrounds, Henri Cordier asserted that Chinese dignitaries were "a backward caste which prevent all progress" and that he believed "the decline of China" had reached "the last period" of its long descent. Cordier's speech was published in Rogers, *Congress of Arts and Science*, 1:86–108. See also Nakamura, *Okakura Kakuzō*, 255.

26 John W. Hanson, *The Official History of the Fair St. Louis, 1904: The Sights and Scenes of the Louisiana Purchase Exposition* (St. Louis, Mo., 1904), 368.

27 The prince was also given a private tour of the fine arts building. See *World's Fair Bulletin*, December 1904, 6. See also "How Japan Has Given the West Lessons in the Art of War," *St. Louis Globe Democrat*, 9 October 1904.

28 *St. Louis Globe Democrat*, 17 February 1904. One of these buttons is in the collections of the Missouri Historical Society.

29 Spurr, *Rhetoric of Empire*, 15–16; Bennett, "Exhibitionary Complex," 79.

30 Hoshi Hajime, "Formosa: An Experiment in Colonization," *Japan and America* 4, no. 8 (August 1904): 31. Hoshi also ran short articles in his journal with titles such as "Formosan Head Hunters Still Resisting" and "Troublesome Native Formosans Suppressed" (January 1903): 16. See also Mark Bennitt, ed., *History of the Louisiana Purchase Exposition* (St. Louis, Mo.: Universal Exposition Pub. Co., 1905), 303–306; Hoshi Hajime, *Prominent Americans Interested in Japan and Prominent Japanese in America*, supplement to *Japan and America* (New York, 1903), preface; Spurr, *Rhetoric of Empire*, 33; Isaac F. Marcosson, "Japan's Extraordinary Exhibit," *World's Work*, August 1904, 5148.

31 The most extensive work on the Ainu at the St. Louis fair is James W. Vanstone, "The Ainu Group at the Louisiana Purchase Exposition, 1904," *Arctic Anthropology* 30, no. 2 (1993): 77–91. See also "Education of the Ainu," *Japan and America* 2, no. 9 (September 1902): 17, and *The Exhibition of the Empire of Japan Official Catalogue* (St. Louis: International Exposition, 1904), 18. The typically racist fair publication is John Wesley Hanson, *The Official History of the Fair St. Louis, 1904: The Sights and Scenes of the Louisiana Purchase Exposition* (St. Louis, Mo., 1904), 385, 391. The frontispiece is from Buel, *Louisiana and the Fair*, vol. 5.

32 Spurr, *Rhetoric of Empire*, 69; Captain F. Brinkley, ed., *Japan: Its History, Arts, and Literature* (Boston: J. B. Millet, 1901), 19.

33 Rutherford Alcock, *Art and Art Industries in Japan* (London: Virtue, 1878), 1–5, 129–130; John Findling, ed., *Historical Dictionary of World's Fairs and Expositions, 1851–1988* (New York: Greenwood Press, 1990), 51. See also Imperial Japanese Commission to the Louisiana Purchase Exposition, *The Exhibition of the Empire of Japan Official Catalogue* (St. Louis, Mo.: Woodward and Tiernan, 1904).

34 Benjamin Lee Wren, "A History of Trade Relations between Japan and the United States in the New Orleans Area" (Ph.D. diss., University of Arizona, 1973), 37–41.

35 Bennitt, *History of the Louisiana Purchase Exposition*, 303.

36 See Ranbir Vohra, *China's Path to Modernization: A Historical Review from 1800 to the Present* (Englewood Cliffs, N.J.: Prentice-Hall, 1987), 83–110; June Grasso, Jay Corrin, and Michael Kort, *Modernization and Revolution in China* (Armonk, N.Y.: M. E. Sharpe, 1997), 34–73; Jonathan D. Spence, *The Search for Modern China* (New York: Norton, 1990), 216–245.

37 All of China's exhibits were organized under the administration of Sir Robert Hart of the Chinese Maritime Customs. See J. K. Fairbank, K. F. Brunei, and E. M. Matheson, eds., *The I.G. in Peking: Letters of Robert Hart Chinese Maritime Customs, 1868–1907* (Cambridge, Mass.: Belknap Press, 1975), 99. See also Stanley F. Wright, *Hart and the Chinese Customs* (Belfast: Mullan and Son, 1950), 399–401. See also Barbara Vennman, "Dragons, Dummies, and Royals: China at American World's Fair, 1876–1904," *Gateway Heritage*, fall 1996, 16.

38 Hoshi Hajime, ed., "Death of Colonel Buck, United States Minister to Japan" and "Minister Takahira and the Japanese Mission," *Japan and America* 3, no. 1 (January 1903): 20–21; Irene E. Cortinovis, "China at the St. Louis World's Fair," *Missouri Historical Review*, October 1977, 59–66. See also "Commissioner-General Barrett," *World's Fair Bulletin*, 3 January 1903, 24; Bennitt, *History of the Louisiana Purchase Exposition*, 290.

39 E. J. Hobsbawm, *The Age of Capital, 1848–1875* (New York: Charles Scribner's Sons, 1975), 285; David R. Francis, *The Universal Exposition of 1904* (St. Louis, Mo.: Louisiana Purchase Exposition Co., 1913), 343; Greenhalgh, *Ephemeral Vistas*, 15, 198.

40 Scottish artists wanted to participate and the British would not allow it. See correspondence between George F. Parker, the fair's representative to the United Kingdom, and Halsey Ives between 1901 and 1904, St. Louis Art Museum Archives (hereafter SLAM); Col. Charles M. Watson to Halsey Ives, 8 June 1903, SLAM.

41 Ives had been involved in the U.S. art exhibit in the 1900 Paris fair and had also been chief of fine arts for the 1893 Chicago fair. See Francis, *Universal Exposition*, 57; Papers of the "Commission on Fine Arts Recommendations in the Louisiana Purchase Exposition Department of Fine Art," box 8, folder 49, SLAM. See also Ives to Shugio, 22 January 1902, SLAM. "You will find at least two old friends in our commission when we come out to St. Louis" (Shugio to Ives, 27 January 1903, SLAM). See also Shugio to Ives, 3 September 1903, SLAM.

42 See correspondence between Halsey Ives and the Japanese Art Commission, 1901 to 1905, SLAM; Kwanjiuro Yamashita, *The Illustrated Catalogue of Japanese Fine Art Exhibits in the Art Palace at the Louisiana Purchase Exposition, St. Louis, MO* (Kobe: Kwansai Shashin Seihan Insatsu Goshi Kaisha, 1904).

43 Ives to Shugio, 22 March 1902, SLAM; "The Department Jury of Awards, September 20, 1904," box 8, folder 53, SLAM; Francis, *Universal Exposition*, 348.

44 Bennett, "Exhibitionary Complex," 93. "Imperial superiority" is taken from Bennett, who cited Peter Stallybrass and Allon White, *The Politics and Poetics of Transgression* (London: Methuen, 1986), 42. See also Frank Parker Stockbridge, ed., *The Art Gallery of the Universal Exposition* (St. Louis, Mo.: Universal Exposition Pub. Co., 1905).

45 For the disappointment of the critics see William H. Low, "The Field of Art," *Scribner's Magazine*, June 1905, 767. See also Francis, *Universal Exposition*, 359; Charles H. Caffin, "The Exhibit of Pictures and Sculpture," *World's Work*, special double exposition, August 1904, 5183–5184.

46 In his note Mitchell wrote that he was "much indebted to Said's work." See Said, *Orientalism*, 160–161, 168, 239; Mitchell, "Orientalism and the Exhibitionary Order," 306 n. 47.

47 "Exhibitionary order" is Timothy Mitchell's phrase. An immense amount of international trade was initiated at the expositions. See Inspector General of Customs, *St. Louis Louisiana Purchase Exposition Catalogue of the Collection of Chinese Exhibits* (1904).

48 Mitchell, "Orientalism and the Exhibitionary Order," 300–301; Edward V. P. Schneiderhahan Diaries, MHSA.

49 See "Draft of list of medals," box 8, folder 57; "Department of Art: Department Jury of Awards," box 8, folder 54; listing of Chinese art dated 23 June 1904, box 9, all in SLAM; Francis, *Universal Exposition*, 317.

50 For the exclusion of China from the catalog see Ives to Bolles, 25 June 1904, SLAM. See also "Table of Exhibits in Department of Art," box 9, folder 6; "Lists of Medals Awarded," box 8, folder 6; Ives to D. Percebois, Secretary of Imperial Chinese Commission, 17 August 1904; "Copy of Report for Department of Art," 31 July 1904, box 9, folder 2; Ives to Francis Carl, 11 March 1904, and to Percebois, 11 August 1904, all in SLAM; Katherine Carl, *With the Empress Dowager of China* (Tientsin: Société Française, 1926). China was allotted only two positions on the prestigious painting jury, and they were not held by Chinese but by Robert Hart's cousins, Kate and Francis Carl. See *Official Catalog of Exhibitors for the Art Section* (St. Louis, Mo.: Louisiana Purchase Exposition Co., 1904).

51 Okakura's speech was published in Rogers, *Congress of Arts and Science*, 4:663–676. Cordier's was in ibid., 1: 86–108.

52 Spurr, *Rhetoric of Empire*, 28.

Objects of Desire: Japanese Collectors and Colonial Korea

Kim Brandt

Japan is one of the few countries in the world where ceramics are widely acknowledged as a major art form, and famous pots and potters alike command
national respect and admiration. While much of this attention is directed at
native pottery traditions, there has long been a special subculture of interest
in the ceramic art of Korea. Japanese fascination with Korean ceramics is
centuries old and can be traced back reliably to the late medieval period,
if not before. Yet the specific character of late-twentieth-century Japanese
appreciation of Korean ceramics owes a great deal to much more recent
history. In particular, only in the 1920s and 1930s did certain categories of
the pottery and porcelain of Korea's Chosŏn period (1392–1910) begin to
achieve the special status they retain in Japan today. Yi dynasty (*Ri chō*)
wares, as these objects are known in Japan, have a peculiar, almost cult-
like following among Japanese collectors and aesthetes that persists into the
present. As one collector has noted, there are those who go so far as to assert

that the appreciation of ceramics "begins with Yi dynasty and ends with Yi dynasty."[1]

There is a faint but unmistakably colonialist air that attaches to the fetish of Yi dynasty wares in Japan. It seems to exhale from the very name Yi dynasty, a slightly archaic term referring to the rule by the royal Yi house of the immensely long period from 1392 to 1910. Koreans and most scholars of Korea today—in Japan as elsewhere—call the period by its formal, rather neutral realm name, Chosŏn. Perhaps it is relevant here that Chosŏn, unlike Yi dynasty, was the name by which the Korean regime chose to be known while it was in power; only after the Yi monarchy lost its authority, with the advent of Japanese colonial rule (1910–1945), did the external, yet oddly familiar and informal perspective implied by "Yi dynasty" gain general currency. In any event, the term persists in Japan, especially in reference to the categories of Korean art and crafts that became increasingly popular during the 1920s and 1930s and that remain salient among collectors and others today.[2]

Yet the relation between Japanese colonial power in Korea and the rising popularity during the 1920s and 1930s of certain Korean objects in Japan was neither simple nor direct. Some sense of the complexity of the problem is suggested by the career of Yanagi Sōetsu (1889–1961), one of the most famous Japanese collectors and promoters of Yi dynasty wares. Yanagi is best known today as the founder and leader of the so-called *mingei*, or folk craft, movement, a loose assemblage of artists, craftspeople, collectors, and others who began promoting the rustic, artisanal aesthetic of Japanese handicrafts in the late 1920s. Yet no small part of Yanagi's continuing celebrity derives from his reputation as a heroic defender of Korean art and culture against Japanese imperialism. During the decade preceding his discovery of *mingei*, Yanagi threw himself into things Korean. Between 1914—when he is said to have fallen in love with a Chosŏn jar—and 1924, Yanagi made as many as ten trips to Korea, often staying for weeks at a time (fig. 1).[3] In addition to assembling his own celebrated collection of Korean ceramics and other objects, Yanagi devoted much of this period to writing numerous articles and even a book on Korean art and related subjects, as well as giving well-attended public lectures in both Korea and Japan. He also joined with friends to organize several art exhibitions in both countries and led a widely

Figure 1 The Chosŏn period jar presented to
Yanagi by Asakawa Noritaka in 1914. It is often
suggested that this is the Korean object that first
alerted Yanagi to the value of Yi dynasty wares.
Collection of Nihon Mingeikan.

publicized campaign to establish a museum of Korean art in Seoul, which
opened in April 1924.

A consideration of Yanagi's early period of Korean activism offers insight
into the process by which Japanese colonialism may be said to have reinvented
Korean art in Japan. Colonial opportunities made it possible for middle-class
cultural elites to define and promote selected Korean objects as high art.
At the same time, the meanings and value that Yanagi and his cohort of
literati-collectors successfully attached to Korean objects were instrumental
in the reproduction of Japanese colonial power. The Korean art museum,
for example, served ultimately to promote the legitimation and therefore
the stability of the Japanese regime in Korea. More generally, the writings
of Yanagi and his fellow enthusiasts of Korean art contributed to a larger
body of colonial knowledge about Korea and Koreans. They praised Yi

dynasty wares and the culture and people that produced them, in terms that made Korea's status as a colonial possession of Japan seem both natural and inevitable.

The particular trajectory of Yanagi's career draws attention as well, however, to the ambivalence of a non-Western colonialism. It is significant that Yanagi turned to Korean art after a youth spent absorbed in the study and appreciation of European (and some American) monuments of literature, painting, and sculpture. During the late 1910s and 1920s Yanagi was only one among a number of cosmopolitan Japanese who turned partly away from Western high culture to celebrate the artistic and spiritual traditions ascribed to the Orient (*Tōyō*), a geo-cultural entity usually identified as comprising China, Japan, Korea, and India. The return to the Orient (*Tōyō e no kaiki*), as later scholars have referred to this fascination with the idea of an ancient Oriental civilization, represented a complex adaptation of Western ideas about the non-West. On one hand, Yanagi and others accepted and employed Western systems of knowledge, including those mechanisms that—like the very idea of an Orient—implied Western superiority. At the same time, however, they sought to refute Western dominance by asserting indigenous Oriental value, and Japanese autonomy in particular.

The significance of the early-twentieth-century Japanese enthusiasm for Korean, Japanese, and other Asian objects must also be understood, therefore, within the context of a world increasingly dominated and defined by Western power. The discovery of Korean art, like the discovery of *mingei*, represented an effort to resist the controlling hierarchies and categories of Western knowledge. Unfortunately the strategy of resistance from within, by means of the selective use of Orientalist terms and tropes, could produce only partial freedom from the oppression of Western hegemony. Japanese literati gained some autonomy, but only by alienating themselves from the Orient they exalted and by reproducing Western-style colonial knowledge and power in Korea, Japan, and eventually through much of Asia.

Canon Revision and the Uses of Colonialism

While Yanagi was certainly among the most prominent and active of those Japanese who took up Yi dynasty wares in the 1910s and 1920s, he was by no means alone. In addition to Japanese residents of Korea such as Asakawa Noritaka and his younger brother Takumi, who tutored Yanagi in the appreciation of Chosŏn arts and crafts, there were others based in Japan who, like Yanagi, were struck by the new aesthetic possibilities to be found in relatively humble objects of Korean provenance. One narrative of Yanagi's discovery of Korean art, for example, suggests that he was introduced to it by his friends Bernard Leach and Tomimoto Kenkichi, artists who had both become ardent admirers of Chosŏn ceramics after viewing some examples at a colonial exposition in Tokyo in 1912.[4]

The young men who began to congregate in Seoul and Tokyo around their shared enthusiasm for later Chosŏn period porcelain and stoneware were also linked by similar social and cultural station. As middle-class intellectuals—artists, writers, university students, and teachers—they shared a somewhat precarious position as members of a cultural elite largely cut off from the monopoly capital that was rapidly producing a new haute bourgeoisie of industrialists and financiers.[5] Yet the opportunities opened in Korea by Japanese colonial power gave Yanagi and his peers the means to contest the increasing sway of bourgeois economic elites in cultural matters, and especially in the highly prestigious domain of art ceramics. By challenging the authority of the tea ceremony establishment in particular, Yanagi and other middle-class literati were able to revise the art ceramics canon in Japan to include the objects they had discovered in Korea. Through their success in promoting novel categories of Korean ceramics, Yanagi and others gained the cultural capital—or the status and authority—that enabled, in turn, their campaign to promote *mingei*.

Korean ceramics have been highly valued in Japan for centuries. Certain types of Korean bowls produced during the late Koryŏ (918–1392) and early Chosŏn periods, in particular, achieved special iconic status during the late sixteenth century within the context of the elite practice of the tea ceremony.[6] The importance of Korean bowls only increased during the 1910s and 1920s with the revitalization of the tea ceremony as a pastime for the very rich.[7] It may not seem surprising, therefore, that Japanese collectors of the early twentieth century were disposed to take an interest in the Korean ceramics rendered increasingly accessible by Japanese colonization. Indeed Yanagi himself often cited the aesthetic tradition of tea in explaining the importance he attached to Korean craft objects.[8]

Yet the enthusiasm of Yanagi and others for Yi dynasty ceramics, not to mention woodwork and other handicrafts, cannot be explained by the tea aesthetic alone. For one thing, the types of pottery and porcelain they helped to bring into vogue during the 1920s and 1930s were distinct from the older Korean bowls admitted within the tea canon. Many of the objects that would later come to epitomize Yi dynasty wares, such as white porcelain (*hakuji*) vases and other objects associated with Confucian ritual practices in Korea or the small, whimsically shaped "water droppers" (*suiteki*) customarily used by Korean literati to wet their inkstones, had no function within the tea ceremony (fig. 2). Moreover, there was a difference between the way objects were understood within the tea ceremony and the way they were approached by young Japanese collectors in colonial Korea. By the nineteenth century the tea ceremony had become a site at which individual objects were appreciated as utterly particular and unique; to participate in the culture of tea was, in part, to accept a highly elaborated, semiapocryphal system of knowledge about a limited number of teabowls and other items. A cherished tea implement (*cha dōgu*), housed like a jewel in layers of custom-made silk bags and inscribed boxes, was surrounded by an aura of iconic originality. Its value was produced largely by esoteric convention, which assigned it a name, a category, and a pedigree of origin, past ownership, and use.

By contrast, the middle-class intellectuals who browsed the antique shops and markets of 1910s Seoul drew on a much more cosmopolitan, self-consciously modern fund of knowledge to evaluate objects. They used universalist standards associated with Western art and science to resist the parochial conventions of the tea world and to assert their own aesthetic authority. Yet at the same time they continued to rely on certain aspects of tea tradition to obtain legitimacy for their efforts to expand the field of collectible objects. Yanagi, for example, claimed that in promoting Yi dynasty (or, later, certain categories of Chinese, Southeast Asian, rural Japanese, and even English handicraft) goods, he was reviving the true spirit of the early

Figure 2 A Chosŏn period "water dropper" (*suiteki*). Collection of Nihon Mingeikan.

tea masters. Later followers of the first geniuses of tea had, Yanagi charged, fallen into an increasingly stylized and imitative formalism. He felt that the tea ceremony as practiced in his own day had lost most of its originally creative character; it venerated the individual objects hallowed by centuries of tradition but failed to recognize the value that also existed in newer or otherwise unfamiliar things.[9]

It should be noted, however, that Yanagi's characterization of the tea ceremony as an increasingly ossified, conservative set of persons and practices was not entirely fair. In fact, during the decades around 1900 the tea ceremony saw one of the more exuberant periods of change and creativity in its long history. Beginning in the 1880s and 1890s, tea was transformed. Formerly a genteel, mostly private pastime for literary men, it became a highly competitive arena for the expression of power, status, and wealth by a variety of rising social groups.[10] Most conspicuously, during the economic boom associated with World War I, a new class of industrialists—particularly those connected with the Mitsui *zaibatsu*, or financial conglomerate—used their wealth to dominate the tea world with a lavish new style of tea that centered on the uninhibited acquisition and display of art objects new to the tea context.[11]

In some ways, in fact, *zaibatsu* tea in the 1910s and 1920s brought a freer approach to tea practice and ideology. Its exponents brushed aside received conventions about the type of art suitable for display in order to introduce new categories of objects—namely those of Buddhist art unconnected to the Zen sects or to tea practice—into the tearoom for the first time.[12] Yet at the same time *zaibatsu* tea reiterated and reinforced selected elements of the tea tradition, particularly as it concerned the canon of famous tea objects (*meiki* or *meibutsu*). The 1920s saw the publication, for example, of the *Taishō meiki kan*, an influential nine-volume photographic catalog of pedigreed tea caddies and teabowls.[13] Its compiler, Takahashi Yoshio, a central figure within *zaibatsu* tea circles, intended the catalog to provide a definitive modern accounting of objects belonging to the category of "celebrated tea implement." Yet with the *Taishō meiki kan* Takahashi actually managed to modify the existing canon even as he reestablished and buttressed its parameters.[14] In so doing he reinscribed a hierarchical ranking of ceramics from the perspective of a tea establishment newly invigorated by the infusion of monopoly capital.

Yanagi's critical attitude toward the modern tea ceremony may have had as much to do, therefore, with the changing nature of the tea world as with its alleged inertia. Nor was he alone in such criticism. The luxurious hedonism that *zaibatsu* tea represented came to seem increasingly irresponsible and extravagant as the interwar Japanese economy slumped and social issues such as those concerning the urban and rural poor acquired new urgency.[15] Moreover, the growing cachet of the tea ceremony as a form of conspicuous consumption drove the tea-goods market to unprecedented heights, richly rewarding the captains of industry who already owned most of the celebrated tea implements but probably disgruntling aesthetes with more limited incomes. As Yanagi wrote in 1928, "Today such things as the making of tearooms with great refinement, at the cost of a thousand yen, must be called contrary to the true spirit of tea."[16]

For men such as Yanagi, colonial Korea offered special opportunities to counter the hegemony, reinforced by big money, of the tea tradition over the production and consumption of art ceramics in Japan. Perhaps the first to exploit these opportunities was Asakawa Noritaka, later known in Japan as the patron saint of Korean pottery (*Chōsen tōki no kamisama*). According to one account, it was Asakawa who presented Yanagi with the fateful Chosŏn jar in 1914.[17] In 1913, three years after Japan's formal annexation of Korea, Asakawa moved to Seoul from his native Yamanashi prefecture, where he descended from a line of literary gentry, to take a position as an elementary school teacher. A tea aficionado himself, Asakawa was frustrated by his inability to afford the types of Korean ceramics favored by most Japanese collectors. Aside from the individual bowls hallowed by tea tradition, the Korean pots admired in Japan, as elsewhere, tended toward the impressive Chinese style wares produced for ruling elites before the Chosŏn period. By contrast, Yi dynasty white porcelain, along with other types of Chosŏn period ceramics, was relatively cheap and plentiful. Asakawa and other Japanese with more taste and information than money—salaried employees of the colonial government-general or of private Japanese enterprise in Korea, scholars, writers, students, and artists—took it up in part because they could afford it.

Akaboshi Gorō, another authority on Yi dynasty pottery and porcelain, later wrote of his early days antique hunting in colonial Seoul (or Keijō, as it was called by the Japanese) that he, like Asakawa, had at first been attracted to green-glazed ceramics ("celadon") from the Koryŏ period but had been unable to pay the steep prices it commanded on the market.

At that time it was Asakawa Noritaka who opened my eyes to the over-looked Yi dynasty things. I jumped at the opportunity to have him take me around to all the Keijō antique shops. What now seem astonishingly good pieces were lying around all over the place. Most of what I now own I obtained in Keijō. . . . In those days there were lots of [Japanese] antique dealers in Keijō. . . . In addition there were a great many Korean antique dealers, who mostly had junk shops and sideline businesses. I would be in front of a shop, and a *yobo* (a laborer) would come carrying a Buddha or a bronze piece or a pot wrapped in a cloth, and then he and the shop owner would begin to bargain. Finally the *yobo* would leave, and then the piece just bought would be priced at a hundred times the amount paid. Until I got used to it, I found this kind of thing truly unpleasant, but because it was clear that the objects would end up being sold somewhere, I had to buy them.[18]

Akaboshi offers here a glimpse into the colonial market relations that made it possible for him and other Japanese of relatively limited means to amass, despite the occasional pang of conscience, what later became extremely valuable collections of Korean art. Even at prices that returned large profits to Japanese (and some Korean) dealers, Japanese collectors found Korean art objects a good bargain.[19]

In addition to collecting ceramics, Asakawa devoted much of his twenty-odd years in Korea to the investigation of hundreds of old kiln sites in an effort to correct the errors of Japanese tea lore about Korean teabowls. His challenge to the hegemonic ideology of ceramics purveyed largely by the tea establishment was not confined to the assertion of independent aesthetic authority that Yanagi, for example, appeared to find sufficient. Yanagi, already famous as a founding editor and writer for the magazine *Shirakaba* [White birch] (published 1910–1923), through which he had helped to introduce canonical elements of Western high culture to Japan, simply dismissed later developments in tea as formalist and narrow decadence. He suggested that his own preferences in art ceramics, like those of the early tea masters, drew rather on a universal realm of aesthetic value to which he, as a recognized expert on Western art, had special access. Asakawa, a provincial schoolmaster, was perhaps less comfortable snubbing the aesthetic conventions of the rich and venerable. Instead, he bolstered his attack on tea knowledge with science. In 1934 Asakawa gave an address in Tokyo on the subject of his pottery investigations:

> Even when the [ceramic] objects that came [to Japan from Korea] in long ago times have written explanations attached to them, these are the judgments made from four-and-a-half mat tearooms by tea people. Because they did not actually know Korea, these judgments are nothing more than flights of fancy. They knew almost none of the facts. . . . If, first, [an object's] place of origin, the period when it was produced, and

the conditions of its transmission become clear, then for the first time it will become a proper historical source. For example, when we talk of the Korean teabowl categories of Ido, Totoya, Soba, Katade, Gohon, these are all conventions derived from superficial observation; what is referred to as correct knowledge about these categories consists of the records made regarding individual bowls, and these are nothing more than conventions limited to the tea world. . . . In these days, which are liberated historically and geographically, I think that it is our work to investigate such things on the basis of a correct foundation.[20]

In this lecture Asakawa noted, moreover, the special advantages of his time and place in colonial Korea. Although he expressed some irritation with the suspicion and resistance he encountered from Koreans during his excavating expeditions, Asakawa stated, "Ever since the annexation, everything [in Korea] has come to light, and things which were buried unused in the ground have appeared here and there; from the standpoint of research, this is the best of times."[21]

Asakawa's findings appear to have troubled the tea establishment. Taka-hashi Yoshio, when compiling the three volumes dealing with Korean teabowls in the nine-volume *Taishō meiki kan*, felt compelled to make re-peated references to Asakawa's investigations in Korea and the new critical light in which they cast many of the received traditions of the tea world.[22] Takahashi resolved his dilemma by regretting that it was too late for him to fully assimilate Asakawa's contributions in the *Taishō meiki kan*: "Because I myself wish to go to Korea after the publication of this catalog is completed, and do research there, for the time being I will base my commentary here on the past sayings of tea people, and hope to elucidate with regard to new facts such as those cited above at some other time."[23] However that elucidation may have been managed, the authority of tea ideology was gradually forced to retreat, in the face of empirical contradiction, from its original monopoly on the truth of Korean-Japanese pottery.

In their resistance to the authority of tea, and in their efforts to draw attention within Japan to previously overlooked categories of art ceramics, Yanagi and Asakawa took part in a more general trend in ceramics apprecia-tion during the 1910s and 1920s. Scholarly groups like the Tōjiki kenkyūkai or the Saikōkai, whose leading members were attached to Tokyo Imperial University, or the Chōsōkai at Waseda University, dedicated themselves to the scientific study and appreciation of old Japanese, Chinese, and other Asian ceramics. Their efforts were inspired in part by the example—and the threat—of European and North American scholars and collectors, whose acquisitions of certain types of Japanese and other Asian art treasures had only been facilitated by the narrow scope of tea taste.[24] At the same time they, like Yanagi and Asakawa, were often collectors of relatively limited means who sought to broaden the field of art ceramics eligible for legitimate appreciation.

But Asakawa, Akaboshi, Yanagi, and the other early collectors of Yi dynasty pottery and porcelain also used the advantages of their position in colonial Korea, in combination with the tools of Western-style knowledge, to force open the categories of collectible art in Japan. They became cultural heroes of a sort for establishing a distinct subfield in the appreciation of ceramics that was both independent of tea taste yet partly informed and legitimated by it. As a measure of the success of the early collectors, Japanese demand for "Yi dynasty" grew rapidly during the 1910s and 1920s, spreading from colonial residents and visiting cognoscenti in Korea to the metropolitan market in Japan. So popular did several types of the Chosŏn period pottery and porcelain first collected by Yanagi and his peers become, in fact there even emerged a lively trade in Yi dynasty fakes, known sometimes as *Taishō Ri chō* (Taishō Yi dynasty).[25]

In successfully revising the canon of Japanese art ceramics, intellectuals and artists such as Yanagi and Asakawa were able to wrest some of the leadership in the prestigious field of art ceramics from bourgeois economic elites, who were bidding for dominance from their new cultural power position within the tea establishment. Colonial opportunities allowed middle-class literati to parlay modest investments into enormous returns in cultural capital. Although the highest prices continued to go to the older, rarer, and safely pedigreed objects of tea, the market value and cultural prestige of the late Chosŏn period objects first bought cheaply in colonial Seoul climbed steadily, bringing both symbolic and actual wealth to many early collectors.[26]

Solving the Korea Problem

The success of Yanagi, Asakawa, and others in revising the Japanese art canon to include novel categories of Korean objects owed much to the immediate and material opportunities opened up in colonial Korea to Japanese of even modest wealth. Especially after formal annexation in 1910, it was a relatively simple matter for Japanese such as the Asakawa brothers or Yanagi to live, work, or travel in Korea, usually with the sorts of privileges monopolized by colonial elites everywhere. For Japanese in Korea, these privileges included the freedom to seek out and appropriate Korean goods of all description at very low cost and to remove those goods—even rare or antique art objects—permanently to Japan.

But colonial power also produced other, less predictable opportunities for Japanese interested in shaping new meanings or identities. Yanagi and his immediate circle were especially active during the years between 1919 and 1924, when Korean nationalist resistance opened new spaces for negotiation and change within the colonial context. They used the relative fluidity and even instability of this period, when Japanese colonial policy and administration were under public review, to promote their own programs for cultural reform. By boldly engaging in the debate on colonial policy, Yanagi gained unprecedented publicity for his own definitions of art generally and of Korean art in particular. He also succeeded in gaining significant public support in both countries for his various projects to improve Japan-Korea relations through the cultural preservation and revival of Korea. There was a critical edge to culturalist reform efforts like Yanagi's, which implicitly or explicitly suggested the inadequacy and immorality of assimilationist colonial policy. Yet it is important to recognize that in Korea during the early 1920s, nationalist cultural reform was a means employed by governing authorities to produce legitimacy and stability for the Japanese regime. Korean art proved very useful to the colonial system that had helped to define it.

Early 1920s Korea was the site for a widely acknowledged crisis in colonial relations. By 1919 a decade of oppressive, even brutal assimilationist rule had produced an uncontainable level of outrage and opposition throughout much of Korean society. The organized mass demonstrations that ensued on 1 March 1919—thereafter sacred to Korean nationalist memory as the

March First Movement (*samil undong*)—terrified and infuriated colonial authorities, who called out the troops. Several weeks of mayhem and some thousands of Korean casualties later, it was clear to many in Japan as well as Korea that something had gone very wrong. Although mainstream Japanese opinion tended to blame Koreans (and Western missionaries) for what were commonly described as riots and insubordination by malcontent Koreans (*futei na Senjin*), it was difficult to escape the reflection that Japanese colonial policy might also bear some responsibility. As a consequence, the "Korea problem" (*Chōsen mondai*) and discussion of its resolution figured large in both colonial and metropolitan publications for several years thereafter.

In this context, Yanagi was one of the few Japanese who dared to publish, repeatedly, opinions sharply critical of Japanese colonial policy. In essays and articles that appeared in newspapers and well-known journals from 1919 through 1924, Yanagi presented himself as a conscientious objector to the inhumanity and philistinism characterizing Japanese attitudes and policy toward Korea. As he put it in "Thinking on Koreans" [*Chōsenjin o omou*], an impassioned four-part article published first in a major Tokyo daily in May 1919,

> If we wish for eternal peace between ourselves and our neighbors, then we must purify and warm our hearts with love and sympathy. But, unfortunately, Japan has dealt with the sword, and offered abuse. Can this possibly give rise to mutual understanding, or create cooperation, or produce union? Nay, all Koreans feel throughout their beings a limitless enmity, resistance, hatred, and separation [*bunri*]. It is an inevitable consequence that independence should be their ideal.[27]

Yanagi especially stressed the efficacy of art as a means of producing the mutual understanding and love necessary for improved Japanese-Korean relations: "I believe it is art, not science, that promotes congress between countries, and draws peoples together. . . . Only religious or artistic understanding can give experience of the inner heart, and from that experience create a limitless love."[28]

The extraordinary power Yanagi attributed to art—its capacity for social and political healing—derived from the Romantic philosophy he embraced, as did many of his colleagues in the so-called Shirakaba school.

Art, in this view, was the key to a transcendent, mystic realm of natural and universal truth, beauty, and humanity. It was opposed, moreover, to the particularistic and divisive, unnatural modes of being associated with modern science and industry, politics, and nationalism. Raymond Williams has pointed out, in the case of the British Romantic poets, that the opposition they perceived between natural beauty and personal feeling, on one hand, and industrial civilization, on the other, has been often misunderstood as a dissociation. But in fact the British Romantics, like their Japanese counterparts of the 1910s and early 1920s, were far from indifferent to politics and social affairs. Rather, their commitment to art and love represented a direct criticism of modern state and society, which they hoped thereby to reform.[29] In this sense Yanagi, the author in 1914 of a massive study of William Blake, was simply extending principles long dear to him and many of his fellow literary youth (*bungaku seinen*) in proposing that the Korean problem might be understood and resolved best by means of art.

Yet by choosing to write regularly on so current and sensitive a topic, Yanagi also ensured that his definition of art generally, and of Korean art in particular, reached a much larger audience than he had ever addressed before. First in Japanese, then in English and Korean translations, his articles on the importance of a proper recognition of the value and meaning of certain Korean objects as Art circulated widely in both Japan and Korea. In a 1921 piece first published in *Shirakaba* and then translated into English for the *Japan Advertiser*, Yanagi wrote, for example, "Who could look at this exquisite figure of Maitreya Buddha with its expression of profound meditation, or at this vase of ancient Korai [Koryŏ] work, and still remain cold toward the nation that could make such things. Art transcends frontiers and the differences of men's minds." Here Yanagi proposed relatively conventional candidates for inclusion within what he called the "universal realm of art."[30] Both ancient Buddhist statuary and Koryŏ period ceramics were already acknowledged within Japan as valuable Korean art products. Elsewhere, however, Yanagi insisted that Chosŏn period ceramics also qualified as "great art" (*idai na geijutsu*).[31] In his 1922 essay "Korean Art," for example, Yanagi again reminded readers of the glories of ancient Korean Buddhist statuary before asserting, "But people must not think that it is only in the distant past that Korea had art and culture. Is not the Koryŏ dynasty immortal for its ceramics? . . . Even from the Yi dynasty, which is thought to be decadent and therefore rarely considered, I have witnessed many immortal works. Some of its woodwork and porcelain are truly eternal."[32]

Yanagi did more than write. Early in 1920 he and his wife, Kaneko, a professional contralto who specialized in German lieder, announced their intention to raise money through a series of benefit concerts in Japan in order to travel to Korea and perform for Koreans. This was to be part of an effort to prove that art and religion, rather than militarism or diplomacy, could more effectively create harmony between the two countries.[33] At this point Yanagi seems also to have been planning the establishment of a literary magazine based on the cooperative efforts of Koreans and Japanese. In May of the same year Yanagi Sōetsu, Kaneko, and British artist and potter Bernard Leach traveled to Seoul for three weeks of welcome parties, concerts, and lectures sponsored by various Korean and Japanese organizations. All concerned pronounced the entire venture a great success.[34] This was the first of many trips Yanagi and Kaneko, accompanied by various people, were to make to Korea during the next few years. By the end of 1920 Yanagi had abandoned his plan for a literary journal in favor of a project to found a museum of Korean art, to be located in Seoul. Much of his activity (and that of his wife and friends) between 1920 and early 1924, when the museum finally opened, was devoted to this end. In addition to fund-raising and promotional concerts and lectures in Korea and Japan, Yanagi and his friends busied themselves with exhibitions of Korean pottery in both countries, a fund-raising drive organized through *Shirakaba*, a stream of publications on Korean art, group art-collecting and kiln research trips within Korea, and complicated negotiations in Korea concerning the site of the museum (fig. 3).

Especially after his death in 1961, Yanagi was eulogized by many Japanese as well as Koreans for championing Korean art and culture during the colonial period. His activist period in the early 1920s came in for special notice by those who held him up as an example of "gently stubborn" resistance to the imperialist Japanese state.[35] Even the Japanese Ministry of Education may be said to have endorsed Yanagi's postwar identity as an advocate for Korean culture against Japanese colonial rule. A 1974 high school Japanese-

Figure 3 Yanagi (front center) and Asakawa Noritaka (far left) at a 1922 exhibition of Korean ceramics in Seoul. The three later Chosŏn period vases in the foreground are all celebrated pieces presently held in Japanese collections.

language (*kokugo*) textbook approved by the ministry included an emotional essay written by Yanagi in 1922 protesting the projected destruction of a historic Seoul landmark by the colonial government-general.[36] Yet as historian Takasaki Sōji has noted, Yanagi's criticisms were directed largely against the heavy-handed militarism and assimilationism that characterized Japanese colonial policy before 1919, and which came in for general disapproval during the relatively liberal era of the early 1920s. It is significant that Yanagi's relations with the new colonial administration, brought in after the March First Movement, were cordial.[37] Indeed, Korea in the early 1920s under the new Saitō government-general was highly receptive to Yanagi's special brand of cultural activism.

Many of the Korean organizers of the March First Movement sought to make use of Woodrow Wilson's statements on the doctrine of national self-determination in order to attract international attention to the issue of

Korean independence. There were even hopes that the Japanese government might be embarrassed into relinquishing its nine-year-old colony.[38] Korean efforts were partly successful. The independence movement, along with the violent countermeasures immediately taken by General Hasegawa Yoshimichi, the governor-general of Korea from 1916 to 1919, received publicity in both Japan and the West. In consequence the Tokyo government felt increasing domestic as well as international pressure to review the evidently unsuccessful policy of "military rule" (*budan seiji*) that Hasegawa and General Terauchi Masatake, his predecessor from 1910 to 1916, had implemented in Korea.[39] Some of that domestic pressure was applied by the few Japanese intellectuals who, like Yanagi, dared publically to condemn the brutality of Japanese rule.

In August 1919 Prime Minister Hara Kei replaced Hasegawa as governor-general of Korea with Admiral Saitō Makoto, who immediately undertook a more conciliatory "cultural" policy, thereby inaugurating the period of so-called cultural rule (*bunka seiji*), from 1919 until approximately 1931, in Korea. But as Michael Robinson has shown in his study of Korean cultural nationalism during this period, Saitō's colonial policy was "a brilliant co-optative maneuver."[40] By expanding the arena of legally permissible political and cultural activity in colonial Korea, Saitō's regime was largely successful both in making Japanese rule acceptable to world opinion and in gaining increased legitimacy within the colony. At the same time, the Saitō administration strengthened the police control apparatus. The result was a split in the Korean nationalist movement between moderate or "cultural" nationalism, which flourished during the early 1920s, and a newer radical, leftist nationalism that came under increasingly effective attack by the Japanese colonial state.[41]

During the early 1920s the museum was Yanagi's central preoccupation in Korea, but at the same time he continued to produce public commentary in both Korea and Japan on the more general theme of Japanese-Korean relations. For the most part Yanagi settled down to write pieces urging cultural understanding between the two countries and adjuring Koreans to focus on the development of cultural rather than political identity and independence. Although Yanagi could occasionally prove something of a gadfly to Japanese in Korea, on the whole his views and activities were as acceptable to the Saitō administration as they were to Korean cultural nationalists during the early 1920s. Much like Yanagi, these Koreans considered political independence a remote goal predicated on gradual, long-term cultural development. They focused on strengthening Korean identity through historical studies, education, a vernacular language movement, and cultural societies, and their programs were based on a policy of nonconfrontation with Japanese authorities.[42] One leading exponent of Korean cultural nationalism even wrote about his movement in 1922 that it was "untainted by politics."[43] This influential segment of elite Korean opinion welcomed and supported Yanagi's endeavors. The *Tonga ilbo*, for example, a Korean-language newspaper founded and edited by prominent moderate nationalists such as Kim Sŏngsu and Chang Tŏksu, actively promoted Yanagi and his projects through articles and reviews as well as the sponsorship of lectures and concerts.

As for the government-general, Saitō's cultural policy corresponded in many ways to the proposals for Korean development outlined by Yanagi as well as many Korean cultural nationalists. The actual reforms Saitō planned in Korea after 1919 were organized around precisely their concerns: the eradication of militarism in Japanese rule, increased educational opportunity for Koreans, freedom of speech, and general respect for Korean culture. In practice, of course, many of Saitō's promises were only half-kept. The gendarmerie was abolished, but only to be replaced by what became a much larger and more comprehensive civilian police force.[44] A civilian governor-general, though held out as a possibility, was never appointed. The public educational system was greatly expanded, and the curriculum was revised to include Korean studies; but it has been argued that the real beneficiaries continued to be the resident Japanese community.[45] Publication controls were relaxed, but only for relatively apolitical materials; socialist or otherwise radically critical opinion was suppressed.[46]

In this context, Yanagi's Korean projects met with approval and even active support from Japanese authorities. In early 1921 Yanagi met with Saitō, who offered to house the proposed Korean folk art museum in a building belonging to the government-general.[47] In 1922 the governor-general was among the twelve hundred persons who attended an exhibit of Chosŏn pottery organized by Yanagi and his friends in Seoul in order to promote the museum. On that occasion Saitō and his right-hand man Ariyoshi Chūichi also donated a large sum of money to the museum fund.[48] It may have mattered that Yanagi's father had been an admiral in the Japanese navy and was, therefore, once Saitō's superior, and that Yanagi's sister was married to a well-regarded bureaucrat within the Korean government-general. Yet these facts alone are not enough to explain the support Yanagi received not only from Saitō but also from the official government-general newspaper, the *Keijō nippō*, as well as other government organizations through the 1920s and beyond.[49]

For Yanagi the opening of the Korean folk art museum in April 1924 marked the end of a five-year period of public engagement in the politics of colonial Korean culture. After 1924 Yanagi's activities in Korea took on a quieter, more conventionally philanthropic and educational cast. Supported by the colonial government, he and his wife made several benefit lecture and concert circuits in aid of, in 1924, Korean victims of the massacre that followed the 1923 earthquake in Japan and, in 1925, victims of a Korean flood. But Yanagi's real interest had moved to Japan, where he was increasingly preoccupied with what would become a lifelong campaign to preserve and revive another culture—his own—against the assimilationist threat posed by Western-style modernization.

Orientalism for the Orientals: Korean Art and the Reproduction of Colonial Knowledge

At the same time that Yanagi endeavored to relocate certain Korean objects within a universal category of world art, where they might take their place alongside such timeless monuments to human genius as classical Greek architecture, Russian literature, and French postimpressionist painting, he and others promoted the idea that Korean achievements also belonged within the alternate category of Oriental art (*Tōyō no geijutsu*). During the late 1910s and 1920s, there developed within Japanese literary and artistic circles a wave of renewed interest in Asian, and especially Japanese, artistic monuments and traditions.[50] Yanagi and other members of the *Shirakaba* set were quick to assimilate the various Japanese, Korean, and Chinese objects they admired within the category of Oriental art, which they usually envisioned as a subset of the wider canon of universal or world art. They helped to promote the idea that "Oriental art" denoted the greatest artistic achievements of the Orient, or *Tōyō*; this was a vaguely defined region comprising China, India, Japan, and Korea, which was often figured in terms that posited the centrality of Buddhism to a once-great and unified ancient civilization.

In adopting the notion of Oriental art as a means of defining and celebrating not only Korean but also Chinese and Japanese ceramics, painting, and sculpture, Japanese collectors, artists, and writers were engaged in a complex interaction with Western as well as Japanese colonial power. By employing Western systems of thought, including Orientalist ideas that functioned to reduce and subordinate the non-West, they seemed to accept the often oppressive categories and hierarchies of a Eurocentric ideology. Yet some of the writers and artists who embraced the idea of the Orient did so partly to revise and even to resist the "common sense" about Asian cultures and especially artistic achievement that derived from the prestige of Western views. The result was an ambivalent form of colonial knowledge, mobilized in part to resist Western power but serving finally to reinscribe it.

Like many of his peers, Yanagi found his way to non-Western, or indigenous, aesthetic value through an initial and abiding preoccupation with Western literature and art. His earliest efforts to promote Korean art were conducted, therefore, within the parameters of a highly European frame of reference. This was true in an institutional as well as epistemological sense; Yanagi first wrote on Korean art in *Shirakaba*, a magazine that gained its celebrity and influence during the 1910s in large part through its dedication to the goal of introducing European (and some American) high culture to Japan. It should not be surprising, therefore, that Korean art was introduced in *Shirakaba* in a manner shaped by several typically Western assumptions about the non-West. For example, the first Korean art featured in the magazine, in the February 1920 issue, was Buddhist sculpture dating from the eighth century and earlier—objects evoking the lost grandeur and mystic spirituality of a remote Oriental past.[51] This, as Yanagi put it in his editorial commentary, was a "second experiment"; the first had been conducted in July of the previous year, when Yanagi selected several details from ancient Japanese Buddhist paintings for reproduction in the magazine.[52]

In both issues Yanagi considered himself to be introducing the readers of *Shirakaba* to Oriental art. In the first he wrote at some length in defense of this innovation, which he expected would surprise and even offend the many readers who had "long adored Western art":

> Just as we looked at the Occident with entirely new demands, so now we have begun to look at the Orient with eyes unlike those of anyone before. . . . We have begun to comprehend the Orient anew, but not from the fixed and academic viewpoint people have taken to date. Rather we comprehend the Orient in a universal sense; or, to put it differently, even though it is the Orient, we comprehend it in terms of universal value, and of truth that transcends the distinction between East and West.[53]

Yet Yanagi's efforts to demonstrate the universal value and truth of Oriental art as it transcended the division between East and West relied on stubbornly Western categories. These included not only the central, unitary category of the Orient, and its irresistible associations with the past splendor of an ancient civilization, but also the category of art itself, as defined preeminently in terms of painting and sculpture.

Yanagi may well have chosen Buddhist sculpture in particular to represent Oriental art because it was already well recognized both in Japan and the West as an important genre of native fine art, distinct from the lower orders of handicraft or industry.[54] Yet art historian Kinoshita Naoyuki has shown that Buddhist artifacts were transformed into artworks only in the late nineteenth century, largely at the behest of government officials determined to effect Japanese "civilization and enlightenment," in conformity to Western standards of cultural and social progress. In their search for an indigenous tradition of sculpture, one of the central genres of fine art within the European West, modernizing elites were quick to discover and promote carved Buddhist images. These seemed the closest counterpart to the monumental statues and busts ubiquitous in the public spaces of nineteenth-century Europe and North America. At the same time Buddhist objects answered well to Western consumers' touristic interest in the Japanese exotic, which Meiji officials could not afford to ignore. By 1900, therefore, the process by which many Buddhist artifacts were removed from temples, where they had functioned as sacred objects, and placed in museums (as well as private collections), where they became art objects in glass cases, was more or less complete.[55] Fifteen years later, Yanagi and other Taishō cosmopolitans found Buddhist sculpture ready-made, by their Westernizing Meiji elders, as Oriental art.[56]

No less than modernizers of the Meiji era, however, the young intellectuals who turned to the Orient in the late 1910s hoped to use Western means to resist aspects of Western hegemony. Yanagi suggested that by introducing Japanese to the magnificence of Oriental art, he might remind them that the West was not the exclusive province of value: "But for Japan today, which is in a strange condition, this sort of elucidation is both meaningful and necessary. For it is a fact that young Japanese are more familiar with things Occidental than with things Oriental."[57] Nor was Yanagi content to accept uncontested all of the implications of the Western categories and definitions he employed. For example, although the first Oriental numbers of *Shirakaba* featured painting and sculpture, it was not long before Yanagi had persuaded his fellow editors to let him devote an issue to Chosŏn period ceramics, which as he insisted at every opportunity, belonged in the category of "great art."[58] Like the early modernists in Europe, of whom he was almost certainly aware, Yanagi was restive with the conventional European distinction between fine and decorative or applied arts. Not only did such a separation imply and reinforce hierarchies of class, according to which the sculptor or painter occupied a position elevated far above that of the engraver or printer, but it projected those hierarchies onto the international stage. In this sense the strong association of East Asian cultures with ceramic, print, and textile arts, for example, could only reinscribe Oriental inferiority.

Most important, Yanagi and his fellow celebrants of Oriental art lost no time in qualifying the essential uniformity implied by the idea of the Orient. In particular, they claimed for themselves, as Japanese, the capacity for active modern consciousness and aesthetic discernment normally monopolized, according to Orientalist thought, by the West. In this sense Japan, especially modern Japan, was different; it was located both within and beyond the Oriental sphere. Of course, the idea that the hybrid nature of Japanese modernity might give it a distinctive role relative to an Orient defined largely in terms of ancient art and spirituality was not new with the *Shirakaba* generation. In his 1903 book on Japanese art, *The Ideals of the East*, art educator Okakura Kakuzō had already informed European and American readers that "Japan is a museum of Asiatic civilization; and yet more than a museum, because the singular genius of the race leads it to dwell on all phases of the ideals of the past, in that spirit of living Advaitism which welcomes the new without losing the old."[59] Okakura concluded by suggesting some of the larger implications of Japan's singular aesthetic genius: "The Chinese War [the Sino-Japanese War of 1894–1895] . . . arouses us now to the grand problems and responsibilities which await us as the new Asiatic Power. Not only to return to our own past ideals, but to feel and revivify the dormant life of the old Asiatic unity, becomes our mission."[60]

Both Okakura and Yanagi appear to have imagined an identity and a role for modern Japan distinct from those of either Orient or Occident. In a sense, writers and artists of Yanagi's generation were able to go some way toward realizing Okakura's vision; the Korean museum opened in 1924, for example, seems an almost uncanny expression of Okakura's notion of Japan's special curatorial role in the preservation of Asiatic civilization. However, Yanagi and his fellows, like Okakura, found it difficult to transcend the models and forms for international relations established by the West—even as they struggled to free themselves from the disadvantages of their own position within a Western-dominated world order. The very idea of a museum was borrowed from western Europe, where its emergence and development were deeply involved in the history of modern imperialism.[61] In their voluminous writings on Korean material culture, moreover, Japanese collectors and critics of the 1920s and 1930s relied on rhetorical strategies of knowing and appreciation that had long been employed within the Western Orientalist literature on the non-West. As with the Korean museum, the result contributed to the reproduction of Japanese colonial power.

In 1922 Yanagi published his classic statement on Korean art, an influential essay that appeared in the magazine *Shinchō*.[62] In it he claimed that Korean geography interacted with Korean history, which he characterized in terms of instability, invasion, and subservience to foreign powers, to make the Korean essence lonely, sorrowful, and spiritual. Yanagi pursued a similar logic to argue that China's size and power created a people and art defined by strength and that the security and comfort of Japan's geographical situation explained an essentially optimistic, playful character. Further,

Yanagi proposed an association between each country and one of the three elements he considered constitutive of all art—form, color, and line. He argued that since the ideal form should be stable, the ideal color bright, and the ideal line long and thin, Chinese art was characterized by stable forms, signifying power; Japanese art, by bright colors, signifying pleasure; and Korean art, by thin, long, curved lines, signifying sorrow and loneliness.

Yanagi suggested that ideal lines and forms—or melancholy and stability—were incompatible, especially in the case of pottery, which he considered the apotheosis of the art of long, curved lines.

> All [Korean pots] are unstable because they are long and narrow, but in them the demand for the element of line is completely satisfied. How inappropriate and fragile the long, narrow part is in use. The people do not have worldly desires. [63]

Yanagi noted further an absence of bright color in Korean art and culture and arrived thereby at his notorious theory of Korean whiteness. He observed that Koreans often wore white clothing and interpreted this to mean, again, that Koreans were an essentially sad people:

> White clothing has always been for mourning. It has been the symbol of a lonely, reverent, and profound heart. The people, by wearing white clothing, are mourning for eternity. I think that the difficult historical experience of the people, who have suffered much, led naturally and inevitably to the clothing they wear. Is not the paucity of color true proof of the absence of pleasure in life? [64]

During the colonial period the idea of essential Korean sorrow brought about by a national history of unceasing disaster was consistent with both scholarly and popular Japanese views of Korea. In his work on the Japanese historiography of Korea, Hatada Takashi has shown that during the 1910s and 1920s Japanese scholarly discourse on Korea and its history centered on the theory of Korean stagnation (*teitairon*). This notion, which has persisted well into the postwar period, brings together several other themes central to the colonial era Japanese study of Korea: the theories of the common origins of Japanese and Koreans (*Nissen dōsoron*), of the original unity of Manchuria and Korea (*Mansen ittairon*), and of Korean subordination to other countries (*taritsuseiron*). In short, the basic argument promoted by Japanese scholars who wrote on Korean history during this period was of the tragic impossibility of independent Korean development.[65] Publications on Korean art and culture by critics and collectors such as Yanagi contributed to a larger discourse that naturalized Japanese colonialism as a normal and even inevitable product of history, geography, and essential Korean identity.

The idea of melancholy as a central aesthetic principle of Korean culture was accepted by many. Various members of Yanagi's circle of friends and acquaintances, such as publisher Kurahashi Tōjirō and artist Tomimoto Kenkichi, took up the theme in their own writings on Korean art and culture.[66] In 1933 Uchiyama Shōzō, another collector and Korean pottery expert, wrote, "When we contemplate Yi period wares, we realize that lonely people are indeed possessed of warm hearts."[67] As suggested by Uchiyama's remark, many who wrote on Korean art during this period also imagined an identity between Korean objects and Korean people. For some the comparison between Koreans wearing white, for example, and the white porcelain of the later Chosŏn period was irresistible. Kurahashi concluded his preface to a 1932 book on Korean white porcelain with a typical conceit: "Those who travel in Korea are likely to see the scene of people in white clothing working slowly on the reddish-brown terrain. Those white-clad Koreans [*Senjin*] are, in sum, the white porcelain of the Yi dynasty."[68]

Japanese writers regularly assumed the position of the colonialist master, or subject, whose consuming gaze rendered everything Korean—landscape, people, and things—into a unified aesthetic object. Often this maneuver was accomplished by means of the same rhetorical strategies that had long been employed in Western texts to subordinate non-Western (including Japanese) others. For example, in 1922 Asakawa Noritaka published a poem called "Tsubo" [*Jar*], which gave vent to a fantasy assimilating Korean women and ceramic objects. After comparing the shape of a Korean waterjug to a girl's breast, "a form born to be loved," he went on to write in vaguely erotic terms of the Korean woman as a "walking Yi dynasty jar."[69] The familiar metaphor of colonial object as woman could also make room—sometimes even in the same text—for another familiar trope: colonial object as child. Asakawa's poem includes the following verses:

Koreans
Do not know what intention is
Rather than self-consciousness and reflection
They have one instinctive way
They make things with the pure heart of a child drawing a picture
And that one feeling continues to the end
An art in which feeling rather than rationality has won
An art in which the same thing cannot be made twice
Children's work made by adults

One bows the head on seeing the drawings of children
And feels astonished shame of one's own impurity[70]

The theme of the childlike Korean unconsciously producing masterpieces of art recurs in texts throughout this period. Yanagi used it, as did his friend Bernard Leach, who wrote in 1960, "The Coreans and their pots are childlike, spontaneous and trusting. We had something akin to this in Europe up to about the thirteenth century."[71]

Another comparison to Europe is apt here. Elisa Evett, in her study of the reception of Japanese art in late-nineteenth-century Europe, notes that critics dwelled on what they saw as the childlike, unconscious, even primitive qualities of Japanese images and, by extension, of the Japanese themselves.[72] In his 1898 *The Soul of the Far East*, for example, Percival Lowell wrote that the Japanese are "still in that childish state of development before self-consciousness has spoiled the sweet simplicity of nature."[73] These perceptions of the Oriental other were linked, of course, to ideas about the imperial European self; the decadent modern West had lost, irrevocably, the innocence and purity of the nobly savage state in which the Japanese were still to be found.[74]

In much the same way, Japanese writings on Korean pottery helped to define and interpret not only the colonial Korean object but also the colonialist Japanese subject. In a sense, Korea offered an opportunity for critical reflection on Japan's modern development. For example, the childlike purity of Korea served to highlight the adult consciousness and corruption of a modernizing Japan. Much as it had for Europeans and Americans contemplating the Far East, this metaphorical figure expressed the power relation between two cultures while it evoked nostalgia for a lost, premodern past. Writings by Japanese critics refer to the "naturalness," "unconsciousness," and "traditionalism" of Korea, Koreans, and Korean art. These were in explicit contrast to the artifice, self-consciousness, and dynamic Westernized modernity of Japan, which the authors generally deplored.[75] As Yanagi wrote of Japanese ceramics in 1931: "Production was poisoned by appreciation. Japanese bowls bear the scars of consciousness."[76] Yet Orientalist strategies of appreciating Korean objects also assigned great creative power and authority to Japanese consciousness, however scarred or impure. Almost every Japanese writing on Korean ceramics in this period stressed the importance and value of the tea masters' discovery of Korean pottery in the sixteenth century and, by extension, of Japanese aesthetic discrimination generally. Occasionally it was even suggested that the Japanese genius lay less in art production than it did in art appreciation.[77] Moreover, that genius was in itself a form of production, and one that was perhaps of a higher order than that of simple manufacture. As Yanagi put it, "The Koreans made rice bowls; the Japanese masters made them into teabowls."[78]

By claiming the power to discern Oriental objects and even to create their proper meanings and uses, Japanese intellectuals self-consciously ranged themselves alongside their Western counterparts as imperial authorities. In his first public reaction to the Korean independence movement of 1919, for example, Yanagi suggested that just as U.S. writer Lafcadio Hearn had "understood Japan better than some of the Japanese," so, too, Japanese like himself might be able to render "the labor of love for Korea" and fathom Korean "inner life as shown in religion and art." "There has been no Hearn for Korea yet," he observed.[79] Yet in claiming the type of authority over Oriental objects monopolized previously by Western subjects, Yanagi and his cohort were bidding for something beyond a mere power-sharing arrangement. They were explicitly engaged, for one thing, in an effort to resist the growing predominance of Western power throughout the world, and particularly in East Asia. As Yanagi wrote in 1923 of the Korean art museum he was planning, "It would be the greatest of pities if the introduction of the material civilization of Europe should lead to the extinction of our cherished Oriental handicrafts, as seems quite likely, so it is my earnest hope that the establishment of a gallery like this may not only serve to preserve the relics of the past, but also to provide a stimulus for new activities in the days to come."[80]

Like Okakura, Yanagi proposed that Japan respond to the Western challenge by means of a museum of past Oriental greatness that would also be, in some indefinite way, much more. In postcolonial retrospect it is perhaps too easy to read imperialist intent into the vague, ambitious vistas opened by Okakura's 1903 mission to "revivify the dormant life of the old Asiatic unity," or even by Yanagi's hope twenty years later of "new activities in the days to come." Certainly Yanagi's museum, which was made possible by Japanese colonial power in Korea and even helped to reproduce it, was both more specific and ultimately more oppressive than the one Okakura only envisioned. Yet Yanagi belonged to a generation much more disillusioned than Okakura's with the imperialist modernizing project of the nineteenth-century nation-state. His aspirations for the future of Japan, Asia, and indeed the world were critical, therefore, and vaguely utopian; only a few years later, for example, he looked toward a "Kingdom of Beauty" that promised humanity a quasi-socialist liberation from capitalist modernity.[81] Nevertheless, the means Yanagi and other Japanese writers and artists employed to produce greater freedom and even love were only too easily turned to a very different account.

Writers and artists in 1920s Japan collected Oriental objects for a variety of reasons. They admired and bought Chosŏn period pottery, for example, because they thought it beautiful or a bargain or novel or exotic or all of these things at once. Motivations are likely to have ranged from the wish to follow current fashion or to emulate certain groups or figures, to an impulse to know more about Korea or simply to engage in an accepted, masculine form of playful consumption. But for those who ranked among the most articulate and influential enthusiasts of Oriental art during this period, the acquisitive appreciation of Korean ceramics was also important as a powerful way to be both modern and Japanese. By using opportunities created in Korea by Japanese rule and by adopting selected aspects of Western-style colonial knowledge, Yanagi and others gained potent forms of cultural and social authority in Japan, Korea, and even the West.[82]

Yet the autonomy that colonial power and knowledge conferred was also curiously confining. Japanese intellectuals could name, define, and manipulate Oriental objects, but only by alienating themselves from the Orient they admired. Yanagi and his peers were largely successful in assigning enormous value and significance to new categories of Oriental art. Between 1920 and 1945, Korean, then folk Japanese, Chinese, Okinawan, "Manchurian," and Ainu material culture all gained new status as objects of metropolitan Japanese desire. Activist collectors such as Yanagi accomplished this feat, however, by separating themselves—as Japanese, as moderns, as members of a privileged social class, and as men—from the premodern, preconscious creativity they celebrated. One consequence was that modern Japanese artistic creativity could only seem somewhat incongruous, in need of deprecation; as Yanagi wrote in 1928 in his founding treatise on folk craft, "Seen as human beings, how much greater cultivated individual artists are than uneducated artisans; yet if we consider the work, how much greater folk-craft is than individualistic creations."[83] But surely the most grievous outcome of all was the role Yanagi and many other Japanese intellectuals eventually found themselves taking within an exploitative, brutal system of colonial relations with fellow Orientals, and even with fellow Japanese. The distress experienced by Japanese intellectuals mobilized by the imperialist Japanese state cannot, of course, compare to the price paid by its victims throughout Asia.

Notes

In revising this essay for publication I was aided greatly by the comments and suggestions of Mark Jones, Gennifer Weisenfeld, Catherine Ciepiela, Janet Gyatso, Andre Schmid, and two anonymous readers for *positions*. I thank them all as well as the many others who have helped me with this project over the years, especially Carol Gluck, Henry Smith, and my parents. Special thanks are due to the Nihon Mingeikan (Japan Folk Crafts Museum) for permission to reproduce the photographs in figures 1–3.

1 Komatsu Shōei, *Ri chō no yakimono* [Yi dynasty pottery], no. 576 in the Color Books series (Tokyo: Hōikusha, 1982), 104.
2 See, for example, two glossy paperback guides to the collection and appreciation of Yi dynasty crafts: *Ri chō o tanoshimu* [Enjoying Yi dynasty] (Tokyo: Heibonsha, 1998), and *Ri chō ni nyūmon* [Introduction to Yi dynasty] (Tokyo: Bunka shuppan kyoku, 1998).

3 Takasaki Sōji, "Yanagi Sōetsu to Chōsen: kankei nenpu" [Yanagi Sōetsu and Korea: A chronological record], in *Chōsen o omou* [Thinking on Korea], by Yanagi Sōetsu, ed. Takasaki Sōji (Tokyo: Chikuma shobō, 1984), 237.

4 Yoshida Kōzō, "Tomimoto Kenkichi nenpu" [Tomimoto Kenkichi: A chronological record], in *Yōhen zakki* [Miscellaneous notes from the vicinity of a kiln], by Tomimoto Kenkichi (Tokyo: Bunka shuppan kyoku, 1975), 198. See also Tomimoto, "Takushoku hakurankai no ichinichi" [One day at the colonial exposition], in *Tomimoto Kenkichi chosakushū* [Selected writings of Tomimoto Kenkichi] (Tokyo: Gogatsu shobō, 1981), 472, cited in Brian Moeran, "Bernard Leach and the Japanese Folk Craft Movement: The Formative Years," *Journal of Design History* 2, no. 2–3 (1989): 139–144.

5 Unlike many of his fellow graduates of Gakushūin, the higher school of choice for aristocrats and members of the imperial family, Yanagi was not independently wealthy. As the second son of a talented former samurai whose mathematical and navigational skills enabled an illustrious career in the navy, Yanagi was born into the Meiji technocratic elite. Although his father eventually achieved the rank of admiral, Yanagi inherited neither landed nor industrial wealth. Throughout his life, for an income he depended on his own activities as a writer, a teacher, an art collector, a fund-raiser, and a public speaker and also on his wife, Yanagi Kaneko, who had a successful career as a professional Western-style singer and voice teacher.

6 On the history and significance of Korean teabowls within the tea context see Louise Cort, "The Kizaemon Teabowl Reconsidered: The Making of a Masterpiece," *Chanoyu Quarterly*, no. 71 (1992): 7–30, and Hayashiya Seizō, "The Korean Teabowl," *Chanoyu Quarterly*, no. 18 (1977): 28–46.

7 Kumakura Isao, in his history of the modern tea ceremony, notes that during the 1910s and 1920s tea caddies (*chaire*) and especially teabowls gained enormously in importance and value relative to other objects used in the tea ceremony, such as hanging scrolls and incense containers. During the period 1924–1926 and again in 1927–1929, Korean bowls fetched the top sums for tea objects sold. See Kumakura, *Kindai chadōshi no kenkyū* [Studies in the modern history of the tea ceremony] (Tokyo: Nihon hōsō shuppan kyōkai, 1980), 265–268.

8 In English see, for example, Yanagi Sōetsu, *Folk-Crafts in Japan*, trans. Shigeyoshi Sakabe (Tokyo: Kokusai Bunka Shinkokai, 1936), 10–12, or Yanagi, *The Unknown Craftsman: A Japanese Insight into Beauty*, adapted by Bernard Leach and trans. Mihoko Okamura (New York: Kodansha International, 1972), 190–196.

9 One of the earliest expressions of these views, which Yanagi was to develop throughout his career and particularly in the postwar period, is in the essays collected as *Kōgei no michi* [The way of craft], first published in 1927–1928. See *Yanagi Sōetsu zenshū* (hereafter YSz), [Collected works of Yanagi Sōetsu] (Tokyo: Chikuma shobō, 1980–1992), 8:205–208. Also see his 1933 lecture "Sadō to kibutsu" [The tea ceremony and utensils], in YSz, 17:503–515.

10 The enthusiasm of early-twentieth-century industrialists and politicians for the tea ceremony recalls, of course, earlier periods when *chanoyu* served similar social, political, and economic

functions for Japanese elites. It was only after 1868, during the first decades of systematic Westernization, that the tea ceremony fell into relative neglect. See Paul Varley, "*Chanoyu*: From the Genroku Epoch to Modern Times," in *Tea in Japan: Essays on the History of Chanoyu*, ed. Paul Varley and Kumakura Isao (Honolulu: University of Hawai'i Press, 1989), 161–194.

11   For a lively study of one of the central figures in this process, with special attention to his legendary art collection, see Christine M. E. Guth, *Art, Tea, and Industry: Masuda Takashi and the Mitsui Circle* (Princeton, N.J.: Princeton University Press, 1993).

12   Ibid., 119–128; Kumakura, *Kindai chadōshi no kenkyū*, 257.

13   Takahashi Yoshio, *Taishō meiki kan* [Taishō catalog of famous tea objects], 9 vols. (Tokyo: Taishō meiki kan hensanjo, 1922–1931).

14   By, for example, stressing the importance of tea caddies and teabowls relative to other, formerly more prominent categories of tea objects. Kumakura argues that the publication of the *Taishō meiki kan* helped to promote the sharp rise in market value of teabowls and tea caddies during the 1920s. See Kumakura, *Kindai chadōshi no kenkyū*, 17, 267–268.

15   Guth, *Art, Tea, and Industry*, 183; Kumakura, *Kindai chadōshi no kenkyū*, 267–268.

16   Yanagi, *Kōgei no michi*, in *YSz*, 8:205.

17   Takasaki, "Yanagi Sōetsu to Chōsen: kankei nenpu," 237.

18   Akaboshi Gorō and Nakamaru Heiichirō, *Chōsen no yakimono: Ri chō* [Korean pottery: The Yi dynasty] (Kyoto: Tankō shinsha, 1965), 26. The Korean word *yobo*, which Akaboshi glosses as "laborer," is in fact a term of familiar second-person address. Akaboshi's usage suggests that it had a different meaning in the colonialist Japanese lexicon.

19   Japanese collectors often refer to the low prices of Korean craft objects and antiques generally, and Chosŏn era Korean ceramics in particular, during this period. See, for example, the comments of another well-known collector of Yi dynasty objects, Kurahashi Tōjirō, in "Chōsen kōgei zakki" [Miscellaneous notes on Korean crafts], *Teikoku kōgei* [Imperial craft] 4, no. 2 (February 1930): 32; also see the reminiscences of another collector, Nonogami Keiichi, in "Ri chō hakuji to watakushi" [Yi dynasty white porcelain and I], in *Ri chō hakuji shōsen* [Selections on Yi dynasty white porcelain], ed. Nonogami and Itō Ikutarō (Tokyo: Sōjūsha bijutsu shuppan, 1984), 142.

20   Asakawa Noritaka, "Chōsen kotōki no kenkyū ni tsukite" [On research into old Korean ceramics], in *Keimeikai kōenshū* [Lectures of the Morning Star Society] 55 (Tokyo: Keimeikai jimusho, 1934), 30–31.

21   Ibid., 37, 35. Many researchers and collectors benefited from the "geographical liberation" of Korean tombs as well as kiln sites under Japanese colonialism.

22   Takahashi Yoshio, "Kaisetsu" [Commentary], in *Taishō meiki kan*, 6:4–5; 7:1–4; 8:1.

23   Ibid., 6:5.

24   For a brief discussion of the "scientific" trend in ceramics study and appreciation in Taishō Japan, and its Western inspiration, see Suzuki Kenji's text in *Tōgei (I)* [Ceramic art], vol. 15 of

Genshoku gendai Nihon no bijutsu [Modern Japanese art in color] (Tokyo: Shogakkan, 1980), 110.

25 Pak Cho, *Ri chō kōgei to kotō no bi* [The beauty of Yi dynasty crafts and old pottery] (Tokyo: Tōyō keizai nippō sha, 1976), 418, 421. Also see Nonogami, "Ri chō hakuji to watakushi," 142.

26 In 1996 a Chosŏn period jar of precisely the type first collected by Yanagi, Asakawa, and their cohort was sold at Christie's for $8.6 million, then the highest price ever paid at auction for an Asian art object. See *New York Times*, 2 November 1996.

27 *YSz*, 6:30–31. The article appeared in the *Yomiuri shimbun* [Yomiuri newspaper]. The verb *omou* in its title, translated here as "thinking," also carries a strong sense of "yearning for," or "loving."

28 *YSz*, 6:31.

29 Raymond Williams, *Culture and Society, 1780–1950* (New York: Columbia University Press, 1960), 30–31, 42–43.

30 Yanagi Sōetsu, "If Japan Understood Korean Art: An Appeal for the Establishment of an Art Gallery," *Japan Advertiser*, 23 January 1921.

31 Yanagi Sōetsu, "Ri chō tōjiki no tokushitsu" [The special character of Yi dynasty ceramics], in *YSz*, 6:165. This essay was first published in the September 1922 issue of *Shirakaba*, then translated in the same year into Korean for a Korean weekly newspaper.

32 Yanagi Sōetsu, "Chōsen no bijutsu" [Korean art], in *YSz*, 6:92. This famous essay was first published in the May 1922 issue of the magazine *Shinchō* [New tide].

33 Yanagi Sōetsu and Yanagi Kaneko, " 'Ongakkai' shuisho" [Prospectus for a concert], *YSz*, 6:172–173. According to Sōetsu's own account in "Kare no Chōsen kō" [His trip to Korea], which appeared in *Kaizō* [Reconstruction] in September 1920, this statement was sent to his friends.

34 Takasaki Sōji, "Yanagi Sōetsu to Chōsen" [Yanagi Sōetsu and Korea], *Chōsen shi sō* [Korean History Series], no. 1 (June 1979): 78.

35 This view of Yanagi's "gentle stubbornness" (*odayaka na gankōsa*) has been given influential expression by cultural critic Tsurumi Shunsuke. See his commentary, or "Kaisetsu," for a 1975 volume collecting Yanagi's writings, in the series *Kindai Nihon shisō taikei* [Modern Japanese thought]; see also his biography of Yanagi, *Yanagi Sōetsu* (Tokyo: Heibonsha, 1976). Another prominent exponent of a similar view has been Ubukata Naokichi, whose influential essay on Yanagi and Korea was first published in the journal *Shisō* [Thought] several months after Yanagi's death: "Nihonjin no Chōsenkan: Yanagi Sōetsu o tōshite" [Japanese views of Korea: Through the medium of Yanagi Sōetsu], *Shisō*, October 1961, 66–77.

36 Nishio Makoto, Usui Yoshimi, and Kinoshita Junji, eds., *Gendai kokugo 3* [Modern Japanese 3] (Tokyo: Chikuma shobō, 1974), 208–220.

37 Takasaki, "Yanagi Sōetsu to Chōsen," 97.

38 Chong-sik Lee, *The Politics of Korean Nationalism* (Berkeley and Los Angeles: University of California Press, 1963), 114–120.

39 Mark R. Peattie, "Japanese Attitudes toward Colonialism: 1895–1945," in *The Japanese Colonial Empire: 1895–1945*, ed. Ramon H. Myers and Mark R. Peattie (Princeton, N.J.: Princeton University Press, 1984), 106; Lee, *Politics of Korean Nationalism*, 124.

40 Michael E. Robinson, *Cultural Nationalism in Colonial Korea, 1920–1925* (Seattle: University of Washington Press, 1988), 4.

41 Ibid., 4–8.

42 Michael E. Robinson, "Ideological Schism in the Korean Nationalist Movement, 1920–1930: Cultural Nationalism and the Radical Critique," *Journal of Korean Studies* 4 (1982–1983): 247–252.

43 Ibid., 254.

44 Ching-chih Chen, "Police and Community Control Systems in the Empire," in Myers and Peattie, *Japanese Colonial Empire*, 222–224.

45 E. Patricia Tsurumi, "Colonial Education in Korea and Taiwan," in Myers and Peattie, *Japanese Colonial Empire*, 303–304.

46 Michael E. Robinson, "Colonial Publication Policy and the Korean Nationalist Movement," in Myers and Peattie, *Japanese Colonial Empire*, 327.

47 Yanagi Sōetsu, " 'Chōsen minzoku bijutsukan' ni tsuite no hōkoku" [Report on the "Korean folk art museum"], *Shirakaba*, February 1921, 130.

48 Takasaki, "Yanagi Sōetsu to Chōsen," 100; "Chōsen minzoku bijutsukan dai jū ichi kai kaikei hōkoku" [Eleventh financial report on the Korean folk art museum], *Shirakaba*, November 1922, n. p.

49 Takasaki, "Yanagi Sōetsu to Chōsen," 100–101.

50 The publication of philosopher Watsuji Tetsurō's *Kōji junrei* [Pilgrimage to ancient temples] in 1919, in which he celebrated the ancient Buddhist art of Nara, Japan's eighth-century capital, is often cited as a key moment in the "return" to Japan and/or Asia. Art historian Kitazawa Noriaki has also noted, in his study of the painter Kishida Ryūsei, the simultaneous rise of interest among painters in a reappraisal of *bunjinga*, a genre of Chinese-style Japanese painting that flourished during the eighteenth and nineteenth centuries. See Kitazawa, *Kishida Ryūsei to Taishō abuangyardo* [Kishida Ryūsei and the Taishō avant-garde] (Tokyo: Iwanami shoten, 1993), 199.

51 See Edward Said, *Orientalism* (New York: Pantheon, 1978), 78–79, for discussion of the classically Orientalist emphasis on the glory of Oriental antiquity, in opposition to the decrepitude of Oriental modernity.

52 Yanagi Sōetsu, "Kongetsu no sashie ni tsuite" [On this month's illustrations], *Shirakaba*, February 1920, 102.

53 Yanagi Sōetsu, "Kondo no sashie ni tsuite" [On the illustrations], *Shirakaba*, July 1919, 108–109.

54 A third "Oriental" issue of *Shirakaba*, put out in July 1920, featured photographs of Buddhist statues from temples in Nara. Moreover, Yanagi's first lengthy essay on Korean art, published

in the June 1919 issue of the magazine *Geijutsu* [Art], dealt with Buddhist sculpture of the Silla period (57 B.C.E.–A.D. 935).

55 Kinoshita Naoyuki, *Bijutsu to iu misemono: Abura-e chaya no jidai* [The spectacle called art: The period of the Abura-e Chaya] (Tokyo: Heibonsha, 1993), 32–34.

56 For an illuminating discussion of both the use of Buddhist "statues" at the world's fairs of the late nineteenth century and the efforts by such Taishō intellectuals as Watsuji Tetsurō to turn Buddhist art to a different sort of account, see Noriko Aso's dissertation, *New Illusions: The Emergence of a Discourse on Traditional Japanese Arts and Crafts, 1868–1945* (Chicago: University of Chicago, 1997).

57 Yanagi, "Kondo no sashie ni tsuite," 110.

58 *Shirakaba*, September 1922.

59 Okakura Kakuzō, *The Ideals of the East with Special Reference to the Art of Japan* (London: John Murray, 1920), 8. Leslie Pincus has discussed usefully the impact Okakura's ideas had on at least one important thinker of Yanagi's generation, the philosopher Kuki Shūzō. See Pincus, *Authenticating Culture in Imperial Japan: Kuki Shūzō and the Rise of National Aesthetics* (Berkeley and Los Angeles: University of California Press, 1996).

60 Okakura, *Ideals of the East*, 208.

61 There is a large and growing literature on the close relationship between Euro-American imperialism and the development of what Tony Bennett has called the "exhibitionary complex" of the modern museum together with various other institutions and practices. In addition to Bennett's suggestive "The Exhibitionary Complex," *New Formations* 4 (spring 1988): 73–102, see also James Clifford, *The Predicament of Culture* (Cambridge, Mass.: Harvard University Press, 1988), esp. chap. 10. Relatively recent examples of works on museums, collecting, and colonialism include Annie E. Coombes, *Reinventing Africa: Museums, Material Culture, and Popular Imagination in Late Victorian and Edwardian England* (New Haven, Conn.: Yale University Press, 1994), and Nicholas Thomas, *Entangled Objects: Exchange, Material Culture, and Colonialism in the Pacific* (Cambridge, Mass.: Harvard University Press, 1991), chap. 4. Among the numerous works dealing with the world's fairs of the nineteenth and twentieth centuries see esp. Robert Rydell, *All the World's a Fair: Visions of Empire at American International Expositions, 1876–1916* (Chicago: University of Chicago Press, 1984), and Timothy Mitchell, *Colonising Egypt* (Berkeley and Los Angeles: University of California Press, 1988), chap. 1.

62 *YSz*, 6:89–109. "Chōsen no bijutsu" was republished later the same year in Yanagi's book *Chōsen to sono geijutsu* [Korea and its art] (Tokyo: Sōbunkaku, 1922).

63 Yanagi, "Chōsen no bijutsu," in *YSz*, 6:102.

64 Ibid., 105.

65 Hatada Takashi, "Chōsen shizō to teitairon" [Representations of Korean history and the theory of stagnation], in *Chōsen to Nihonjin* [Korea and the Japanese] (Tokyo: Keisō shobō, 1983), 66–92.

66 See, for example, Kurahashi Tōjirō, "Chōsen tōki ni tsuite" [About Korean ceramics], in *Keimeikai dai ni jū kyū kai kōenshū* [Lectures of the twenty-ninth meeting of the Morning Star Society] (Tokyo: Keimeikai jimusho, 1928), 37–38; also Tomimoto Kenkichi, "Ri chō no suiteki" [Yi dynasty water droppers], *Shirakaba*, September 1922, 23.

67 Quoted in G. St. G. M. Gompertz, *Korean Pottery and Porcelain of the Yi Period* (London: Faber and Faber, 1968), 7.

68 Kurahashi Tōjirō, ed., *Tōki zuroku: Ri chō hakuji* [A pictorial record of ceramics: Yi dynasty white porcelain] (Tokyo: Kōseikai shuppanbu, 1932), n. p. The Japanese word *Senjin* is an informal, usually pejorative contraction of the term *Chōsenjin* (Korean) that was often used during the colonial period in particular.

69 Asakawa Noritaka, "Tsubo," *Shirakaba*, September 1922, 57, 61.

70 Ibid., 59.

71 Bernard Leach, *A Potter in Japan, 1952–1954* (London: Faber and Faber, 1960), 161.

72 Elisa Evett, *The Critical Reception of Japanese Art in Late Nineteenth Century Europe* (Ann Arbor: University of Michigan Press, 1982), 35–40.

73 Quoted in ibid., 40.

74 Ibid., 42–46.

75 See, for example, Asakawa's essay on Chosŏn period ceramics, "Ri chō tōki no kachi oyobi henzō ni tsuite" [On the value of and changes in Yi dynasty ceramics], *Shirakaba*, September 1922, or Tomimoto Kenkichi's 1925 essay on Seoul, "Keijō zasshin" [Keijō thoughts], in *Yōhen zakki*, 75–89.

76 Yanagi Sōetsu, "'Kizaemon Ido' o miru" [Looking at the "Kizaemon Ido"], *Kōgei* [Craft], no. 5 (May 1931): 15–33; reprinted in Yanagi, *Chōsen o omou*, 198.

77 See, for example, Asakawa, "Ri chō tōki no kachi oyobi henzō," 5.

78 Yanagi, *Chōsen o omou*, 196.

79 Yanagi Sōetsu, "An Artist's Message to Koreans: Japan's Mistaken Policy and Korea's Sad Fate," *Japan Advertiser*, 13 August 1919. This is an abridged translation of "Chōsenjin o omou," which appeared several months earlier in the *Yomiuri shimbun*.

80 Yanagi Sōetsu, "If Japan Understood Korean Art," *Japan Advertiser*, 23 January 1923. The article was first published as "'Chōsen minzoku bijutsukan' no setsuritsu ni tsuite" [On the establishment of the "Korean folk art museum"], in *Shirakaba*, January 1921, 180–184.

81 See, for example, Yanagi's founding statement of *mingei* theory, *The Way of Craft* [*Kōgei no michi*], first published serially in 1927 and 1928 in the magazine *Daichōwa* [Great harmony]. See *YSz*, 8:61–279.

82 It was as an expert on Oriental art and religion that Yanagi, for example, accepted an invitation to teach at Harvard University for the 1929–1930 academic year.

83 Yanagi, *Kōgei no michi*, in *YSz*, 8:170.

Touring Japan-as-Museum: *NIPPON* and Other Japanese Imperialist Travelogues

Gennifer Weisenfeld

JAPAN is indeed a "Land of Color, Culture and Charm." It is the land where East and West meet in perfect accord, where the modern culture of the Occident harmonizes with Oriental civilization. Available throughout Japan are the latest travel facilities from automobile to airplane, plus home comfort and snug hotel accommodation, which assure the tourist a delightful trip at minimum expense of time and money. —Board of Tourist Industry, Japanese Government Railways, advertisement, 1939

Okakura Tenshin, the prominent turn-of-the-century cultural ideologue, envisioned Japan as a museum, both the repository of Asian culture and a living exhibit of this legacy functioning in the contemporary world.[1] The illustrated, Western-language, promotional quarterly *NIPPON* (1934–1944) was an invitation to tour this museum. Touting the magazine as a representation of "actual life and events in modern Japan and the Far East," *NIPPON*'s designers used a host of sophisticated modernist visual techniques, including an array of stunning photomontages, as a means of enticing the Western tourist to authenticate Japan by experiencing "the world-as-exhibition," about which Timothy Mitchell has so eloquently written.[2] This "world-as-exhibition," explains Mitchell, was "not an exhibition of the world but the world organized and grasped as though it were an exhibition." Like the dioramas and live exhibits at the Parisian world's fair in Mitchell's analysis, *NIPPON*'s Japan was a world set up as a picture. It was "ordered up as an object on display to be investigated and experienced by the dominating European [Western] gaze."[3]

As an instantiation of Japan-as-museum, *NIPPON* deserves consideration as "a privileged arena for presenting self and 'other.' "[4] Jeanne Cannizzo has argued that the museum is a "cultural text, one that may be read to understand the underlying cultural or ideological assumptions that have informed its creation, selection and display."[5] In keeping with the museum metaphor, I will consider the magazine layout as an analogue to gallery installation and the designers as curators of the exhibition experience, the magazine text becoming a kind of expanded wall label that explains the cultural practices and artifacts being presented. Yet the question of who controls the means of representation still remains. Everything in a museum is put under the pressure of a "way of seeing," according to Svetlana Alpers, and it is the purpose of this essay to elucidate the mechanisms by which *NIPPON*'s director Natori Yōnosuke (1910–1962) and his stable of skilled commercial designers and photographers at the publishing firm/design studio Nippon Kōbō (Japan studio) constructed a way of seeing Japan.[6]

The Nippon Kōbō members were already individually well known for their work in photojournalism (*hōdō shashin*) and advertising (*kōkoku*) before they launched the journal. Their integrative techniques effectively blurred the line between avant-garde art, reportage, advertising practice, and national propaganda (*kokka* or *kokusaku senden*). As I will discuss below, the blurring of boundaries extended to the line between metropole (*naichi*) and colonies (*gaichi*), between essays and advertisements, and between culture and industry, visually simulating the literal annexation of Japan's colonial subjects into the empire and establishing industrial and commercial interests as fundamental components of Japanese modern cultural identity.

What should not be forgotten in the analysis of this periodical is the intended audience: the Western viewer. Implicit in *NIPPON* is the display of one culture by its self-appointed representatives to another culture (or in this case many other cultures, to disaggregate "the West"). Michael Baxandall reminds us to consider the "status of the viewer as an agent in the field of exhibition," pointing to the relationship between presenter and presentee as an integral factor in the configuration of the means and mode of representation.[7] It can be said that since its forced opening to Commodore Matthew Perry in 1853, Japan has maintained an ambivalent relationship to the West in terms of its status in the world imperialist theater. Although never a formal colony of any Western nation, Japan still figured prominently in Orientalist and primitivist representations of Asia. Many foreign travelers, such as American Howell Reeves, who visited Japan in 1926, expressed their expectations of an exotic Orient while writing disparaging accounts of their experiences that expressed only patronizing contempt for the country's backwardness:

> I wonder if it will be all that our imagination has created? The land of sunshine and flowers—of romantic rain—of oriental mists—of rumbling volcanoes—of thrilling earthquakes—of gardens and bamboo—of rice and silk—of swiftly moving rickshaws—of queer slant eyed people, courteous and quiet. . . .
>
> If you consider Japan as a nation emerging from barbarian, or a semi-civilized condition then you are filled with enthusiasm and admiration for the progress that has been made. If, however, you view Japan as the Japanese insist upon your viewing it—as a first class civilized nation— then the picture presents an entirely different aspect. . . . It may be a "long, long way to Tipperary" but the distance is short indeed compared to that which the Japanese must travel, mentally, morally, and materially to stand abreast of "western civilization."[8]

Japanese intellectuals and state officials internalized many aspects of Western imperialist culture in the process of negotiating a modern national identity. *NIPPON* was a part of Japan's ongoing dialogic response to this Western

Orientalizing and primitivizing perception, as it launched an unceasing campaign to gain cultural legitimacy in the eyes of the West. The magazine's imploring tone was often filled with a certain degree of melodrama and genuine anxiety over increasing world political tensions concerning Japan's economic practices and aggressive expansion into Asia in the 1930s that were leading to rising anti-Japanese sentiment abroad.[9] The prominent cultural critic Hasegawa Nyozekan, previously a champion of socialism but later a convert to the nationalist cause in the 1930s, wrote an essay for the magazine titled "What Do the Japanese Want?" beseeching Western countries to appreciate Japan.

> What do we Japanese ask of the people of the world? Those who know Japan well, fully understand that we are not all anaemic in any sense of the word, and that we are full of life.... We would like to be "respected" by good people, men and women, of the world.... Some psychopaths living in an illusory world of extreme egoism or suffering from a superiority complex, would greatly exaggerate their own importance. Worse than that, what can be so ridiculous as to see a little monkey with a silk hat on his head wanting to be saluted by the onlookers! Those, who look upon our case as anything analogous to these above instances, may laugh at us to their heart's content, and reap their own benefit. To those friends who show their friendly attitude toward us without hesitation, how shall we repay their gentleman-like action? The least we can say is that we are prepared to return to them tenfold of what we receive.[10]

In *NIPPON* the invitation to understand Japan was offered on both a diplomatic and a touristic level. Or perhaps it is more accurate to say that tourism was seen as an integral component of international relations, designed to faciliate cross-cultural understanding by acclimating the Western viewer to the foreign context of Japan, at the same time adjusting Japan to suit the comfort level of the visitor. Thus, in this paper I will argue that by offering a means of "specular dominance" over Japan, *NIPPON* was both an attempt by state-sanctioned representatives of the Japanese empire at self-representation *and* an invocation to the Western viewer to colonize the country through a kind of touristic gaze.[11]

Natori Yōnosuke, Photojournalism, and the Origins of *NIPPON*

Inaugurated in 1934, *NIPPON* published thirty-six issues over the course of a decade, only folding in 1944 at the end of the Asia Pacific War. It was available in at least eight countries and was published regularly in four and sometimes as many as six languages; most articles were translated multilingually in each issue.[12] The editor-in-chief of the magazine, Natori Yōnosuke, graduated from the regular division of Keio Gijuku Daigaku (forerunner of Keio University middle school) and then went to Germany, where he studied applied crafts, commercial art, and photojournalism from 1928 until 1932. In Berlin he met designer Erna Mecklenburg (1901–1979), who soon became his wife, mentor, and collaborative partner in design activities. Natori and Mecklenberg's work was quickly recognized by Herman Ullstein, owner of the Ullstein Verlag, a publishing house that produced a variety of photojournalistic publications, including the *Berliner Illustrirte Zeitung* [Berlin illustrated news]. Natori was hired as a contract photographer for the press in late 1931.[13] Among his various assignments for Ullstein, Natori covered the Manchurian Incident and its subsequent military skirmishes, for which he stayed in China for three months in 1933. Unable to return to Germany afterward due to restrictions on foreign immigration imposed by the Hitler government in the interim, he instead returned to Japan, where he acted as Ullstein's Japan correspondent.[14]

After his return to Japan, Natori founded Nippon Kōbō in August 1933 with designers Hara Hiromu (1903–1986) and Okada Sōzō (1903–1983), photographer Kimura Ihee (1901–1974), and photography critic Ina Nobuo (1898–1978). Natori regarded photography more as "a visual language" than as an art form. He soon established himself as a pioneer in the functional use of photography and photojournalism in Japan, zealously advocating the "educational" possibilities of these modes and establishing strong links to propaganda production.[15] This period marked a significant shift in the perceived role of photography among practitioners in Japan, reflecting similar changes occurring around the world. Ina Nobuo's now-famous manifesto in the first issue of the modernist photography journal *Kōga* [Shining picture], titled "Return to Photography," concluded with the statement, "Those who hold the camera must never forget that they are social beings." This declaration represented a radical departure from the art photography (*gei-jutsu shashin*), art-for-art's-sake mentality of certain Japanese photographers, such as Fukuhara Shinzō and Fuchigami Hakuyō, to a more documentary, socially engaged role for the photographer.[16]

The translation of the term *photojournalism* (encompassing the implications of reportage and documentary photography) into Japanese as *hōdō shashin* was actually done by Natori himself. This new term marked a distinction from the more generic category of press photography, as it implied a more active and journalistic role for the photographer, whose work was seen as paralleling written copy but with the narrative constructed of images—in essence a photoessay.[17] Photojournalism was, therefore, a construction of multiple photographs (*kumi shashin*), either a series of related photographs, a photocollage, or a photomontage.

Concerning the important truth-telling power ascribed to photography at the time and how this was capitalized on in *hōdō shashin*, Ina wrote in 1935, "It has generally become common perception that what is expressed through the eye of the camera actually exists. Due to this attitude, 'hōdō shashin,' which made possible mass communication by being printed, is the greatest weapon for ideology formation."[18] Photojournalism's claims to reportorial accuracy, however, belied the extent to which the photographs were actually manipulated to produce the sensation of "unmediated reality." At the very minimum, we know that Natori did extensive shooting to find the perfect image for any one particular feature, as amply demonstrated by archival evidence of his photo shoots.[19] Moreover, many of the Nippon Kōbō photographers were concurrently affiliated with modernist photography associations, showing an allegiance to avant-gardist manipulation of the photographic medium and fostering what photography historian John Roberts has called the "dialectical permeation" or the "shared cultural space of the photographic document and the avant-garde."[20]

The work and theories of photography discussed among these artists reflected two powerful trends emerging in German photography in the 1930s: New Objectivity (Neue Sachlichkeit) and Bauhaus photography, represented most iconically by photographers Albert Renger-Patzsch and Laszlo Moholy-Nagy, respectively. The Japanese photography community had exceptionally strong ties to Germany both theoretically and in terms of actual practice, as many Japanese photographers as well as Natori studied there during this period. The debates between these two groups hinged on the definition of realism. Renger-Patzsch argued for photography as fact (commonly known as "factography"), and Moholy-Nagy championed a modernist version of realism that took into account a transformation in visual perception. The issues debated by these two groups of photographers were generated originally by the photography of the Russian Revolution, exemplified by the work of Gustav Klutsis, El Lissitzky, and Alexander Rodchenko, who according to Roberts, saw photography as a "source of cognitive transformation."[21] This attitude was most clearly evident in the incorporation of the everyday as a subject with socially transformative potential and in the shift to montage aesthetics, which both simulated a revolution in perception to incorporate the multiperspectival viewpoint and served as a synecdoche of collective experience.[22]

While photographers themselves may have seriously doubted the transparent truthfulness of documentary photography, they still acknowledged that it was received by the general public in such a manner. Nippon Kōbō took its commitment to the promotion of documentary photography very seriously, mounting a groundbreaking exhibition in this area during its first year and publishing a pamphlet titled *Concerning Photojournalism* [*Hōdō shashin ni tsuite*]. However, due to internal conflicts among the members (principally between Natori and the others), the first incarnation of the studio folded in early 1934.[23] Natori soon reestablished it with a new group of associates and began publishing *NIPPON* in October (the studio changed names in mid-1939 to become the International News Company, or Kokusai Hōdō Kōgei Kabushikigaisha).

The main purpose of the journal was to publicize Japanese culture to the rest of the world; thus it served as a quasi-governmental organ of national propaganda. In this capacity Nippon Kōbō received support from state agencies such as the Japan National Board of Tourist Industry and the Society for International Cultural Relations (Kokusai Bunka Shinkōkai, forerunner of the Japan Foundation), a nonprofit organization established under the auspices of the Ministry of Foreign Affairs in 1934. The self-described main objective of the society was "the international exchange of culture and in particular the enhancement of Japanese and Oriental culture abroad, thereby to contribute toward the advancement of civilization and the promotion of human welfare."[24] It was joined in supporting the studio by representatives of industrial capital, in particular the textile company Kanegafuchi Bōseki (Kanegafuchi spinning company), known as Kanebo, whose new president Tsuda Shingo provided a substantial loan to bankroll the launching of *NIPPON*. In light of the magazine's state and private support, its integrated vision of Japanese politics, culture, and industry is no coincidence.

The publication was a total collaboration between photographers and designers, not to mention important textual contributions by well-known ideologues and intellectuals, cultural figures, politicians, and high-ranking military officials. The visual and the textual mutually amplified each other in *NIPPON* to form a single, symphonic, orchestrated expression of identity. The magazine's effectiveness as a means of persuasion was due in large part to the extraordinary talent of its contributors, including some of the foremost Japanese photographers and designers of the twentieth century. Most prominently the roster included photographers Domon Ken (1909–1990), Horino Masao (b. 1907), Kimura Ihee, Watanabe Yoshio (b. 1907), Fujimoto Shihachi (also known as Yonpachi; b. 1911), Matsuda Masashi (b. 1916), Numano Ken (b. 1912), and Furukawa Narutoshi (b. 1900). The chief designers were Yamana Ayao (1897–1980), Kōno Takashi (b. 1906), and Kamekura Yūsaku (b. 1915).

Each designer alternated as art director, a job that involved determining the overall layout of the magazine. Each was also responsible for designing several of the eye-catching array of cover designs. The designer's overall vision unified each issue, transforming the publication into a visual tour de force.

After studying in Osaka at the Akamatsu Rinsaku Institute of Western Painting, Yamana began working for the publishing company Platon-sha, where he did detailed line-drawing illustrations reminiscent of the work of Aubrey Beardsley for the popular magazines *Kuraku* [Pleasure and pain] and *Josei* [Women], while producing illustrations for numerous small literary magazines. Yamana is undoubtedly best known for his work as the principal designer for the Shiseidō cosmetics company where he worked from 1929 to 1932, 1936 to 1943, and 1948 to 1980. Yamana's design activities were so widespread that they connected to almost every major area of publishing during this period.[25] As a pioneer of commercial design, he was also instrumental in the establishment of the earliest professional organizations for commercial designers in Japan, beginning with the Tokyo Association of Advertising Art (Tōkyō Kōkoku Bijutsu Kyōkai) in 1931. He is credited with being the first in Japan to employ the professional title "art director," which appeared on the masthead of the third issue of *NIPPON*. With powerful connections throughout the prewar design world, Yamana brought considerable expertise to Nippon Kōbō endeavors. He was in charge of graphic design layouts and advertising design for *NIPPON* and worked with the magazine through its entire run despite his resignation from Nippon Kōbō in 1936. The following year he began lecturing on design at the Tama Imperial Art University (Tama Teikoku Bijutsu Daigaku, now Tama Art University). In 1940 he was appointed chairman of the Society for the Study of Media Techniques (Hōdō Gijutsu Kenkyūkai).[26]

Kōno Takashi had a similarly illustrious career in design after graduating in 1930 from the Tokyo School of Fine Arts (Tōkyō Bijutsu Gakkō), where he studied crafts and illustration. He soon went to work producing advertising and set designs for the Shochiku Motion Picture Company. Kōno initially served as a freelance graphic designer on *NIPPON* and was eventually hired to work as principal art director on a number of Nippon Kōbō publications. Like many Nippon Kōbō members, Kōno was convinced by Natori in the late 1930s to take up work in China in the studio's Shanghai-based press operation, which functioned under a variety of different organizational designations as it expanded into the Japanese colonies and onto the war front to serve as the official press union for the imperial army propaganda department.[27]

Considered one of the most influential designers of the postwar era, Kamekura's prewar and wartime work has been less studied. As a young designer Kamekura came under the guidance of Ōta Hideshige. As former director of the advertising division of the Kao Soap Company, Ōta had distinguished the company's advertising with his highly experimental techniques, such as using Kimura Ihee's gritty photographs of Tokyo daily life in Kao newspaper advertising. Kamekura joined Ōta's newly established Kyōdō Kōkoku (Collaborative advertising) design firm while he pursued his design education at the New Academy of Architecture and Industrial

Arts (Shin Kenchiku Kōgei Gakuin) in Tokyo, established in 1931 on the model of the Bauhaus by Kawakita Renshichirō.[28] Kamekura worked in the art department of Nippon Kōbō from 1938, taking over for Natori as chief art director of *NIPPON* in 1940 after the latter left for Shanghai to establish the studio's sister organization.

On 28 September 1940 Japan signed the Tripartite Alliance with Germany and Italy that formed the Axis powers of World War II, which was heralded in *NIPPON* as leading "Toward a New World Order" (*shintaisei*).[29] Not surprisingly, *NIPPON* added Italian to the languages of the magazine. Soon after the alliance was formed, and with the bombing of Pearl Harbor in 1941, subscriptions to *NIPPON* in the United States dropped off dramatically. The magazine's tone shifted to one of more overt wartime propaganda, and the journal published several issues on daily life on the home front and in the colonies. The magazine was published less often and more erratically thereafter, averaging only about three issues per year. This is understandable in light of the additional projects in which the members became involved on the continent. The majority of the material I analyzed for this essay appeared prior to the beginning of the Pacific War in 1941, when the use of propaganda to ameliorate world political tensions was still considered a possibility and tourists from non-Axis countries could still visit Japan.[30]

Staged Authenticity

NIPPON was certainly not the only Japanese photojournalistic promotional magazine that emerged at this time. There was a range of similar periodicals, including the national policy journal *Shashin shūhō* [Photographic weekly], published weekly by the Cabinet Information Office from 1938 until 1944 and which utilized evocative photographs by Nippon Kōbō associates Domon Ken and Kimura Ihee, among others. Concerning the function of *Shashin shūhō* in the context of photojournalism, Izumi Reijirō commented,

> Of course, *Shashin-Shūhō* is, at least for the present, an instrument of national propaganda, and thus, its contents are more than pure photojournalism. They play a major role as publicity photographs. While in principle news photographs naturally contribute to the objective of

presenting powerful publicity, unlike photojournalism, which reports events which actually occurred, publicity photographs must be published in advance (using models for instance) in order to facilitate public relations and convey the message, "It should be like this. We wish it were like this."[31]

Despite positioning itself as a news source reporting on events that actually occurred rather than as a publicity organ, *NIPPON* displayed a modus operandi strikingly similar to that of *Shashin shūhō*. As Dean MacCannell has noted in his pioneering study *The Tourist*, sightseers are often "motivated by a desire to see life as it is really lived," to have an "authentic, demystified experience."[32] But the very act of representing culture (as in *NIPPON*) inserts a mediating presence between the tourist and the sight. Ironically, the representations of a sight are usually the initial enticement spurring the tourist's desire for contact. Touristic representations are coded with "markers," that is, any information about a specific sight that defines it. Some of these markers take on a particularly symbolic status; in the case of Japan, Mount Fuji is the example par excellence. Recalling his expectations prior to visiting Japan in the mid-1910s, Englishman Frank Lee wrote,

> I had, of course, read quite a number of books about Japan and had, as I confidently thought, a most complete knowledge of the country and of its people. From picture post-cards, N.Y.K. [Nippon Yusen Kaisha, Japan's largest shipping company] and Tourist Bureau posters, etc., I was thoroughly conversant with Mount Fuji from every aspect, with *geisha*, cherry-blossoms, snow scenes, planting rice, paper lanterns, paper umbrellas, *geta*, temple gates, *torii*, and all the other things which make people in Europe and America believe Japan to be a veritable fairyland, without trams or trains or taxis, but only magic carpets wafting the traveller to spots of beauty where, on alighting, he will be served by fair women with the choicest tea in the most dainty little cups.[33]

According to MacCannell, the tourist attraction is generated in the relationship between the sight, its markers, and the tourist. Attempts are made to obscure any glimpse of the mediation of markers by the offering of "truth markers"—markers that set themselves in opposition to other markers deemed somehow less authentic. But an anecdote recounted by American Carol Bache about her trip to Rinnoji Temple soon after she arrived in Japan in the early 1930s pithily expresses the elusiveness of the so-called authentic experience of Japan:

> There was the sound of water falling over rocks, and we could hear the monks' voices in the temple chanting sutras. The lower garden lay in darkness, but the shadows sparkled with tiny points of light as the fireflies wove their way in and out of an elaborate ballet. It was so warm that the lattices had been pushed back, and in one of the rooms I saw a young monk seated at a low table, bending over his work. Light from a standing lantern fell upon his shaven head and intent face, and I could imagine the miracle of calligraphy—the Lotus Sutra perhaps—that was taking shape under his writing brush. The scene was perfect; it was natural; not staged for eager tourists, as we had come upon it quite by chance; and I had a strong intuitive feeling that what I had been seeking since my arrival lay close at hand—a glimpse of "the real Japan." At that instant the temple bell boomed. . . . It filled the night, drowning my footsteps and another sound as well, the rapid click-clack of the typewriter on which the monk was writing, using all of his fingers in the touch system. It was a bitter blow, but what a paradox! . . . For years now, I have been diligently collecting [these paradoxes], spurred on, I suspect, by the secret hope that if enough paradoxes could be laid out end to end, the sum total of them all might be that ephemeral thing we are all still seeking—the real Japan.[34]

Well aware of this pervasive touristic desire to share "the life behind the scenes," *NIPPON* offered itself as a view of "*actual* life and events" in order to satisfy the tourist's search for demystified experience—a factographic representation of the everyday. Once again, however, I must return to Mitchell's assertion that since the world itself is a form of exhibition, the positing of authentic versus mystified experience is necessarily an artificial bifurcation. But in this case it sets off the purported authenticity of one view by positing the existence of false views. *NIPPON*, then, sets the record straight.

To quote Spencer Crew and James Sims, "Authenticity is not about factuality or reality. It is about authority"—an authority that *NIPPON* possessed as both a seemingly unmediated news source and a government-sanctioned publication.[35] It should be mentioned, however, that perhaps as significant as what was included was what was omitted. In sections where *NIPPON* extols the virtues of the countryside, the ongoing domestic agrarian crises are never mentioned. The topic is only raised in the context of the promotion of modern industry and colonialism, which are posited as solutions to the state of chronic agricultural depression, Japan's overpopulation, and the enforced restriction on foreign immigration. While rising international tensions are not absent from the pages of the magazine and form an important backdrop to the entire production, the tensions between Japan and its colonies, which included continuous raids on Japanese settlers in Manchuria, never appear. The omissions speak volumes.

Resonance in the Land of Color, Culture, and Charm

NIPPON's kaleidescopic view of the Japanese empire promoted a timeless land with verdant peaks, typified by the national symbol of Mount Fuji; friendly natives (the idealized "happy" people of the countryside and the colonies); and refined cultural sensibilities. At the same time, it presented an urban, industrialized, expansionist imperial power that had rapidly annexed Taiwan, Korea, and Manchuria and was setting its sights on the rest of China. Articulated just when Japanese military and colonial bureaucracies were becoming literal custodians of land and people on the continent, the magazine's presentation of Japan-as-museum assimilated images of Asianness derived from imperial colonial acquisitions. The visual language for metropole and colonies was skillfully blended to obscure internal boundaries and mute the cultural violence implicit in Japanese imperialism.

The *NIPPON* designers provided an ethnographic presentation of Japan and its imperial subjects constructed to produce a sense of "resonance" in the viewer, an effect defined by Stephen Greenblatt as "the power of the displayed object to reach out beyond its formal boundaries to a larger world, to evoke in the viewer the complex, dynamic cultural forces from which it has emerged and for which it may be taken by a viewer to stand."[36] This was, of course, a deliberately cultivated sense of resonance that was channeled into particular areas. The topics covered in the magazine ranged widely, often oscillating between the contemporary and the traditional, or preservation of the latter in the former as evidenced, for example, in the lifestyles and activities of people on the periphery of metropolitan Japan, such as the agrarian countryside. A careful symmetry was maintained between the rural and the urban, the folkish and the cosmopolitan, and the historical and the contemporary. Each element was portrayed as a symbiotically linked part of a larger whole, a notion pithily expressed by Yamana Ayao's montage cover design for the first issue of the magazine (fig. 1). The image of a bright red, kimono-clad Japanese female folk doll is superimposed on Watanabe Yoshio's black-and-white photograph of a modern steel-reinforced concrete building, an emblem of the Japanese modernist architecture that was transforming the urban landscape. The images are balanced in a curious manner, with the doll positioned on a sharp diagonal to the left, solidly anchored in the right angle of the building structure, the partial image of which is shown clearly slanted to the right. The images visually interlock and interpenetrate, the transparency of the red form revealing the building behind. The components that constitute "Japan" may be divergent, but they are inseparable.

A striking two-page spread titled "At the Foot of Mt. Fuji" (fig. 2) employs six differently sized photographs skillfully arranged in an asymmetrical composition to present country people and their majestic environment near Japan's primary spiritual symbolic marker, Mount Fuji.[37] The layout expresses a visual dynamism through the juxtaposition of close-ups of people's faces and rural homes and wide-angle shots of the landscape and Mount Fuji, which presides majestically in the distance. Three angelically smiling figures—two young girls and a woman—are situated in a triangular composition in the center anchoring the piece through human interest. They appear as if caught in the midst of their daily activities; the photographs capitalize on the aesthetic of the snapsnot. The accompanying text reads,

> In the country surrounding the base of Fuji-san a community of farming people continues to live whose faith in life is inspired by the lovely landscape about their homes and the ancient traditions symbolized by the noble mountain. Their eyes are ever smiling for they are privileged, unlike others, always to gaze upon lofty Fuji with its unmelting snow, and

Figure 1 Yamana Ayao, cover design, *NIPPON*, no. 1 (1934). Harvard College Library.

their laughter is ever innocent, for they are free from the cares and strife of the distant cities—distant, it may seem to them, far more than ordinary distance can measure. The spirit of the mountain is their guide in life, its mysterious influence fills their days with happiness from childhood to old age, and they are never discontented, nor forget to thank Fuji-san for the deep comfort it gives.[38]

In addition to the metropolitan fascination with the simplicity of the countryside, it is the sheer "everydayness" of the scenes that is so inviting. Writing

Figure 2 "At the Foot of Mt. Fuji," *NIPPON*, no. 6 (1936): 22–23. Private collection.

in *NIPPON*, Kabayama Ayské explicitly identified the realm of the everyday as a space for preserving culture: "In Japan, one can find the very highly developed culture of the East preserved carefully, not only in museums, temples and shrines, but also in the home, and in the daily lives of the people."[39] The message of the layout is clear: people in the countryside remain spiritually connected with their auratic landscape, thus preserving essential Japanese culture, *and* they are sheltered from the oppressive cares of the modern world by a benevolent national government.

Another lively photo-essay displaying the agrarian periphery is a more direct invocation to the tourist. "Un Week End à Izu" [A weekend at Izu] is accompanied by a series of letters written by Iijima Minoru to an unidentified Monsieur K.[40] Through this style of personal address, the author is able to speak directly to the reader as well. Iijima recounts his short vacation jaunt to the ocean. Just three hours from Tokyo, Izu provides a brief escape from the torrid heat of the metropolis and all the hectic responsibilities associated with urban life. The author is in Shizuura, on the western coast of Japan near the Izu Peninsula. He describes leaving far behind the tumultuous sounds of the capital to contemplate the radiant sky and the intense blue ocean; he arrives in an agreeable mood to view the active and peaceful life of the local fishermen and their families. The spectacle of the fishermen's labor with their catch of sardines writhing on the decks of the boats enchants him. He explains to his friend that one must go to Izu "to reclaim contact with Japan." At the same time, however, its natural beauty earns Izu the honorary title of "the Riviera of Japan"—the resort connotation is not lost on anyone. This is augmented by an enumeration of basic geographical information about the area read directly from a tourist guidebook.

The first image that greets the eye is a large, dramatic shot of two men rowing a boat photographed from below as if seen from the ocean itself.[41] The figures are highly abstracted, and the overall visual impact is enhanced by the stark contrast between the bright, sunlit bodies and the dark underside of the boat. Below to the right sits a small, distant photograph of men pulling in their net while fishing in the ocean; read in series, this photo contextualizes the more fragmentary image above. On the next two pages (fig. 3), four vibrant images of young boys in loincloths (*fundoshi*) fishing and frolicking in a local river express intense visual excitement. One boy exclaims with arms raised in triumph, "*Look* at my big *yamame* [salmon]!" Another boy bent over and peering into the water with his friend, their nearly naked rears to the viewer, yells at the fish, "*Just* try and get away from me this time...." The photographs are composed without sharp separation (the image to the left even extends across the binding divide); one picture bleeds quickly into the next to mirror the liveliness of the scene. The water splashes so vividly that the reader almost feels the spray. The caption comments, "Playing in the midst of their natural blessings, these children seem like the sun in their brilliant joyousness." At the end of this adventure, as he contemplates returning to his life in Tokyo, with its new tramways, buses, and the elevator

Figure 3 "Un Week End à Izu," *NIPPON*, no. 8 (1936): 20–21. Private collection.

to his office on the seventh floor, Iijima admits, "After 3 days of only staying in the countryside, I begin to feel a little nostalgia for the capital."[42]

The crossover between urban and rural Japan is frequently expressed in the pages of *NIPPON* through the figure of the Japanese woman. Special features on all aspects of Japan's female imperial subjects abound; whether she is dressed as a geisha, a modern housewife, or a textile laborer, the Japanese woman is another significant marker for Japan as tourist site. *NIPPON* author Sugiyama Eisuke reinforced this notion in his statement that "Japanese women seem to have an instinctive capacity for hospitality."[43] When viewers see a Japanese woman, therefore, they should feel invited.

Issue number 10 (1937) is devoted to the topic of Japanese women, with features on the activities of young girls, the housewife, female factory workers, country women, women entertainers, female artists, women's organizations, and women's health. The panoply of subjects and their visual representation in many perspectives reflect the invocation by well-known author Yosano

Akiko in the opening essay, "A Talk on Japanese Women," to observe Japanese women from every angle (fig. 4).[44] This also incorporates a view of Japanese women from the perspective of a foreigner. As is true throughout the magazine, the gaze of the foreigner is not only implicit in the function of the magazine but literally integrated into the content. It is always clear that the Japanese are not only evaluating themselves but are being evaluated by others.

"First Steps towards Being a Perfect Housewife," an instantiation of the "good wife, wise mother" (*ryōsai kenbō*) ethic that was part of Meiji period nation-building ideology, tells the story of a young woman being groomed to take her rightful place in Japanese society as the title suggests, as "the perfect housewife."[45] Text by Iijima Minoru tells the readers that Japan has "a family system strictly adhered to from ancient times . . . , and a large family generally lives together. . . . So whether the home is a soothing resting place in life or not depends much on the clever management of the housewife." She must cultivate a variety of skills: sweeping, cooking, washing, sewing, personal grooming, caring for younger siblings (and by extension her future husband and in-laws), and maintaining good physical fitness. At the same time, the girl is a citizen of the world and must devote part of her time to reading books so that she may "keep up with the times and with modern culture." She also occasionally eats out at a restaurant, visits the theater, and goes *alone* to a party to meet young men. The layout of the piece presents a series of photographs of various sizes scattered in different orientations across the page and depicting the woman's activities in sequence with the textual commentary. Text and pictures are set against a partially patterned background of floral textile motifs, presumably referring to the kimono, an easily recognizable emblem of Japanese femininity and tradition. Dramatic high and low angles are juxtaposed to animate the display. The organically shaped background patterns not only visually link discrete images and draw the eye through the narrative; they are also meant to evoke the aesthetics of Japanese womanhood, particularly a close sympathy with nature.

Specific attention was given to the aesthetic aspects of Japanese culture as evidence of the nation's overall civilization. In "Life and Art," Hasegawa Nyozekan asserts, "No nation is capable of producing supreme art without some refinement in the very life of her people. The artistic curves of physical

Figure 4 "First Steps towards Being a Perfect Housewife," *NIPPON*, no. 10 (1937): 14–15. Harvard College Library.

arts are defined by the curves in the movements and gestures in daily life."[46] In addition to theater, music, and the fine arts, Japanese handicrafts were specifically featured in the magazine. Crafts had served the nation-building project exceptionally well by representing Japanese culture on the prominent imperialist stage of international world's fairs, beginning with their spectacular reception in Vienna in 1873. This practice continued unabated. Of the two special issues on handicrafts (nos. 11 and 13), the former reported on the Japanese submissions to the 1937 international exposition in Paris. A montage illustrating this issue shows selected examples of Japanese handicrafts (fig. 5). Bamboo and straw baskets, lacquerware, metalwork, and ceramics are organized in a circle around their descriptive text in the center. Crafts were heralded in the pages of *NIPPON* for displaying the Japanese people's adroitness at adapting the cultural achievements of other nations (in this case, China, Korea, and Western countries). They were a testament

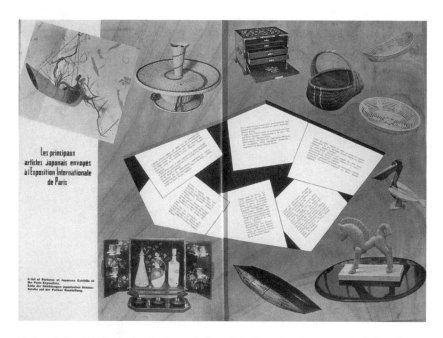

Figure 5 "Les Principaux Articles Japonais Envoyés à L'Exposition Internationale de Paris," *NIPPON*, no. 11 (1937): 34–35. Private collection.

to the Japanese ability to harmonize the two opposing forces of Oriental and Occidental culture. Aesthetic but functional objects showed the strong connection between crafts and the life of the people, implying a high level of refinement in the everyday life of regular Japanese folk, a notion that came right out of the ideology of the Japanese folk craft movement (*mingei undō*) as articulated by Yanagi Sōetsu. The decorative alcove (*tokonoma*) in the Japanese house was lauded as a kind of altar to aestheticism.

Later in the same issue, the article "Pottery: How to Appreciate Its 'Japanese' Traits" proves the profound Japanese commitment to aesthetics by explaining that historically warriors have even been willing to give up fiefdoms or sacrifice their lives for tea ceramics. Moreover, the article states that "the Japanese have prized and appreciated ceramics with love, for they have always been objects of adoration among us. Are there any people who take delight in a flaw in porcelain? The Japanese with an eye for beauty have prized even a flaw as a sort of picturesque addition. . . . They find in a flaw an ornament or something that speaks of the history of the pottery."[47] Japanese aesthetic tastes are thus not only refined but unique in their high valuation of flawed wares and, by extension, show appreciation for the life of the object, whose history is reflected in its cracks and uneven glaze. Pottery, in this case, is almost reified into a living being.

At the end of the issue, a feature on a provincial "Village of Pottery" shows ceramic production as communal labor and therefore representative of common values, in some sense staging Japanese labor to prove both the inherent aesthetics of daily life and its authenticity. The repeated staging of Japanese labor in *NIPPON* reveals an acute awareness of the tourist's desire for demystification. The magazine's designers had struck on an effective way of seeming to reveal the inner workings of Japanese culture by staging what MacCannell calls a "back region." Analogous to restaurants revealing the kitchen to their clientele, it is a gesture toward authenticity that is still in actuality equally mystified.

> A mere experience can be mystified, but a touristic experience is always mystified. The lie contained in the touristic experience, moreover, presents itself as a truthful revelation, as the vehicle that carries the onlooker behind the false front into reality. The idea here is that a false back is more insidious and dangerous than a false front, or an inauthentic demystification of social life is not merely a lie but a superlie, the kind that drips with sincerity.[48]

Examples of such a back region include extensive scenes of staged industrial or agricultural labor, whether in domestic textile factories or on peasant farms in Manchuria. This staged labor serves two purposes: it presents the "actual Japan" at work engaged in everyday activities that have a factographic function, and it promotes the integral role of industry in Japanese culture (including industries being developed in the colonies that were indistinguishable from those in the metropole). The latter purpose had a corollary objective, to assuage international fears about Japanese trade practices by presenting a wholesome image of Japanese labor.

The enlistment of representations of labor to justify state policies, even evoking a kind of wartime mobilization mentality well before Japan was engaged in the Pacific War, is pointedly indicated in a dynamic photomontage layout on Kanebo textile production where two large close-up photographs of spinning machinery open to an interior four-page spread that reveals the company's productive female labor force and all the inner workings of the factory environment. The piece incorporates the following statement, probably penned by Natori (something that could as easily have been written in the mid-1980s as the mid-1930s):

> The phenomenal rise of Japanese merchandise in world markets has affected the industrial life of so many foreign lands that this country now finds herself engaged in perhaps the bitterest trade war known to history—the weapon of which is the prohibitive tariffs, import quotas, patriotic propaganda, "anti-dumping" legislation and, in addition, every other strategic device known to commercial defense.
>
> Meanwhile, due to an almost uncanny combination of low prices and superior quality, Japanese textiles continue to maintain their leading export position, and continue to serve as [sic] basic commodity in the spectacular offensive. . . .
>
> A feature of the [Kanebo] company is its ideal management. Its staff of 41,000 workers is controlled in the manner of a huge single family, fostered in the "Kanebo spirit" of harmony and co-operation. For the benefit of employes [sic] an elaborate welfare organization is maintained, the special fund reserved for this amounting to more than ¥40,000,000.[49]

In April 1938 Nippon Kōbō began producing for the Japanese Central Trade Organization (Boeki Kumiai Chūōkai) the multilingual promotional journal COMMERCE JAPAN, which reused many of the same photographs published in NIPPON and featured the same stories, with an added emphasis on statistical information on various sectors of Japanese production and trade. The journal placed heavy emphasis on convincing the United States that Japanese imperialism was good for U.S. export trade, as it produced an expanded market for goods. In NIPPON itself, the intermingling of advertisements sponsored by industry and promotional articles about industry mirror the visual blurring of publicity and photojournalism.

Images and themes from NIPPON spilled over into a vast array of contemporaneous cultural projects as Nippon Kōbō associates expanded their activities. As part of a series of publications put out by the Society for International

Figure 6 Advertisement for *NIPPON: The Nation in Panorama*, *NIPPON*, no. 14 (1938). Harvard College Library.

Cultural Relations, the studio issued a special book-length publication also titled *NIPPON*. Touting the book as "The Nation in Panorama" and offering "a comprehensive photographic résumé of the changing life and institutions of Japan in a *de luxe* album of montage," the advertisement in the magazine (fig. 6) showed representative interior photomontages from the album arranged in a contiguous circular pattern surrounding the copy (uncannily similar to the layout of craft goods in fig. 5).[50] The art direction and photomontage compositions were handled by lesser-known *NIPPON* graphic designer Kumada Gorō using photographs by studio associates.[51] The individual photographs would have been familiar to any regular *NIPPON* reader, as they appeared in different layouts in previous issues, but their reconfiguration took the use of montage aesthetics to a new crescendo.

The book-length collection included over thirty-three montages representing the same kaleidoscopic view of Japan as the magazine. Two examples from the album amply demonstrate the great assortment of themes and the expressive dynamism of the collection as a whole. One image represents a Shinto shrine (fig. 7); the other, the Japanese navy (fig. 8). The image of

Figure 7 Kumada Gorō, montage composition, Shinto shrine, in Kokusai Bunka Shinkōkai, *NIPPON: The Nation in Panorama* (1937). Avery Architectural and Fine Arts Library, Columbia University in the City of New York.

the shrine shows the same scene viewed from two perspectives, simulating a spatial progression through the shrine gate (*torii*) up to the inner sanctuary. Multiperspectival visual axes are constructed through the positioning of the stone lantern in the middle that both links and divides the two views. An enormous guardian stone dog (*koma inu*) standing at the front of the gate is boldly foregrounded, accentuating its function as enunciator and protector. In the distance, people are seen bowing in prayer in front of the shrine. "As a method of cojoining and disjoining symbolic elements, of the asymmetrical disruption of the symmetrical, montage's break with the conventional unities of time and space," argues Roberts, "allows art to claim a verisimilitude of the synecdochal, or part *for* the whole, as well as a verisimilitude of the discontinuous, the accumulation of disparate parts into wholes which imply the unfinished/expansive/transitive nature of reality."[52] The skillful collage of multiple images thereby stands in for the multiperspectival viewpoint of the modern spectator.

Moreover, montage allows the designer to establish new hierarchies within the image through manipulation of scale, particularly through dramatic foregrounding, as seen in the deployment of the symbolic marker of the

Figure 8 Kumada Gorō, montage composition, Bluejackets, in Kokusai Bunka Shinkōkai, *NIPPON: The Nation in Panorama* (1937). Avery Architectural and Fine Arts Library, Columbia University in the City of New York.

Shinto *torii*.[53] This same visual device is employed on the graphically rendered cover of *NIPPON* number 20 (fig. 9), designed by Takamatsu Jinjirō, where a massive Shinto *torii* stands over the entire landscape of Japan expressing the all-encompassing sphere of Japan's native creed, which had become the state-sanctioned national religion of the country. Like the aesthetics of pottery, Shinto spirituality, it was claimed, deeply permeated the daily life of the people.[54]

The montage of the Japanese navy, known as the "Bluejackets" (originally in *NIPPON*, no. 9 [1936]), greets the viewer with a spectacle of military fanfare. Two discrete but seamlessly woven views of the sailors at attention create a sharply receding perspectival view of the entire corps; the viewer is addressed directly as the figures stand at attention on the deck of their ship under the resplendently waving rising-sun flag. Two foregrounded, fragmented images of the same bugler from different angles echo the multiperspectival viewpoint. This is perhaps one of the most engaging images in the collection because the open deck of the ship draws the viewer into the pictorial space. Roberts notes that unlike discrete photographs, which represent completeness, montage requires the viewer's cognitive interaction

Figure 9 Takamatsu Jinjirō, cover design,
NIPPON, no. 20 (1939). Private collection.

to complete and interpret the image. In this sense it "addresses the spectator conversationally."[55] The use of montage in both the magazine and the album provides the sensation of touring living, interactive exhibits.

Akin to many of their colleagues abroad in the mid- to late 1930s, the Japanese became infatuated with montage aesthetics as a quintessentially modern form of expression and displayed large-scale photomurals at their world's fair pavilions beginning in Paris in 1937 and continuing through the San Francisco Golden Gate International Exposition in 1939 and the New York World's Fair in 1939–1940. In its coverage of the San Francisco fair, *NIPPON* presented the travel and communications section of the Japanese pavilion decorated with photomurals sponsored by the Japanese Government Railways, the Ministry of Communication, and the Japan Broadcasting Association. The murals consisted of photographs commissioned by the Society for International Cultural Relations and were edited by *NIPPON* graphic designer Kōno Takashi. Under the title "Hallo America!" the spread presents the enormous figure of an American girl in the foreground curiously staring out at a series of disembodied photomurals surrounded by cutouts of assorted fairgoers floating through the empty space while viewing the exhibits (fig. 10).[56] By incorporating the Western viewer directly into the image, the magazine self-reflexively manifests Japan's presentation of its "national strength, national character and national significance" for Western consumption.[57] The same year, also under the sponsorship of the Society for International Cultural Relations, Bauhaus-trained artist and *NIPPON* contributor Yamawaki Iwao (1889–1987), using stunning photographs by Domon Ken, designed five spectacular large-scale photomurals titled "Advancing Japan" ["Yakushin Nippon"] for the Japanese exhibit at the New York World's Fair's Hall of Nations.[58] Each montage was fourteen feet high and nine feet wide—in effect, *NIPPON* writ large. Or rather, the serial photographs and montage layouts in the magazine formed a virtual diorama that directly paralleled the exhibition environments constructed for the fairs. Yamawaki declared that the photomurals were the culmination of a Bauhaus ideal of fusing photography and space.[59]

Staging the Colonies: "Up and Coming Manchoukuo"

NIPPON's subtle interweaving of colonial subjects into the fabric of Japan went a long way in legitimizing the imperialist agenda. The cover of issue 27 from 1941, designed by Kamekura Yūsaku, exemplifies the embodiment of Japan's expansionist vision in visual culture (fig. 11). It displays the upper torso of a healthy, smiling, young Japanese boy upon whose body has been superimposed the red outlines of a map of Japan and its surrounding territories, with a directional compass to the left of his head. Peninsular and continental lands are presented as a borderless expanse linked to the Japanese archipelago through the body of the youth. As he gazes optimistically beyond the frame of the image, the boy stands with folded arms, unambiguously conveying his readiness for the task of realizing the visionary Japanese project in the colonies.

As a metonym for the Japanese nation, eponymous *NIPPON*'s regular incorporation of colonial holdings under the overarching canopy of "Japan"

Figure 10 "Hallo America!" San Francisco Golden Gate International Exposition, 1939, *NIPPON*, no. 17 (1939): 48–49. Harvard College Library.

served as a form of cultural annexation.[60] A special issue from 1939 (no. 19) on the Japanese puppet-state of Manchukuo is one of the most visually interesting of the entire run of the magazine. It begins with an eye-catching cover design, also by Kamekura, showing a series of cut-out photographs of individual figures from the interior layouts—men and women, farmers, soldiers, and city dwellers—superimposed on a boldly colored orange map of Manchukuo (fig. 12). The figures are identifiable by costume as Japanese, Manchurian, Korean, Mongolian, and White Russian, the so-called *quinque* racial population of Manchuria.[61] The mutual cooperation among diverse races in Manchukuo is quickly established as a defining feature of the region, although admittedly it was not always as easily achieved as hoped. The visible map of Manchukuo rests in a yellow frame, metonymically representing its debt to the Japanese, the people of the sun. The *NIPPON* title over the yellow frame reinforces this association. Kamekura's cover attempts to express the utopian excitement of Japanese policies toward Manchuria. A

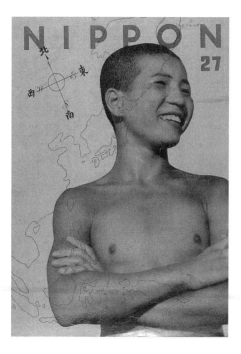

Figure 11 Kamekura Yūsaku, cover design,
NIPPON, no. 27 (1941). Harvard College Library.

soldier, most likely Japanese—the only figure who stands completely outside
the bounded area of the map—points to the visible map with great purpose.
In the white space around the map, figures either gaze, walk, or gesture
toward the mapped landscape. Two women in kimonos seen walking from
behind allude to the influx of Japanese women into the colonies as part
of the governmental policy of intermarriage between Japanese and native
inhabitants as a strategy of colonial integration (a policy employed in all
Japanese colonial regions). Two soldiers holding shovels sitting to the right
are revealed inside the magazine to be assisting in the reclamation of arable
land that is transforming Manchukuo's agrarian economy. To the upper
left, a soldier standing in defense of the realm looks beyond the border
with binoculars. To his right in the north, mounted riders lead the eye to a
Manchurian woman and her small child; the mother points out toward the

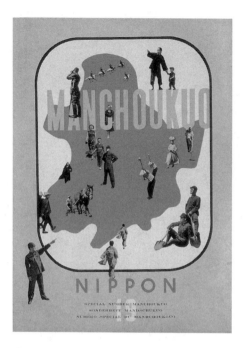

Figure 12 Kamekura Yūsaku, cover design, Manchukuo special issue, *NIPPON*, no. 19 (1939). Private collection.

land, indicating to the next generation the future to come. Manchukuo is a dynamic place.

Use of the visible map to define Japanese spheres of interest is given an interesting twist in an advertisement for "Kanebo in Manchoukuo," where the same map is shown blanketed by the company's textiles (fig. 13). In lieu of its residents, the region is dotted with pinned pieces of paper that indicate Kanebo production facilities.

In the Manchukuo special issue, one is immediately confronted with a bold, two-page spread displaying a series of Manchurian flags with an inset of the emperor of Manchukuo. The magazine contains a series of strongly worded texts underscoring the benevolent rule in Manchukuo, careful not to assert that it is, in fact, Japanese rule.[62] Repeated mention is made of the desire for the ruler and the ruled to be "morally united into one harmonious whole,

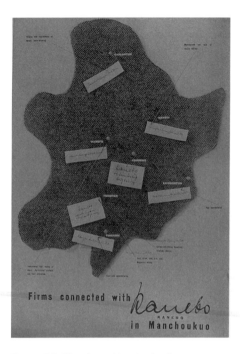

Figure 13 "Kanebo in Manchoukuo"
advertisement, *NIPPON*, no. 19 (1939): 62.
Harvard College Library.

advancing with one purpose to attain the final goal of the state"—a task
achieved at least visually in *NIPPON*.[63] The magazine incorporates several
four-page foldout spreads that present an integrated exhibition of Japan's
imperialist goals. A few of the main themes represented are cooperative
government, immigration work, the five-year industrial development plan,
defense, resources, (land) reclamation, the past (Manchuria's history), mass
communication, and standard of living. All of the special issues on Japanese
colonial territories state repeatedly that if Western detractors would only visit
these utopian regions of modernization, they would see the benevolence of
Japanese imperialist policy.

   The section on cooperative government displays two pages with five large,
individual portraits of representatives of the major racial groups (fig. 14).
The Japanese face in the center links them. The spread literally opens in the

Figure 14 "Cooperative Government," *NIPPON*, no. 19 (1939): 16–17. Harvard College Library.

middle of the man's face; his big smile and tilted head beckon the reader to read further. The man is presumably an immigrant settler who is part of the Japanese government's twenty-year project to resettle one million households (five million Japanese immigrants) in Manchuria, a policy established in 1936. Even though the caption describes the Manchurians as the nucleus of Manchukuo, this statement is undermined by the placement of the Japanese figure in the center of the layout to form the visual nexus of the piece. Inside is a four-page spread on land reclamation. Here the two soldiers with shovels from the cover are foregrounded to the right as they survey a series of photographs of agricultural labor and some explanatory text about the thirty thousand members of the Young Farmers' Volunteer Corps that had immigrated to the region in 1938.

Next is a photomontage display of Manchukuo's industrial resources: iron, coal, and hydroelectricity (fig. 15).[64] An oversized figure of a laborer stands grinning proudly as he grips his tool and looks out across the vista of indus-

Figure 15 "Resources," *NIPPON*, no. 19 (1939): 25–26. Harvard College Library.

trial development that is constructing a new infrastructure in Manchuria. Expanding behind him are images of different kinds of heavy machinery and busy scenes of labor, all of which stand out against the dramatic black background of the layout. Once again the dynamism of Manchukuo is reaffirmed.

The notion that Japan's relationship with Manchuria is special, not exploitative like the associations forged between Western nations and their colonies, is repeatedly asserted. Historical ties are documented as a means of certifying long-standing cultural connections between the two countries, and the archaeological evidence is displayed in a museological framework somewhat akin to the layout of a display case. The end of "The Excavation of the Ruins of P'o-Hai's Palace," quickly segues from the historical past to the concerns of the present. The last paragraph of the text reads, "Discovery of Japanese 'Wadokaichin' coins, of the Nara era, among the relics [at the palace] was held especially significant as indicating the ancient kingdom's relationship with Japan."[65] Halfway through, the article begins to share a split page with another essay on the region, this time on contemporary Manchuria, titled "Growing Manchoukuo." The same archaeological objects are then represented in the special issue on Manchukuo as part of a montage with the title "Past" (fig. 16). Ancient stupas, architectural details, Buddhist sculpture, and other cultural objects are exhibited in lavender frames of different sizes that simulate the relative size of wall displays as they recede in the white space. The large face of a Manchurian woman looms from the left edge of the image and surveys the artifacts on display. Mirroring the technique used in the San Francisco World's Fair layout, cut-out figures of Asian and Western viewers are scattered about the page and appear to be wandering through the exhibits. Both the present and the past are served up as a picture, the world-as-exhibition.

Conclusion: "Japan Becomes Comfortable"

In the same manner that L'Exposition Coloniale Internationale de Paris in 1931 claimed to take you "round the world in one day," *NIPPON* could claim to satisfy the exotic tastes and quest for adventure of the Western traveler.[66] A 1939 issue (no. 17) even provided a "One Month Tour of Japanese Culture," aided by a series of detailed illustrated maps that, in fact, closely mirrored the tour routes taken by foreign visitors recorded in their publicly and privately published travel accounts (fig. 17). The first two-page spread suggests touring the modern and historical monuments in Tokyo—the Imperial Diet Building, the Imperial Palace, Yasukuni Shrine, and Ueno Park—before departing the city for scenic sights in Nikkō, Yokohama, Kamakura, and Utsunomiya. For trout fishing, Lake Chūzenji and Lake Towada are recommended; a foreign couple with their fishing rods are shown in the center of the image to underscore this leisure activity. The tour then veers sharply to the north, as the traveler is guided up to Hokkaido, first to Hakodate "the most up-to-date city of Northern Japan," then to Daisetuzan National Park, which "can show the tourist everything in the way of mountain scenery; high peaks, deep forests, and mountain flowers make a nature lover's and botanist's Paradise." The tourist is further informed that "in ancient days a

Figure 16 "Past," *NIPPON*, no. 19 (1939): 43–44. Private collection.

primitive race lived in Daisetuzan National Park, and archaeologists consider this district to be one of the finest sources of prehistoric flint tools."
Below, another primitive race in Hokkaido is identified as the Ainu, the
"curious and dwindling race" of whom there are only about fifteen hundred
members left. The text explains that "the Ainu are characterized by bodies
and features similar to those of the white race, and in ancient times possessed
a great spiritual culture, which is now disappearing."[67] As one American
visitor sarcastically noted after speaking with John Batchelor, the Christian missionary who devoted his life to protecting the Ainu, Batchelor had

successfully "preserved one of the nation's top tourist attractions."[68] The association between exhibiting culture and travel was undeniable. They were both impulses to explore and, most important, to chart the unknown—the desire to satisfy a persistent classificatory impulse.

Japan was hailed as the perfect synthesis of East and West. The nation was "more than herself," according to Nitobe Inazō; "Asia and Europe in one."[69] This harmonious synthesis profoundly affected the invocation to the Western traveler, who was assured of familiar and civilized accommodations throughout the country. After all, this was "Japan, the land of silk and also the land of RAYON!" as the *NIPPON* advertisement for Toyo Rayon Kaisha extolled.[70] Japanese modernization had transformed the country enough to

Figure 17 "One Month Tour of Japanese Culture," *NIPPON*, no. 17 (1939): 26–27. Harvard College Library.

make it a "comfortable" experience for any Western visitor, as attested to in the feature "Japan Becomes Comfortable," which ran in the Board of Tourist Industry periodical *Travel in Japan*, published from the spring of 1935.[71] The magazine employed many of the same young modernist photographers as *NIPPON* to create a parallel promotional tool explicitly for encouraging tourism.[72]

Seen in tandem with *Travel in Japan*, *NIPPON* reads as a virtual travelogue, an image reinforced by periodic features on topics concerning the Board of Tourist Industry, Japanese Government Railways. Occasional advertisements for the organization, which replicated the interior montages, were emblazoned on the inside back cover of the magazine. One particularly evocative board advertisement in *NIPPON* number 20 (1939) employs a montage of iconic symbols of Japaneseness pastiched together using the soft and inviting images of cherry blossom petals to create almost a halo around the various sights (fig. 18). Two athletes reaching energetically for a

Figure 18 Board of Tourist Industry, Japanese Government Railways, advertisement, *NIPPON*, no. 17 (1939): inside back cover. Harvard College Library.

ball are enveloped in cherry blossoms in the center roundel. To the left are the mountains; to the right, the *torii* of a Shinto shrine. Various images of a woman playing the koto, bicyclists, farmers with a horse-drawn wagon, and butterflies float in the sea of blossoms. On the upper right sits the text quoted in the epigraph to this essay.

After the nationalization of the Japanese Government Railways (Tetsudōshō) in 1906, the agency cofounded the Japan Tourist Bureau in 1912, together with other service providers in the tourism industry (private railways, steamship companies, and hotel owners) as part of its mission to promote tourism to Japan among Europeans and Americans. The Board of Tourist Industry (Kankōkyoku) was later established in 1930 as an oversight agency for the development and management of tourism initiatives. One of its central responsibilities was the sponsorship of multilingual publications, such as *NIPPON* and *Travel in Japan*, to publicize tourism to Japan.[73] Japanese tourism officials also gradually expanded their emphasis in the 1920s–1930s to include the promotion of domestic tourism and Japanese tourism to the colonies.[74]

In the early 1930s, when the board was establishing itself and the world economy was still feeling the effects of the depression, tourism to Japan remained stagnant and even slightly decreased, as it did elsewhere. The fiscal year 1931–1932 saw a total of 27,273 foreign visitors to Japan. Chinese accounted for 46 percent, Americans were second at 23 percent, and British tourists made up 13 percent. Yet among those who identified their travel objective as sightseeing and spent less than three months in the country, Western travelers were a much higher percentage. The money spent by foreigners on sightseeing in Japan also dipped from a high in 1929–1930 of ¥39,932,000 to ¥23,317,000 in 1931–1932.[75] From 1933 to 1935, however, the board recorded an annual 20 percent increase in foreigners visiting Japan. In 1935, according to estimates by the Ministry of Finance, ¥96,019,000 was spent by foreigners in Japan, ¥70,242,000 of which came from tourists. This amount nearly equaled the Japanese export trade in silk textiles, valued at ¥77,000,000.[76]

Familiar food and comfortable transportation and accommodations were a constantly voiced concern among Western travelers, and the ability of the Japanese to provide these amenities was often the litmus test of the country's civilization. Japanese tourism authorities understood this well and concentrated on providing "first-class" facilities both within Japan and in the colonies. Frederica Walcott, an American traveling to Japan via Korea in 1915, remarked on Japan's progress:

> When finally late in the evening we drew up at the South Gate Station of Seoul it seemed as if Aladdin and his lamp must have been there since my last visit, for in no other way did it seem possible to account for so many changes as had taken place in the old lazy-going capital of my 5-year-old

recollection. Instead of a dark, gloomy station we found a roomy modern building, where we were met by hotel runners in uniform, who escorted us to an American motor-car in which we drove rapidly through well paved electrically lighted streets, where formerly had been dark, muddy roads in fearful condition of filth and lack of repair, to a modern hotel. . . . The new Chosen Hotel . . . has been built by the Japanese-controlled Railway Board with the evident intent of drawing tourists to Korea and popularizing the route to Europe by way of Korea and Manchuria. It certainly deserves success, for it is most comfortable in all its appointments, the meals are excellent and the manager is most obliging.[77]

A large proportion of travelers to Japan relied on national tourism authorities to plan their trips, as remarked upon by American John Patric in the account of his trip to Japan in 1934: "A number of American young women schoolteachers had their complete four-week Japanese itinerary mapped out for them by the Japan Tourist Bureau, a trip that was to take them to most of the show places of Japan. They showed it to me. It included rooms and meals in fine European hotels where, they said, 'water will be safe and we won't have to worry about the vegetables.' From the way they talked, I knew they'd miss the real Japan."[78] Patric's travel objective was to have the true, demystified experience of Japan, in this case, not so much for cultural education but to understand the motivations of a potential enemy in war. Upon his disembarkation from the ship he noted,

Every visitor, including me, seemed to be startled by the large number of taxis and the fewness of the rickshas. This indicated a dangerous lack of information about a highly significant thing in modern Japan. I attribute it to photographers and writers, both amateur and professional. Because every travel picture, every travel story, every American home movie or travel album seems to have one *must* when it was prepared. That was: "Get a ricksha in it somewhere prominently, as something exotically symbolic—like geisha girls and blossom festivals—of a strange oriental land." . . . The net result has been to give eye-minded American armchair travelers a wholly false impression of a "colorful Japan," an impression pretty general in America.[79]

To bring the perception of Japan into the twentieth century but still maintain the carefully cultivated image of picturesqueness, the Board of Tourist Industry sponsored a series of books, originally envisioned as having over one hundred volumes, known collectively as the Tourist Library, published by Maruzen beginning in the 1930s. The series booklets began with the following editorial note: "It is a common desire among tourists to learn something of the culture of the countries they visit, as well as to see their beautiful scenery. To see is naturally easier than to learn but flying visits merely for sightseeing furnish neither the time nor the opportunity for more than a passing acquaintance with the culture of any foreign people. This is specifically true of Japan and her people." In other words, the library, *Travel in Japan*, and by extension *NIPPON* all served as supplementary virtual guides to Japanese culture essential for the tourist to cultivate a full understanding of the country that was often more comprehensive (and certainly more controlled) than an actual visit.

Still, like countries all over the world, Japan appreciated the significant monetary benefits of the tourist trade and sought to capitalize on it in any way possible. One important plan was to host the Twelfth Olympic Games in Tokyo in 1940 (later canceled due to increased world political tensions), which coincided with the celebration of the 2,600th anniversary of the founding of the Japanese nation. *The Japan Year Book* announced in 1937, "The [Japanese] governmental authorities and the civilian organizations concerned are energetically devising ways and means to promote the tourist industry in conformity with the exceedingly favourable situation [the prospect of having increased tourism due to the Olympics]. . . . The establishment of an international sea-bathing resort has been proposed and some organizations are sponsoring the creation of better facilities for the study of Japanese culture by means of museums, art galleries, etc."[80]

Representatives of Japan recognized what Alpers rightly notes, that "to be represented in a museum is to be given recognition as a culture."[81] The effort and creativity that went into producing *NIPPON* is a testament to a persistent belief in the potent sociopolitical effect of displaying Japan for Western consumption. By examining the conceptual framework in which *NIPPON* functioned as an official representation of imperial Japan abroad and by analyzing its visual strategies, I have tried to elucidate how the magazine produced the image of Japan-as-museum, waiting for the tour to begin.

Notes

1   Karatani Kojin, "Japan As Museum: Okakura Tenshin and Ernest Fenollosa," in *Japanese Art after 1945: Scream against the Sky*, by Alexandra Munroe (New York: Abrams, 1994), 33–39.

2   Statement on the cover of *NIPPON*, no. 5 (1935).

3   Timothy Mitchell, "Orientalism and the Exhibitionary Order," in *Colonialism and Culture*, ed. Nicholas Dirks (Ann Arbor: University of Michigan Press, 1992), 296, 293.

4   Ivan Karp, "Culture and Representation," in *Exhibiting Cultures*, ed. Ivan Karp and Steven Lavine (Washington, D.C.: Smithsonian Institution Press, 1991), 15.

5   Quoted in Tim Barringer and Tom Flynn, introduction to *Colonialism and the Object*, ed. Barringer and Flynn (London: Routledge, 1998), 5.

6   Svetlana Alpers, "The Museum As a Way of Seeing," in Karp and Lavine, *Exhibiting Cultures*, 29.

7   Michael Baxandall, "Exhibiting Intention: Some Preconditions of the Visual Display of Culturally Purposeful Objects," in Karp and Lavine, *Exhibiting Cultures*, 40.

8   Howell Reeves, *Wanderings in Nippon* (Tokyo: privately printed, 1927), 13, 14.

9   Increased political tensions had already led Japan to withdraw from the League of Nations in 1933. The Japanese were particularly concerned to maintain amicable relations with the United States as evidenced in the extensive U.S.–Japan Friendship display that the Japanese government mounted in 1939–1940 in the country's pavilion at the New York World's Fair, which visually documented the long-standing cultural amity between the two countries.

10 Hasegawa Nyozekan, "What Do the Japanese Want?" *NIPPON*, no. 5 (1935): 15.

11 The terms *specular dominance* and *controlling vision* are used by Tony Bennett in "The Exhibitionary Complex," *New Formations* 4 (spring 1988): 79. As John Urry has explicated, all forms of the gaze are "socially organized and systematized," with the aid of "many professional experts who help construct and develop our gaze." In the case of *NIPPON*, the prominent intellectuals who took on the role of spokesmen for Japan, such as Hasegawa Nyozekan, and the national tourism association (Board of Tourist Industry) were just a few examples of such professionals. Of course, as Urry also notes, there was no single tourist gaze, as the touristic experience was "constructed in relation to its opposite, to non-tourist forms of social experience and consciousness" (Urry, *The Tourist Gaze* [London: Sage, 1990], 1–2). Another equally important component of the tourist experience in Japan was the foreign traveler's perception of difference between Western civilization and the exotic Orient—the expectation of encountering an exotic other—while at the same time yearning for the comforts of home and judging Japan by a perceived lack of amenities.

12 *NIPPON* was available in the United States, Canada, Mexico, Germany, Switzerland, France, Brazil, and Italy. On average about five thousand copies were published for each issue.

13 For a basic chronology of Natori's career see Iizawa Kōtarō, *Natori Yōnosuke*, Nihon no shashinka 18 (Tokyo: Iwanami Shoten, 1998), 68–69.

14 In 1936 Natori returned with Mecklenberg to Germany to cover the Berlin Olympics. His work was picked up by *Life* magazine, and he traveled to New York to continue shooting photographs for *Life*. After driving cross-country to the West Coast, he flew to Beijing to cover the war in China in September 1937.

15 Okatsuka Akiko, "The Founding and Development of Modern Photography in Japan: Consciousness and Expression of the Modern," in Tokyo Metropolitan Museum of Photography, *The Founding and Development of Modern Photography in Japan* (Tokyo: Metropolitan Museum of Photography, 1995), 24.

16 Ina Nobuo, "Shashin in kaere," *Kōga* 1, no. 1 (May 1932). Quoted and translated in Tokyo Metropolitan Museum of Photography, *Founding and Development of Modern Photography in Japan*, 173.

17 In this respect, Natori and his colleagues distinguished their work from the press photography that appeared in other graphic magazines that were extremely popular at the time and run by newspaper companies such as *Asahi graph*. See Ishikawa Yasumasa, *Hōdō shashin no seishun jidai* [The early years of photojournalism] (Tokyo: Kodansha, 1991), 240.

18 Quoted in ibid., 239–240.

19 For examples see ibid., 30, 34, 40–41, 60, 92–93.

20 John Roberts, *The Art of Interruption* (Manchester: University of Manchester Press, 1998), 3. For example, the Association for the Study of New Photography (Shinkō Shashin Kenkyūkai) formed in 1930 included Horino Masao, Watanabe Yoshio, and Furukawa Narutoshi, all photographers who contributed to Nippon Kōbō publications. The group that published the innovative photography journal *Kōga* (1932–1933) counted among its members Ina Nobuo and Kimura Ihee.

21 Ibid., 20.

22 For an extensive discussion of the definition and importance of daily life for the development of modern photography see ibid.

23 After the dissolution of the first Nippon Kōbō, Hara, Kimura, and Okada founded their own group, called Chūō Kōbō (Central studio).

24 *NIPPON*, no. 22 (1940): 52. From its inception the society worked closely with the Board of Tourist Industry. See Foreign Affairs Association of Japan, *The Japan Year Book, 1935* (Tokyo: Kenkyusha, 1935), 720.

25 Yamana not only created posters, newspaper advertisements, and packaging design for Shiseidō, but he also worked as a book designer for the two major publishing houses, Shinchō-sha and Chūō Kōron-sha.

26 For a full chronology of Yamana's career see Meguro Prefectural Museum, *Yamana Ayao-ten* [Exhibition of works by Yamana Ayao] (Tokyo: Kodansha, 1999).

27 For a brief biographical sketch of Kōno Takashi see Ishikawa, *Hōdō shashin no seishun jidai*, 63.

28 For a brief biographical sketch of Kamekura Yūsaku see ibid., 81.

29 The Axis was later joined by Hungary, Rumania, and Slovakia. See *NIPPON*, no. 24 (1940): 11.

30 After the bombing of Pearl Harbor all resident foreigners in Japan from non-Axis countries were interned and eventually repatriated. Published travel accounts indicate, however, that there was still a sizable contingent of travelers to Japan from Germany, which included official tours by Hitler youth organizations and other Nazi representatives. For example see Marie Luise von Gronau, *In Kimono und Obi* (Stuttgart: K. Thienemanns, 1944).

31 Quoted and translated in Okatsuka, "Founding and Development," 24.

32 Dean MacCannell, *The Tourist* (New York: Schocken, 1976), 94.

33 Frank H. Lee, *Days and Years in Japan* (Tokyo: Hokuseido Press, 1935), 5–6.

34 Carol Bache, *Paradox Isle* (New York: Knopf, 1943), 3–4.

35 Spencer Crew and James Sims, "Locating Authenticity: Fragments of a Dialogue," in Karp and Lavine, *Exhibiting Cultures*, 163.

36 Stephen Greenblatt, "Resonance and Wonder," in Karp and Lavine, *Exhibiting Cultures*, 42.

37 The photographs are credited to the unknown, presumably German photographer Fritz Henle. The textual commentary and layout, however, were probably created by the editorial staff and art director Yamana Ayao.

38 "At the Foot of Mt. Fuji," *NIPPON*, no. 6 (1936): 22–23.

39 Kabayama Ayské, "What Has Japan in Store?" *NIPPON*, no. 3 (1935): 7.

40 Iijima Minoru, "Un Week End à Izu," *NIPPON*, no. 8 (1936): 19–22.

41 The photographs are generically credited to Nippon Kōbō.

42 Iijima, "Un Week End à Izu," 22.

43 Sugiyama Eisuke, "Chats on Manchoukuo," *NIPPON*, no. 13 (1937): 23.

44 Yosano Akiko, "A Talk on Japanese Women," *NIPPON*, no. 10 (1937): 3.

45 Iijima Minoru, "First Steps towards Being a Perfect Housewife," *NIPPON*, no. 10 (1937): 12–15.

46 Hasegawa Nyozekan, "Life and Art," *NIPPON*, no. 11 (1937): 5.

47 "Pottery: How to Appreciate Its 'Japanese' Traits," *NIPPON*, no. 11 (1937): 27, 42.

48 MacCannell, *The Tourist*, 102.

49 *NIPPON*, no. 1 (1934): 33.

50 Advertisement over the table of contents in *NIPPON*, no. 14 (1938).

51 Natori, Kimura, Horino, Watanabe, Domon, Fujimoto, Okada, Sakamoto Manshichi, and several others worked on this publication.

52 Roberts, *Art of Interruption*, 30.

53 For essays on the various uses of montage see Matthew Teitelbaum, ed., *Montage and Modern Life* (Cambridge, Mass.: MIT Press, 1992).

54   "Shrines in Shintō Life," *NIPPON*, no. 20 (1939): 19–21.

55   Roberts, *Art of Interruption*, 35.

56   "Hallo America! Some of Our Exhibits at the Golden Gate World Fair," *NIPPON*, no. 17 (1939): 48–49.

57   Ibid., 48.

58   Yamawaki actually designed another, entirely new display for the hall in 1940 when the New York fair was extended for an additional year.

59   For a detailed discussion of this project see Kawahata Naomichi, "Fusing Photography and Space: Iwao Yamawaki's Photo Murals for New York World's Fair," in *Kolloquium über Bauhausfotografie* (Kawasaki: Kawasaki City Museum, 1997), 124–133.

60   Three special issues of the magazine appeared on China, Korea, and Manchukuo: *NIPPON*, no. 14 (1938); *NIPPON*, no. 18 (1939); and *NIPPON*, no. 19 (1939), respectively.

61   Sugiyama, "Chats on Manchoukuo," *NIPPON*, no. 13 (1937).

62   "Up and Coming Manchoukuo," *NIPPON*, no. 19 (1939): 4–6.

63   "Cooperative Government," *NIPPON*, no. 19 (1939): 14.

64   "Resources," *NIPPON*, no. 19 (1939): 25–26.

65   Far Eastern Society of Archaeology, "The Excavation of the Ruins of P'o-Hai's Palace," *NIPPON*, no. 8 (1936): 43.

66   Patricia Morton, "The Civilizing Mission of Architecture: The 1931 International Colonial Exposition in Paris" (Ph.D. diss., Princeton University, 1994), vols. 1–2.

67   *NIPPON*, no. 17 (1939): 26–33.

68   John Patric, *Why Japan Was Strong* (New York: Doubleday, Doran, 1943), 72.

69   Nitobe Inazō and Others, *Western Influences in Modern Japan* (Chicago: University of Chicago Press, 1931), 1.

70   *NIPPON*, no. 4 (1935).

71   Frank H. Hedges, "Japan Becomes Comfortable," *Travel in Japan* 2, no. 1 (1936): 40–44.

72   Watanabe and other members of the International Photojournalism Association (Kokusai Hōdō Shashin Kyōkai) worked for this publication. Incidentally, this was the same group of photographers who worked on the large-scale photomurals displayed in Japan's pavilion at the Paris World's Fair in 1937.

73   The board's activities included "business concerning statistics and investigation; business concerning propaganda abroad; better accommodation and improvement of tourist points and sightseeing facilities; development of the hotel business and improvement of hotel accommodation; overseeing of guides and persons coming in direct contact with foreign tourists." In addition, the Government Committee of Tourist Industry was formed as an auxiliary organ. It was comprised of representatives from shipping firms and hotels, government officials, and scholars. See Foreign Affairs Association of Japan, *The Japan Year Book, 1931* (Tokyo: Kenkyusha, 1931), 297. In 1931 the board set up another subsidiary agency, the Kokusai

Kankō Kyōkai (International Tourism Association), devoted entirely to producing publicity abroad. See Foreign Affairs Association of Japan, *The Japan Year Book 1935*, 720.

74 For a fascinating discussion of the travel industry developed around Manchuria see Louise Young, *Japan's Total Empire* (Berkeley and Los Angeles: University of California Press, 1998), 259–268. For an equally absorbing consideration of the exoticization of Japan for promoting domestic tourism in the postwar period see Marilyn Ivy, *Discourses of the Vanishing* (Chicago: University of Chicago Press, 1995), particularly 29–65. By 1941, under the auspices of the board, the Japan Tourist Bureau had international offices in London, Berlin, Los Angeles, New York, Shanghai, Beijing, Hong Kong, Manila, and Buenos Aires.

75 The total monetary expenditure in 1931–1932 by foreign sightseers, crews of foreign ships, foreign students, missionaries, and for diplomatic services was ¥42,603,000. This, of course, does not include money spent in Japan's colonies, through which many tourists traveled en route to Japan. See Foreign Affairs Association of Japan, *The Japan Year Book, 1933* (Tokyo: Kenkyusha, 1933), 745–747.

76 Statistical information also indicates that there was a "remarkable upward tendency" in the number of tourists coming from Manchukuo and other East Asiatic countries. See Foreign Affairs Association of Japan, *The Japan Year Book, 1937* (Tokyo: Kenkyusha, 1937), 663–665. The latest statistics for foreign tourism in the prewar period that I could locate are for 1939, when 32,951 tourists visited Japan. It is interesting to note that while U.S. and British tourists were still at the top of the list, Germans moved to third, increasing their numbers from 1,523 in 1935 to 2,447 in 1939. See Foreign Affairs Association of Japan, *The Japan Year Book, 1940–41* (Tokyo: Kenkyusha, 1941), 587–588.

77 From the privately published travel account of Frederica Walcott, *Letters from the Far East* (Woodstock, Vt.: Elm Tree Press, 1917), 38. I would like to thank Simon Partner for bringing to my attention the travel accounts in the Duke University Library Special Collections, Durham, N.C.

78 Patric, *Why Japan Was Strong*, 26.

79 Ibid., 44.

80 Foreign Affairs Association of Japan, *Japan Year Book, 1937*, 664.

81 Alpers, "Museum As a Way of Seeing," 30.

Savage Construction and Civility Making: The Musha Incident and Aboriginal Representations in Colonial Taiwan

Leo Ching

In 1911 Japanese colonial officials led forty-three selected aboriginal leaders from Taiwan on one of the seven "tours to Japan proper" (*naichi kankō*). The tours were organized in conjunction with the initial stage of military subjugation of the natives after the pacification of the Taiwanese-Chinese islanders. Four such tours took place between 1911 and 1912 at the height of the military campaign under the directives of the fifth governor-general, Sakuma Samata. Previously, the colonial government had only sponsored one tour in 1897 and, since 1912, only two tours, in 1918 and 1925, respectively. These tours presented a calculated structure of visibility. The visuality of Japanese metropolitan grandeur was to complement the brutality of Japanese colonial force in the larger colonial "enterprise of governing the savages" (*rihan jigyō*).[1] The visiting savages (*banjin*) were directed to and shown various industrial and military facilities, the imperial palace, and Shinto shrines. These carefully orchestrated itineraries were intended to

positions 8:3 © 2000 by Duke University Press

impress upon the aborigines Japanese military dominance and cultural superiority. Thus, despite being the "subjects of seeing," the aborigines, unable to initiate the action of seeing spontaneously under the technological and discursive arrangements of colonial power, remained deprived of the ability of "seeing as subjects." To a large extent the tours succeeded in constructing a field of vision in which the aborigines succumbed to the sights/sites of colonial power.[2] However, the seemingly indestructible colonial relationship was at least momentarily disrupted nineteen years later when Monarudao, one of the young tribal leaders on the 1911 tour, led a violent and bloody rebellion against the colonial authority in what came to be known as the Musha Incident.

The uprising and its subsequent merciless quelling by the authorities effected a necessary rearticulation of Japanese colonial governmentality whereby acculturation, in the form of imperialization (*kōminka*), emerged as the privileged sphere in which colonial power was exercised and consolidated. The incident was hotly debated in the Japanese Diet, and criticism of the colonial government was voiced from both within Japan and abroad. As a result, rather than the crude political operations that had thus far characterized the colonial relationship between the ruling Japanese and the ruled natives, in the post-Musha period the Japanese attempted to maintain their legitimacy through a discourse of incorporation and assimilation. I argue in this essay that after the Musha Incident, we encounter a visible shift in aborigine representations in the circulation of the culture of colonialism. The aborigines are no longer the savage heathen waiting to be civilized through colonial benevolence; they are imperial subjects assimilated into the Japanese national polity through the expressions of their loyalty to the emperor. This shift in representations, I argue, does not constitute a real or radical transformation. Despite colonialist intention and authorization, it is instead a transfiguration that remains trapped and inscribed within the relationality and dichotomy of savagery and civility. The problematic that I address here is akin to what Etienne Balibar has questioned regarding the notion of a "neo-racism."[3] On one hand, are we seeing a new historical upsurge in representations and policies toward the Taiwanese aborigines that can be explained by a crisis conjuncture or by other causes? On the other hand, in its themes and its social significance, is what we are seeing only a new colonial discourse, irreducible to earlier models, or is it a mere tactical adaptation?

I will consider two popular representations of aborigines from the 1910s and the 1930s, "The Story of Gohō" and "The Bell of Sayon," respectively, that best delineate this shift from natural savages to national subjects.[4] "Gohō" is the Japanese adaptation of a Chinese folktale that narrates the benevolence and self-sacrifice of Gohō, a Ch'ing official who supposedly convinced the aborigines to give up their head-hunting practices. "Sayon" is a colonial dramatization and commemoration of an aboriginal girl, Sayon, who drowned in a torrent while shouldering luggage for a Japanese draftee. On one hand, "Gohō" represents the initial colonialist strategy of negation for the construction of savagery, where the aborigines were denied their subjectivities and representations other than the practice of head-hunting. On the other hand, "Sayon" constitutes a post-Musha tactic of idealizing primitivity in the making of civility. Where "Gohō" narrates the aborigines' self-realization and self-condemnation of their own barbarism through the benevolence of colonialism, "Sayon" dramatizes the aboriginal redemption and devotion to the Japanese nation through self-annihilation—a transfiguration from a remorseful savage to a patriotic imperial subject. I contend that one of the ideological intentions of "Gohō" was to intensify the preexisting antagonism between the Taiwanese-Chinese and the aboriginal population during the early years of aboriginal subjugation. In "Sayon," however, the irreducible differences among the colonized are homogenized under the auspices of the Japanese nation for the purpose of total mobilization during the Pacific War. This time the aborigines and the Taiwanese-Chinese are no longer played *against* each other in opposition but are played *off* one another in affiliation for their respective dedication in becoming loyal imperial subjects.

The Unseasoned Blooming of the Musha Red Blossoms

In the morning of 27 October 1930, the thirty-fifth year of Japanese colonial rule, the annual sports day in Musha, a reservation for the unassimilated (*seiban*) aborigines in the mountainous region of central Taiwan, was about to begin. The autumn field event was one of the most festive and important occasions for this regional headquarters of aboriginal settlement. On this day the usually segregated children from the primary school (*shōgakkō*) for the Japanese, the common school (*kōgakkō*) for the well-to-do Taiwanese, and the aboriginal education centers (*bandō kyōikusho*) were brought together for competition. The event also coincided with the visit of the colonial provincial governor and police officials, with many guests, their families, servants, and porters. At around eight o'clock, with great fanfare and excitement, the Tayal aborigines, the Taiwanese, and the Japanese, together numbering four hundred or so, began to sing the national anthem in unison as the Japanese flag was raised. Just then, a shriek akin to that of a wild beast broke out as the crimson head of a middle-aged Japanese man was catapulted into midair against the blue autumn sky—the moment of demise for Sugano Masae, the commissioner of Taichūshū Police Bureau. As if coming out of nowhere, approximately three hundred aboriginal men in native attire and armed with rifles, guns, and swords surged onto the school ground yelling in their native tongue, "Do not spare any Japanese!" The Tayal women rushed to usher their children away as the heads and bodies of Japanese men, women, and children lay strewn on the once orderly ground. It was a moment, recalls Pihowaris, one of the few surviving aborigine witnesses who was then fifteen, when "suddenly the red blossom of Musha made its unseasoned blooming."[5] Altogether, 134 Japanese were slain, making this one of the largest and most notorious uprisings against the Japanese in the country's colonial history.[6]

The uprising was devastating to both the colonial authorities in Taiwan and Japanese colonial rule in general. This "immense scandal" and "surprise of all surprises" shocked imperialist Japan for several reasons. First, the perpetrators came from what the colonial officials had praised as the most "enlightened and compliant" of all aboriginal territories, with relatively high living and education standards. Second, two distinguished aborigine police, Dakkisnobin and Dakkisnaui (Japanese names Hanaoka Ichirō and Hanaoka Jirō, respectively), who were lauded as symbols of Japanese colonial benevolence and tutelage, committed suicide instead of forewarning the authorities or persuading the rebels to surrender. Third, the killing appeared to have been premeditated and methodical because of preliminary attacks on strategic police stations peripheral to Musha and the indiscriminate slaying of Japanese nationals, regardless of age and gender. Finally, the rebellion occurred in the midst of a global economic crisis that further strained the viability of Japanese capitalism and its overseas colonial enterprise. Many metropolitan and colonial officials feared that the Musha Incident would spark nationalist movements and stimulate class antagonisms not only in colonial Taiwan but also in colonial Korea and perhaps in Japan itself.[7] The incredulity and agitation caused by the insurgence consumed the colonial authority to the extent that the subsequent subjugation campaign mobilized approximately three thousand military and police forces (against three hundred rebels) and deployed internationally banned poisonous gas with the clear aim of decimating the rebelling population.

There is considerable literature that speculates on the causes of the Musha Incident, and it is not my intention here to provide another account. Instead, I suggest that the Musha uprising, despite its predicted failure, constituted a historical event that, on one hand, signaled an unprecedented intransigence and resistance by the colonized that deeply shook, if not momentarily destablized, Japanese rule. On the other hand, the uprising also effected a radical shift in Japanese colonial governmentality in which specific forms of imperial incorporation emerged as the primary ideological apparatus whereby colonial power reconstituted itself. It is within this historically specific subaltern resistance and colonial accommodation that we can better understand the persistence of aboriginal representations between savagery and civility.

The Savage Without, the Savage Within

Ōshika Taku's "The Savage" ["Yabanjin"] is arguably one of the most representative texts of the relationship between Japanese and the Taiwanese aborigines in the post-Musha era, and it marks a radical shift in how the categories civilization, barbarity, Japanese, and savage were interpreted in the Japanese colonial consciousness.[8] As Kawamura Minato correctly points out, in an earlier historical moment, at the dawn of Japanese imperialism, the discovery of savages in the exteriority substantiated Japan's identification with civilization as a modern nation-state. With the ensuing incorporation of the savages into the Japanese empire, the discovery of the savages ironically also meant the discovery of barbarity *within* the Japanese themselves.[9] "The Savage," published in the February issue of *Chūo Kōron* in 1935, was selected as prizewinner over some 1,218 other entries. Although the text does not deal with the Musha Incident directly (it takes up an earlier subjugation effort against another aboriginal group in colonial Taiwan), it is hard to believe the events surrounding the Musha Incident had no bearing on Ōshika's work.[10]

"The Savage" chronicles the transformation of the protagonist Tazawa from a Japanese man to a subjugated savage. The son of a mine owner in Japan, Tazawa is banished to colonial Taiwan by his father for inciting the miners during a labor dispute. "Partly desperate and feeling defiant and disdainful," Tazawa gravely requests that the chief of the Savage Rule Section send him to the aboriginal territories. Upon arriving at the assigned post near Musha, Tazawa is attracted to two "savage women" who are sisters of the wife of Ino, the head of the police office. While being teased and warned of the aborigine women's single-mindedness in pursuing Japanese men, Tazawa "finds their demeanor and expressions similar to that of the women in Japan," but with a different "wildness and simplicity." As predicted, Taimorikaru (the older of the sisters) courts Tazawa incessantly. Although attracted by her "innocent spirit," Tazawa finds himself unable to consummate the relationship, feeling an unbridgeable gap between them. On a mission to suppress the rebel aborigines at the Saramao settlement, he unconsciously beheads an aborigine that he has just killed with a rifle. When the severed head is brought back to the police station and shelved with other "enemy heads," Tazawa is struck by the jubilation and calmness displayed by Taimonamo (the younger sister) toward this "cruelty" and is reminded of his own "mental weakness." He says to himself,

> It does not seem that her mind is controlled only by these violent customs. It feels as if one has breathed in a stifling smell of savagery that has been passed on from blood to blood. No, one can't simply call it savagery. It is a savagery that is like the solemn pulsation of a grand tree infused by the spirit of defiance; a grand tree that widens its bosom while being oppressed by the mercilessness of Nature and yet kept alive by its bitter compassion. The sap flows through its pulses, gushing out even to the tips

of the small branches. Compared to that, I am only a small tree that has just been transplanted.[11]

To Tazawa, he cannot reciprocate Taimorikaru's passion because his "savagery is only half-hearted." He tells himself, "Be savage, I must become a savage!" Tazawa's desire to become a savage is equally compelled by his desire to return Taimorikaru to her primordial state of barbarity. He scolds her for learning to eat with chopsticks; he yells at her for powdering her face with white makeup; he berates her for wearing a kimono. His transformation to savagery is completed when Tazawa puts on aboriginal clothes, marks his face with ash, and brandishes an aboriginal sword, imagining himself hunting with the native men. With the crowd roaring and applauding "Savage! Savage!" he finds himself overwhelmed by an inexplicable excitement. "Like a beast who has just been placed in a cage," Tazawa mutters to himself, "I am a savage too! I will be second to none!"

It seems almost too obvious to suggest that this imagining of the native is an operation of power; the transformation of a petit bourgeois Japanese man from civility to savagery is incumbent upon the prohibition of native transgression. The obsession for an imaginative identification with the savages is intertwined with the disavowal of the horrific figuration of a semi-assimilated "Japanese" woman. This discovery of the savage within is no different from the colonial projection of the savage without.[12] Apprehension, definition, and subordination are caught up together in a process of representation that can be traced to the workings of imperial power in the specific context of the relationship between the Japanese and the aborigines, where categories of class, race, and gender emerge in intimate relation to one another. The failed attempt at labor struggle in metropolitan Japan is first displaced onto the racial antagonism between Japanese colonial rule and aboriginal resistance. The desire for transcendence is then projected onto the genderized conflict between Tazawa, who seeks savagery, and Taimorikaru, who becomes civilized. What is crucial for the final transfiguration, however, is that the process must necessarily reverse itself. The consummation between the Japanese man and the aboriginal woman is predicated upon the denial of colonial/racial transgression, that the colonial difference between civility and savagery must be restored and reaffirmed. For the sight of a "mimic" woman only reminds Tazawa of his own incompleteness, a distorted figure of an otherwise essentialized being. Finally, class conflict in the metropole is symbolically resolved through the phantasmatic identification with the savages and Tazawa's empathetic realization of the "suppressed enthusiasm of the oppressed."

What needs to be underscored here is that in the post-Musha era, the aboriginal issues can no longer be situated outside Japanese consciousness. These issues entail not only colonial administration and aboriginal rule but also the fundamental contradiction of Japanese colonial modernity itself. The generic title of "The Savage" seems to underscore the savagery displayed by the supposedly civilized Japanese nation and its civilizing colonial mission. However, as I have argued, the self-reflexive gesture—the discovery of the savagery within—is premised upon the consolidation and extension of the savagery without. Despite the effort to locate the savagery within civility, the binary construction of the two terms, which are not the effect of but the fundamental constitution of colonial modernity itself, remains intact and is thereby reinforced.

Self-Condemnation at the Margin of Civility

In the wake of the Musha Incident, Japanese colonial attitudes toward the aborigines marked a conspicuous shift whereby the ideology of imperialization, rather than military subjugation or economic servitude, emerged as the dominant form of colonial control. This is not to suggest, however, that oppressive apparatuses entirely ceased, labor exploitation vanished, or colonialism's culture enacted an unprecedented role. The near decimation of the entire rebelling population attests to the continuing use of brutal armed force. Cultural practices have long since defined and demarcated the boundaries between the colonizer and the colonized, civility and savagery, and self and other. I argue here that in the post-Musha era, we encounter a radical shift in the representation of aborigines in the circulation of colonial culture. The aborigines were no longer the savage heathens waiting to be assimilated; they were now imperial subjects acculturated within the Japanese national polity. This transformation from savagery to civility, I argue, was partially an attempt by the colonial government to contain the irrepressible contradictions exemplified by the Musha uprising. It also represented an equally urgent need to mobilize aboriginal conscript labor for Japan's war effort. This process of interpellation, or what has come to be known as imperialization, points to the tenacity of Japanese colonial rule as much as to the desire of the aborigines to insert themselves as active agents into the making of history. In this self-affirmation we might view the desire to become Japanese not simply as the substantiation of false consciousness but, rather, as the coming to terms with the trauma and tragedy of the Musha Incident. Warispiho, one of the few surviving aborigine soldiers, with his Japanese name, Yonekawa, tatooed onto his right wrist, defended his decision to volunteer for the war: "By becoming a Japanese soldier, I thought to remove the disgrace that has been attached to the Musha Incident. By enlisting, I would achieve the same honor as the Japanese. I have never feared death."[13]

It is an understatement to say that the Musha Incident rocked the colonial administration and shocked all segments of informed opinion in Japan. Not only did Ishizuka Eizō, the governor-general at the time, resign under pressure to take responsibility, but the origins of the rebellion and its violent suppression by the colonial forces were also hotly debated in the Japanese Diet. More important, the Musha Incident provided the opportunity for the colonial administration to reevaluate and overhaul its aboriginal policies in general. In his *Outline for Savage Rule* published in December 1931, Ōta Masahiro, the succeeding governor-general, called for a fundamental shift in colonial management and attitude toward the aborigines. The *Outline* states,

> The goal of savage governance is to enlighten and educate the savages, to secure their livelihood, and to immerse them in the imperial virtue of equality. Although there have been some changes in the savage governing policy, its ultimate goal has always been to enact the imperial wish of equality and to honor them with imperialization [Japanization]. This has always been the consistent and fundamental spirit.[14]

Despite the authority's pronouncement of the consistent and fundamental spirit of its policy of assimilation regarding the aborigines, the very act of its restating only confirms the exigency and necessity of a new set of colonial rationales as remedial measures in the post-Musha era. The new and primary directive was to enlighten and educate (*kyōka*) them in becoming loyal imperial subjects. Whereas civility had previously existed only in a universal opposition to savagery, now civility was conjoined with the particularity of Japanese nationality, with specific reference to loyalty to the emperor. By June 1935 the colonial government had abolished the use of the term *seiban* (raw savages) and began using the more generic appellation *takasagozoku* (literally, the tribal peoples of Taiwan) when referring to aborigines.

I would like to consider two popular representations of aborigines that best delineate the shift from savage to imperial subject and to note how these representations designate a remarkable site for identity construction and the workings of colonial ideology. One of the most widely circulated narratives regarding Taiwanese aborigines is undoubtedly "The Story of Gohō" (Wu Fang, in Chinese reading) as it is featured in colonial and Japanese elementary school textbooks. The story goes as follows: Gohō, a Ch'ing official, is the sole liaison between the Chinese settlers and the native savages on the island of Taiwan. For years Gohō is able to prevent the killing of the Chinese through various negotiations and manipulations. But eventually he exhausts all means to appease the savages' insatiable demand for human heads to be used in their sacrificial rituals. Reluctantly, Gohō promises the headhunters a prize: a man in red will appear in a particular place at a specific time, and the tribesmen can kill him and take his head. On the agreed-upon day, a man wrapped in a red gown with his face covered by a red hood rides on a white horse to the prearranged site. Following Gohō's instruction, the headhunters ambush and kill the man immediately. As they eagerly unveil the red hood to sever the head, they are stunned to see the tranquil countenance of Gohō. Upon discovering that the man they have just murdered is none other than their respected Gohō, the savages repent in tears and vow never to kill another Chinese again. The moral of the story is not only that Gohō has sacrificed himself for the well-being of others, but that his death has brought civility to the savages, who remorsefully give up their barbarous customs.

The story of the confrontation between the Ch'ing Chinese and the savage aborigines is a Japanese colonial rewriting of an already existing folktale in the beginning of the twentieth century. What looms behind the story of Gohō, the encounter between civility and savagery, culture and nature, and benevolence and ignorance, is the Japanese colonial authority, which by virtue of its very absence in the narrative authors and authorizes a complex reconstruction and rearticulation of colonial ideology.

Like most folklore that exists in a heteroglossic process of appropriation and deletion, elaboration, and condensation, "The Story of Gohō" had several variants before the "official" rendition was completed by the colonial administration. According to Komagome Takeshi, there are at least six variations: four in the Chinese script and two recorded from the aboriginal oral tradition.[15] While all these versions retain the same basic narrative structure—a confrontation between Chinese and aborigines, the killing of a Chinese, the aborigines' vow to end killing—there appears to be no reference to Gohō as a self-sacrificing agent worthy of emulation in any of these earlier accounts. For instance, in most of the Chinese versions, although head-hunting is the main cause of conflict that leads to Gohō's confrontation with the aborigines, the killing of Gohō, contrary to the unintended mistake in the colonial version, is an intentional act by the tribesmen. Gohō has simply confronted the aborigines and engaged in a battle. The aborigines knew exactly whom they were killing. And it is the unexorcised spirit of Gohō following the skirmish that incurs a curse that brings an epidemic killing hundreds of natives and leads to the final resolution, with the aborigines renouncing their head-hunting practices, henceforth substituting round stones for human skulls in their worship. The supernatural elements of the earlier Chinese versions are omitted in the colonial rewriting, most likely corresponding to the overall colonial policy to rid Taiwan of all superstitions and ancient beliefs.

In the aboriginal account of the story, head-hunting is never mentioned as the reason for the conflict. Rather, the killing is an act of retaliation for continuous plundering and harassing by some Ch'ing officers under Gohō's jurisdiction. Gohō, however, is mistakenly murdered. After his death, a mysterious disease spreads among the natives, resulting in many deaths. Fearing the ensuing epidemic as retribution for the murder of Gohō, the tribesmen try to appease Gohō's wrath by promising never to kill another Chinese. The rewriting by the Japanese colonialists largely followed the Chinese versions while augmenting the previously nonexistent sacrificial aspect of Gohō. It is important to underscore that in the colonial revision, the aborigines have renounced their head-hunting practice not through some supernatural curse but through the moral endeavor of a cultured being: Gohō himself. It is this colonial insertion (while retaining the unintentionality of the killing) that ultimately made possible the impossibility of the aborigines' reversion to incivility. It is through a human deed—an act of moral superiority—that the savages are brought into civilization, a narrative indicating existing colonial practices.

One of the textual strategies adopted by the Japanese in the rewriting of Gohō's story is the reemphasis on the savagery of the aborigines through the head-hunting motif commonly found in the Chinese variants. This re-making of barbarism is not only important in accentuating the grandeur of Gohō's nobility, but it is also indispensable in justifying Japan's colonial civilizing mission. The colonial text describes the head-hunting practice as follows: "As the custom of the Arisan savages, they must offer a human head during their religious rituals. As a result, many of those who pass by the savage territories have often met misfortune."[16] This simple and matter-of-fact way of describing head-hunting conceals more than it reveals about the practice itself. This is a "true" account of the aborigines as far as such customs have been witnessed and recorded. However, this is also an ideolog-ical account that performs a symbolic exclusionary tactic through its casual narrative tone. The horror of the Others in their savagery is spoken about as a given and accepted fact. This is where the insistence on the boundary between self and other, civility and barbarism, and culture and nature is established. The simple and brief description glosses over the practice of head-hunting as a specific cultural function within the larger structure of aboriginal social relations—for instance, as a means of establishing antag-onistic relationships between tribes or other nonaboriginal entities, such as the Chinese and the Japanese, or as the practice of initiation for aborigi-nal men. It simply becomes a trope for savagery and cruelty. In the later transcriptions of "The Story of Gohō" into textbooks for colonial educa-tion and its eventual appearance in the textbooks of imperialist Japan, the ritualistic and social purposes of head-hunting are entirely left out. Head-hunting becomes naturalized; the aborigines are by nature immoral and destructive. The irony, however, is that the headhunters cannot be *com-pletely* naturalized; they cannot be regarded as inhuman because if they were animals, their behavior could not provoke such outrage and fear. Therefore, the aborigines must be placed on the very border of humanity, capable of transgression and salvation, but only from their preassigned degraded moral state.[17]

Any political reading must interpret the narrower textual conflict in terms of larger politico-narrative units. "The Story of Gohō" is no exception. The reconstructing of preexisting narratives into an authoritarian colonial discourse is, of course, part and parcel of a larger colonial practice that can only be understood within the specific historical context of colonial Taiwan. When the Japanese first took hold of Taiwan, they were met with unanticipated heavy resistance from the Taiwanese-Chinese population (most noted was the brief proclamation of the Republic of Taiwan that lasted three weeks). Most of this armed resistance was small in scale and sporadic, yet it persisted into the early years of Japanese colonization. As a result, from the first to the fourth reign of the governor general, the colonial administration was preoccupied with subjugating armed uprisings and containing social upheavals in the plain (*heichi*) territories where most Taiwanese-Chinese lived. The aborigines, who were forcibly pushed up to the mountainous (*sanchi*) regions as the result of centuries of infringement by the Chinese settlers, were not of primary concern to the colonial government. As the Taiwanese-Chinese insurgents in the plains were gradually pacified through military force, the colonial government, eager to exploit the rich natural resources in the mountain regions, embarked on a massive mobilization effort to control the aborigines. It is therefore not a coincidence that the colonial rewriting of Gohō's story appeared during the five-year military expedition of the fifth governor-general, Sakuma Samata, against the northern aboriginal tribes, beginning in 1910. The expedition required financial assistance and manpower beyond the capability of the colonial government. As a result, it had to turn to the indigenous Taiwanese landlord class for support and collaboration.[18] The invention of a self-sacrificing Chinese and the reconstruction of head-hunting aborigines in the Gohō narrative functioned, therefore, as colonial ideology that attempted to widen and sharpen the preexisting antagonistic relation between the Taiwanese-Chinese and the indigenous population. The appropriation of "The Story of Gohō" into the colonial discourse is therefore a concomitant incorporation of the already colonized Taiwanese-Chinese into the colonial practice of the military expedition. Textual violence is materialized into actual practice.

The abjection of the aborigines had consequences beyond its immediate and local "savage management" by encouraging Taiwanese-Chinese cooperation. It also acted as an overall trope for asserting the Japanese civilizing mission, thereby rationalizing and celebrating Japanese colonial accomplishments—a symbol of Japan's modernity. As Nitobe Inazo puts it succinctly in *The Japanese Nation*, "Modern nations vie with one another to express their greatness and splendour in territorial expansionism, or else in ethnic colonisation."[19] *The Japanese Nation*, as well as *Bushido* and Okakura Kakuzō's *The Ideal of the East* and *The Book of Tea*, are texts that were written in English in the early twentieth century attempting to articulate (and to justify) Japan's newly attained colonial position to a Western readership. In a chapter titled "Japan As Colonizer," Nitobe cites colonial Taiwan as a prominent example in the continuous education of the Japanese nation in the "art of colonisation." Together with the pacification (or extermination) of rebels, the banning of opium smoking, and the improvement of public health, Nitobe points out the subjugation of the aborigines, especially the head-hunting tribes, as the four major accomplishments of colonial Japan. He describes the aborigines as follows: "They are in a very primitive state of social life. . . . They have scarcely any clothing; a few tribes wear none. Their houses are usually built of wood, bamboo and are roofed with slate or straw. . . . In character, they are brave and fierce when roused to ire; otherwise, friendly and childlike."[20] In this constellation of images of deficiency, nakedness, and infantilism, a rhetoric of underdevelopment is established—their lack of material sustenance and their emotive inclination—both as a justification for Japanese intervention and as the necessary iteration of a fundamental difference between the colonizer and the colonized. As for the head-hunting practice of the aborigines, Nitobe writes,

> What concerns us most dearly in their manner of life, is their much-venerated custom of consecrating *any* auspicious occasion by obtaining a human head. If there is a wedding in prospect, the young man cannot marry unless he brings in a head, and the susceptibility of the human heart being much the same in savagery as in civilization, this is a tremendous

spur to head-hunting. . . . Indeed *all* celebrations of any importance must be graced with it. *Where a bouquet would be used by you, a grim human head, freshly cut, is the essential decoration at their banquet.* [21]

What is striking about the above passage is that, first, while recognizing head-hunting as a cultural construct and a social practice, it also suggests an almost randomness and indifferent casualness to such practices. The casual usage of "any" and "all" and the equating of a skull to a flower denote this generality. Second, it is precisely by appealing to a common *humanity* (the affinity between "us" and "them") that their actions seem *in*human compared with ours, making an obligatory distinction between civilized and barbaric practice. However, by confirming their humanity, Nitobe affirms the savages' potential for civilization and that the progress of civilization depends on the suppression or the outright elimination of savage life (colonization). My point here, of course, is not to endorse head-hunting or to call for cultural relativism. Rather, I mean to bring to light the contradictory mechanics of colonial discourse, which, through the very designation of debasement and abjection, the delimitation of a boundary between self and other, civility and savagery, and categories of good and evil is constructed. Yet the Other cannot remain an absolute Other outside the colonial economy; the boundary must be firm but negotiable. The natives are to become the distorted and negative images of colonialists; they are the same as us but not quite like us.[22] Put differently, only through the discovery (if not an invention) of the natives' incivility can the colonizers locate their own civility, as we have seen in the earlier discussion of "The Savage." The presence of the heathen Other is instrumental in colonialism's perpetual need for self-affirmation through demonstrations of moral superiority. Similarly, only through the incorporation of savagery into its empire, and the manifestation of Japan's own savagery, can the Japanese state become a civilized and modern nation, joining the ranks of the Western powers. The contradiction was anticipated by Okakura Kakuzō in 1906:

The average Westerner, in his sleek complacency, will see in the tea-ceremony but another instance of the thousand and one oddities which constitute the quaintness and childishness of the East to him. He was wont to regard Japan as barbarous while she indulged in the gentle arts of peace: he calls her civilised since she began to commit wholesale slaughter on Manchuria battlefields.[23]

Redemption at the Margin of Nationhood

If the pre-Musha story of Gohō represents the initial colonialist strategy of negation for the construction of savagery, "The Bell of Sayon" constitutes a post-Musha tactic of idealization in the making of civility within Japanese nationality. And if "The Story of Gohō" narrates the aborigines' self-realization and self-condemnation of their barbarism through the benevolence of colonialism, "The Bell of Sayon" dramatizes the aboriginal redemption and devotion to the Japanese nation through self-annihilation. In short, the latter illustrates a transfiguration from a remorseful savage to a patriotic martyred imperial subject. "The Bell of Sayon" is the story of Sayon, a seventeen-year-old aboriginal woman from the Ryōhen settlement, population 340, in eastern Taiwan. In September 1938, with the escalating Japanese war in China, Takita, the police officer in charge of the settlement and also Sayon's teacher, is drafted to the front. Sayon, with ten other aborigines, is to carry the departing officer's luggage to the foot of the mountain. On 27 September the entourage descends the precipitous mountain path of thirty-four kilometers amid a torrential typhoon. As they cross the rising water on the makeshift log bridge, Sayon slips and is swept away by the rapid current. Even after a month of diligent searching, Sayon's body is never recovered. It is reported that at the time she was carrying three large suitcases on her back with a strip of cloth wrapped around her forehead.

Sayon's accident was only casually mentioned in the *Taiwan Daily News* (*Taiwan nichinichi shimpō*) in its 29 September edition, with the heading, "Aborigine Woman Missing after Falling into Stream."[24] For three years the story of a drowned seventeen-year-old aborigine woman remained obscure and insignificant. Once again, the reclamation of Sayon as a patriotic body requires the authorship and the authority of the colonial government. In the spring of 1941, after learning of Sayon's good deed (*zenkō*), Governor-General Hasegawa Kiyoshi presented the Ryōhen settlement with a bell inscribed with the following phrase: "The Bell of the Patriotic Maiden Sayon." The commemoration reverberated throughout the island, especially among the aborigines, and generated a media sensation with a number of paintings of Sayon, a popular song, and eventually a film based on her story.[25] More important, the bell is said to have been used to summon aboriginal patriotic youth groups (*seinendan*) and inspired many to "follow the steps of the patriotic maiden" and join the war effort.[26] What is important here is not whether Sayon was truly patriotic or whether the colonial government was opportunistic in misrepresenting a common aboriginal woman from a remote mountain tribe.[27] Rather, we should be concerned with the emergence of an entirely new representation of the aborigine; the emotive symbol Sayon represented to the aborigine population only encouraged patriotism during the period of war mobilization.

The paintings, a popular song, and a film starring a renowned Japanese idol formed the discursive and visual strategies by which the Japanese colonial discourse re-presented the aborigines as imperial subjects to be mobilized. The multimedia events recast a tragic accident into heroic destiny, where the aboriginal maiden replaces the Ch'ing official as the essential mediator between the colonizer and the colonized, between civility and savagery. Subsequently there were other forms of representation and dramatization that glorified the patriotic deeds of aboriginal men in combat, especially in terms of their courage and loyalty. The virginal image of Sayon, however, was crucial in substantiating, if not actually enabling, the transformation of the aborigines from an unruly population to patriotic subjects in the post-Musha era. Put differently, much like the discursive arrangement of the colonial myth of Pocahontas in the British context, Sayon occupies an exceptional place in the "crossing of the cultural rift" between the colonizer and the colonized, between the ideological expectation of colonialism and the historical occurrence of an unfortunate incident.[28] However, unlike the adventures of Pocahontas, Sayon's crossing of boundaries is not predicated on the successful "rescue" (what Peter Hulme has called "the norms of reciprocity") of John Smith; her later marriage to another colonialist, John Rolfe; or her final acceptance of colonial culture and Christianity. Sayon's crossing, like her unsuccessful crossing of the torrent during the storm, is incomplete and fatal. But it is precisely this failure and her inevitable death that made possible other subsequent crossings by her fellow aborigines. Sayon's aborted crossing is not a demonstration (as in Pocahontas) of a highborn savage who is not cruel or unlearned but in fact gentle and potentially cultured. Nor is Sayon the embodiment of an assimilated native successful in her desire to become Japanese. Rather, the ideological affectivity of the story of Sayon lies in the colonial construction of her extraordinary dedication to die performing her duty as an *ordinary* subject of the empire.

Sayon's plebian characteristics are accentuated in the colonialist media in terms of her youthfulness and innocence. In one of the watercolor portraits, *The Bell of Sayon*, for instance, we see a stoic Sayon sitting on what appears to be a boulder or a large mound of dirt. There is an intended portrayal of primitivity here. Dressed in indigenous garb with a distinctive hair band, she seems to be in an expressionless daze, her gaze directed nowhere. Her left hand rests on the ground for support, and her feet are set firmly against the mound. Her disproportionately large hands and bare feet bear witness to her earthiness and primitiveness, which distinguish her from the acculturated aborigine women in Japanese kimonos that were common in this period of cultural imposition. She is not only grounded in place but also frozen in time. Despite the title of the painting, the bell is conspicuously absent, and there is no narrative about her exemplary deed. In this impressionistic painting, Sayon exists as a nonthreatening, nonsexualized maiden with an utterly pristine and primitive manner.

If the heroics of Sayon are delimited by the aesthetic form of the painting, the popular song *The Bell of Sayon* poetizes her story in close affinity with the colonialist composition. Sung in the form of the traditional Japanese *enka* style, the song begins with Sayon in the midst of the typhoon:

> Storm rages, the foot of the mountain   [arashifukite mine no fumoto]
> Dangerous current, a log bridge   [nagare ayauki marukibashi]
> Who's the one crossing, the beautiful maiden   [wataruwa darezo
>   uruwashiotome]
> The reddened lips, ah . . . Sayon.   [akaki kuchibiru ah—sayon]

The second and third verses describe Sayon shouldering the luggage of her affectionate (*natsukashiya*) mentor (*shinokimi*) in the rainstorm and her sad disappearance (*kiete kanashiki*). The song ends with the final verse:

The purity of a maiden, and her sincerity [kiyokiotomeno magokorowo]
In whose tears, will she be remembered [dareka namidani shinobazaru]
The southern island, deepening twilight   [minamino shimano
                                                    tasogarefukashi]
The bell rings and rings, ah . . . Sayon. [kanewa narunaru ah—sayon][29]

One of the features of the Sayon myth is the ideal of cultural harmony and
selfless devotion through romance. Her unrequited love for the Japanese
officer who was also her teacher is expressed but never substantiated through
Sayon's dedication and willingness to carry his luggage through the raging
storm as he is drafted into the military and presumably is willing to die
for his country. Inseparable from Sayon's love for the officer in the colonial
discourse is her recognition of the importance of the national mission over
personal desire.

The virginal and primitive image of the beautiful Sayon in her purity
and sincerity and with her unconsummated love for one Japanese man is
important in positioning Sayon as a mediator between two communities,
constructing a different relationship between aborigine women and Japanese men. One of the initial colonialist strategies for aboriginal pacification was to encourage marriages between Japanese officers and aborigine
women, usually daughters of prominent leaders. However, these devised
marriages often failed and led to the discontent of both parties. In fact, after the Musha Incident the colonial government became quite fastidious in
monitoring and discouraging any amorous relationships between Japanese
police officers and aborigine women. Many officers were transferred out of
their posts once such a courtship was detected. With the prohibition against
miscegenation, Sayon's unsexualized and unrealizable "romance" in terms
of idolization and chastity provides an instrumental interrelation between
colonizing men and aborigine women. No longer is the relationship between
men and women, husbands and wives, with the possibilities of impropriety
and divorce, but rather, it is rearticulated in a platonic affiliation between
mentors and students, authority and subordinates, based on loyalty and obedience. It is for this purpose that Sayon must remain primitive and innocent
in the post-Musha colonial discourse where the ideology of subordination

and dedication has replaced the instrumentality of transgression and assimilation.

Sayon's mediation through subordination is the dominant motif in the
1943 national policy (*kokusaku*) film *The Bell of Sayon*. It is in the cinematic
narrative that a historical event involving an aborigine woman and the colonial invention of a patriotic martyr collude to complete the specter of Sayon
for war mobilization. Although the film highlights the tragic drowning of
Sayon in its climactic scene, she is not shown dutifully shouldering the exces-
sive luggage of the Japanese officer that must have been partially responsible
for her death. Rather, her duty as an aborigine woman in the colonial empire
is recast as a supporter and intermediary for the impending "volunteer" system of the aborigine men. The film adds two aborigine protagonists, Saburo
and Mona (perhaps a canny reference to Monarudao, the leader of the Musha
uprising), vying for Sayon's affection. One day Mona receives a notice to en-
list in the first Takasago Patriotic Army (*Takasago teishin hōkokutai*) to join
the war effort. As all the young men cheer with encouragement and envy,
Saburo sulks in disappointment. Sayon admonishes him with the following:
"Saburo, why are you so dejected? Isn't today the departure of the Takasago
Patriotic Army? Isn't today the departure of your friend? Even if you weren't
summoned the first time, there will be second, third, fourth, and fifth times.
Eventually you will receive your calling." Soon after, the Japanese officer
receives his draft notice, and Sayon drowns while sending him off, as the
film ends. The grossly didactic juxtaposition between Sayon's tragic death
and the aborigine volunteers' patriotism is choreographed to instill a sense
of loyalty to the Japanese nation during the end of the Pacific War, when
conflict was most intense. Through the various colonial representations, the
death of an ordinary aborigine woman is elevated to the symbol of the patriotic maiden Sayon. What Japanese colonialism conceals in its representations
of Sayon, however, is the historical fate of many of the aborigine volunteers
who would follow her in their journey of no return.

There are a number of obvious differences between "The Bell of Sayon"
and "The Story of Gohō." First, whereas the narrative of "Gohō" is motivated by the *confrontation* between the aborigines and the Chinese, the
dramatization of "Sayon" is undergirded by the *collaboration* between the

aborigines and the Japanese. The conflict is then displaced from that of cultural differences (as between head-hunting and civility) and reconstituted as that between natural forces and human deeds, between the unrelenting storm and the determined Sayon. Second, although both texts resolve their narrative tensions through the deaths of their respective protagonists, their implications are drastically different. Gohō's death is predicated on his self-sacrifice for the good of all (*satsushinjōjin*). Not only were the Chinese spared from being head-hunted, but the savages were also brought closer to civility by renouncing their barbaric practices. Sayon's death, on the other hand, is restricted to the narrative of loyalty to the nation (*jinchūhōkoku*). Her accidental demise, regardless of her intentions and circumstances, is quickly subsumed under the larger moral of selfless dedication to the Japanese nation. Whereas "Gohō" has inspired various versions and revisions, with a significant amount of ambivalence and equivocality, "Sayon" has inspired no such ambiguity. Her story is crystal clear: she died for the country. Finally, if "Gohō" was intended primarily for Japanese and Taiwanese Chinese readers, "Sayon" was definitely composed for aborigine and Taiwanese Chinese consumption. As I have suggested earlier, one of the ideological intentions of "Gohō" was to intensify the preexisting antagonism between the Taiwanese Chinese and the aboriginal population during the early years of aboriginal subjugation. In "Sayon," however, the irreducible differences among the colonized are homogenized under the auspices of the Japanese nation for the purpose of total mobilization for the Pacific War. This time the aborigines and the Taiwanese Chinese are no longer played *against* each other in opposition but are played *off* each other in competition for their respective dedication in becoming loyal imperial subjects. The transformation should not be interpreted in terms of a positive evolution that simply reflects the changing historical moments, although it must be contextualized as such. The shift in aboriginal representation must be understood as an ideological strategy of containment in the post-Musha era in which the aborigines were incorporated into the Japanese national body politic when the previous dichotomy between savagery and civility was perceived as no longer productive. It is in this sense that savagery and civility are not fixed categories where the ontological status of the colonizing Japanese or colonized natives is defined in terms of cultural/racial transgression or individual identity struggle.

Rather, they are part and parcel of a singular colonial operation and imagination that attempts to legitimize, naturalize, sublimate, and control the oppressions, violence, and evisceration of colonialism itself.

Notes

1   For a concise analysis of Japanese "savage management" in the years prior to the Musha Incident as a process of early capital accumulation for Japanese capitalism through land investigation, land appropriation, and labor commodification see Kojima Reiitsu, "Nihon teikokushugi no taiwan sanchi shihai" [Japanese imperialism in the highlands of Taiwan], in *Taiwan musha hōkijiken: kenkyū to shiryō* [Taiwan Musha uprising: Research and primary material], ed. Tai Kuo-hui (Tokyo: Shakai shisōsha, 1981), 47–83.

2   Watan-amoi, one of the participants in the fourth tour to Japan, remarked on the overwhelming quantity of Japanese people in Tokyo and associated their numbers with military prowess. He observed that "like leaves on the trees, the number of Japanese are countless; the number of bullets owned by the savages is incomparable to the sheer number of Japanese soldiers" (quoted in Uno Toshiharu, "Taiwan ni okeru 'banjin' kyōiku" [Educating the "savages" in Taiwan], in Tai Kuo-hui, *Taiwan musha hōkijiken*, 92). The ambivalent relationship between the colonizer and the colonized, between civility and savagery, was not entirely lost on the Japanese writer Nagai Kafu, who happened to come across the 1918 entourage. He wrote, "The seven or eight [Japanese] police who were leading the [Taiwanese savages] with swords on their sides, had the arrogant look of 'we are the truly civilized people.' Compared to the Japanese officials, the raw savages all had the look of gentility and were by no means insidious. They didn't seem to know that in this day and age there are people far more terrifying than cannibals" (quoted in Suzuki Akira, *Takasagozoku ni sasageru* [For the Takasago aborigines] [Tokyo: Chūo kōron sha, 1976], 112).

3   Etienne Balibar and Immanuel Wallerstein, *Race, Nation, Class: Ambiguous Identities* (New York: Verso, 1991), 17.

4   For a cogent discussion of academic constructions of the natives in the Southern Islands and their complicity with Japanese colonial discourse see Tomiyama Ichirō, "Colonialism and the Sciences of the Tropical Zone: The Academic Analysis of Difference in 'the Island Peoples,'" in *Formations of Colonial Modernity in East Asia*, ed. Tani Barlow (Durham, N.C.: Duke University Press, 1997), 199–221.

5   Pihowaris (Kao Yun-ching), *Musha hizakura no kuruizaki* [The unseasoned blooming of the Musha red blossoms], ed. and trans. Katō Minoru (Tokyo: Kyōbunsha, 1988), 11.

6   In 1930 there were 157 Japanese residing in the Musha reservation. But with the annual field day and the visiting colonial dignitaries, it was said that the Japanese numbered 227 at the time of the uprising. Two Taiwanese (a man and a child) who were mistaken for Japanese because

of their clothing were also killed. The total population of the six groups that participated in the uprising numbered 1,373. Of those, only 551 survived; the rest were killed by the subsequent Japanese subjugation or committed suicide. The population was further depleted when the colonial administration conspired and launched an assault on the internment camp with the pro-Japanese aboriginal groups the following April, widely known as the Second Musha Incident. Overall, only 153 men (few above age fifteen) and 145 women survived the attack. The six rebel groups were reduced to one with two-thirds of their population gone.

7   Tai Kuo-hui, "Musha hōki to chūkoku kakumei" [Musha uprising and Chinese revolution], in Tai Kuo-hui, *Taiwan musha hōkijiken*, 203.

8   Ōshika Taku, "Yabanjin," *Chūo Kōron*, February 1935, 67–101.

9   Kawamura Minato, "Taishū orientarizumu to ajia ninshiki" [Popular orientalism and the perception of Asia], in *Kindai nihon to shokuminchi* [Modern Japan and colonies], vol. 7 (Tokyo: Iwanami shoten, 1993), 119.

10 Ōshika spent his early years in colonial Taiwan and published a number of short stories on the Taiwan aborigines: "Tatsutaka dōbutsuen" [The Tatsutaka zoo] (1931), "Banfu" [The savage woman] (1933), "Yokubō" [Desire] (1935), and "Okuchi no hitobito" [The inland people] (1937). Furthermore, Ōshika's sister was married to Kawano Mitsu, who authored two anti-official reports on the Musha Incident.

11 Ōshika, "The Savage," 84.

12 See, for example, Kawamura, "Taishū orientarizumu to ajia ninshi Ki," 118–121, and Kawahara Isao, "Nihon bungaku ni arawareta musha hōki jiken" [Musha rebellion in Japanese literature], in Tai Kuo-hui, *Taiwan musha hōkijiken*, esp. 182–187. Neither Kawamura nor Kawahara mentions the very gender-specific operation within the transformative process.

13 Quoted in Hayashi Eidai, ed., *Shashin kiroku: Taiwan shokuminchi tōjishi, sanchi genjūmin to musha jiken, takasago giyūtai* [Photo record: The history of colonial rule in Taiwan, the indigenous people and the Musha Incident, and the Takasago volunteer army] (Tokyo: Azusa shoin, 1996), unpaginated.

14 Quoted in Kondo Masami, "Taiwan sōtōfu no 'rihan' taisei to musha jiken" [Taiwan colonial general's "savage management" and the Musha Incident], in *Kindai nihon to shokuminchi*, vol. 2 (Tokyo: Iwanami shoten, 1992), 35–60.

15 Komagome Takeshi, "Shokuminchi kyōiku to ibunka ninshiki" [Colonial education and cultural difference], *Shisō*, no. 802 (1991): 104–126. According to Komagome's study, the most likely authorial text on Gohō was produced in 1912 by Nakada Naohisa and titled *Satsushin jōnin, tsūji Gohō* [The self-sacrificing official, Gohō].

16 Komagome, "Shokuminchi Kyōiku to ibunka ninshiki," 114.

17 The case in point here is the distinction—anticipating Claude Levi-Strauss's reading of food preparation in society—between the "raw" (*seiban*) and the "cooked" (*jukuban*) savages. The raw savages are those who have not been subjugated and therefore are considered dangerous

and uncivilized. The cooked savages are those who have crossed the boundary between nature and culture and therefore are considered tamed and closer to civility.

18   Komagome, "Shokuminchi kyōiku to ibunka ninshiki," 108.

19   Nitobe Inazō, *The Japanese Nation: Its Land, Its People, and Its Life* (New York: Knickerbocker Press, 1912), 231.

20   Ibid., 248–249.

21   Ibid., 249; emphasis mine.

22   At one point Nitobe actually speaks of the affinity between the Japanese and the aborigines. He writes, "These Malay tribes resemble the Japanese more than they do the Chinese, and they themselves say of the Japanese that we are their kin and that the Chinese are their enemies" (ibid., 251).

23   Okakura Kakuzō, *The Book of Tea* (Tokyo: Kōdansha International, 1989), 31.

24   Saotome Katsumoto, *Taiwan kara no tegami: musha jiken, sayon no tabi kara* [Letters from Taiwan: From the Musha Incident and the journey of Sayon] (Tokyo: Kusanome shuppankai, 1996), 96–97.

25   The prominent artist Shiozuki Tōho did the paintings. One of the paintings portraying Sayon holding the bell was displayed in Tokyo at the War and Art Exhibit. The song was sung by Watanabe Hamako and composed by the famous Saijō Yaso and Koga Masao. The song became an instant hit in Taiwan. The movie *The Bell of Sayon* (1943) was a collaboration between Shōchiku, the Taiwan colonial government, and the Manchuria Film Association and starred the internationally renowned Ri Kō-ran (Yamaguchi Yoshiko). Ironically, the picture was filmed at Musha.

26   Saotome, *Taiwan kara no tegami*, 113, 120–121.

27   From his interview with Sayon's cousin, Saotome was able to learn that in fact Sayon was ordered to accompany the police officer and that Sayon also saw this as an opportunity to purchase some necessities for the family in the foothill town. See ibid., 119.

28   For a discussion on the colonial construction of Pocahontas see Peter Hulme, *Colonial Encounters: Europe and the Native Caribbean, 1492–1797* (New York: Routledge, 1986), 137–173.

29   Saotome, *Taiwan kara no tegami*, 99–100.

Commentary

Pan-Asianism and the Pure Japanese Thing:
Japanese Identity and Architecture in the Late 1930s

Cherie Wendelken

The formation of the architectural profession in Japan in the late nineteenth century was based on a repertoire of foreign skills, technologies, and representational conventions. The rejection or retention of Japanese identity was therefore a central problematic for architects, widely debated until well after World War II. National identity in architecture is of course closely linked to political concerns, nowhere more so than in Japan in the turbulent 1930s. But because of the lingering political effects of war and defeat, a general climate of intellectual amnesia has made the architectural history of this period, like the larger political history, difficult for Japanese historians to examine. Only in the 1980s have the major monuments of the Japanese colonial period been given attention by scholars.

Like all forms of artistic representation, political meaning in architecture is discursive—dependent on culturally defined interpretations of form—not inherent in form itself. In studies of European architecture of the 1930s,

positions 8:3 © 2000 by Duke University Press

Georgio Ciucci, Diane Ghirardo, and others have demonstrated that the relationship between architectural form and specific political agendas is complex and unstable. The formal vocabulary of national monuments commissioned in the 1930s by fascist regimes and designed by architects such as Albert Speer in Germany or Giuseppi Terragni in Italy has been hotly debated around two central issues: the mechanisms of political meaning in specific vocabularies and the culpability of individual architects as participants, even through the act of design, in larger political events. As regards the first issue, even in the case of state-commissioned public buildings the inherent political meaning conveyed by scale, massing, symmetry, or iconography has been questioned. Architects such as Peter Eisenman have argued for the autonomous, value-free nature of architectural paradigms such as neoclassicism, claiming it as an equally fitting vocabulary for socialist, fascist, or democratic monuments.

If the agency of architects like Speer and the political content of even Terragni's public monuments are being questioned, can anything be said about the political meaning of buildings outside the realm of national monuments?

In the case of 1930s Japan the issue is further complicated by an implicit questioning of the nature of Japanese identity in the modern world. Here we will look at what I propose as two distinct paradigms of Japanese self-conception in the prewar years and their possible meaning. As cultural and architectural paradigms these could remain intact, even while their particular political implications evolved over time. Because issues surrounding state monuments in the 1930s have been so discussed in recent years, I would like to focus on two other realms of architecture where Japanese identity and tradition have been of great concern to architects: the modern Buddhist temple and the modern home.

The first generation of academy-trained architects in the late nineteenth century saw their task as mastery. The reproduction of European neoclassical revival styles and the use of the latest imported engineering technology were in service to a state engaged in "catching up" with foreign powers. After the Russo-Japanese War, however, came a change in the political climate and a corresponding change in national self-conception. Now Japanese cultural identity was described in relation to both the West and Asia. Many of the same architects and intellectuals who first studied and traveled extensively in Europe later traveled and worked in an Asia colonized by Japan. The resulting new paradigm of Japanese identity was synthetic and inclusive. Japan was superior because it represented the culmination of East and West, a privileged site between and above its cultural roots in both worlds. Japan's kinship to Asia justified the displacement of European domination there and legitimated Japan's own colonial presence. But another cultural paradigm saw Japan as unique, neither Asian nor Western. This Japan was sacred and pure, intrinsically superior and separate, and destined to rule. These, then, were the two competing cultural positions of the 1930s: purity versus hybridity or, to put it another way with more meaning for architecture, originality versus skill at appropriation.

Architect Itō Chūta (1867–1954) is remembered as the first historian of Japanese architecture and as an important architect. He was one of the designers responsible for the first modern national style, the *shajiyō*, based on the study of ancient Japanese shrines and temples. In 1902 Itō set off on what would be a three-year journey across Asia that took him to Peking; through China to Burma; to India, where he stayed one year; and on to Egypt, Greece, and Turkey. He eventually made his way to Europe and the United States and finally returned to Japan in 1905, just after the Russo-Japanese War. While in Peking, Itō had met Otani Kozui, abbot of Nishi Honganji, the head temple of the Jōdō Shinshu or Shin sect, also known as the True Pure Land sect. Otani was to prove one of Itō's most important clients, and Itō's contact with him and other Japanese priests involved in the pan-Asian Buddhist movement active in Calcutta, as well as Tagore and Okakura, was to have a profound effect on his architecture.

Before his trip, Itō had designed traditional-style shrines and temples closely based on historical forms in Japan and Taiwan. When he returned from his world tour, his approach changed. Instead of historical indigenous models, he called for a new national style for Japan that would reflect its broader cultural origins in Asia. In most simplistic terms, Itō felt he had found a model for Japanese masonry and reinforced-concrete design in China and India, as both countries had historically used combinations of masonry and wood, and Japan had incorporated aspects of Indian and Chinese culture. The *teikan yōshiki*, or Imperial Crown style, was what he called "evolutionary," meaning that Japanese culture reflected a developmental progression from India through China to its culmination in Japan, and through India, Japan was linked to the West. Itō believed that Japanese architecture needed to reclaim and express this history in order to achieve what he called the next stage of development. He described this as "Eastern architecture adjusted to Japanese needs."

One of Itō's first projects after his return from Asia was a private summer-house outside Kobe, the Niraku-dō of 1908, an eclectic mixture of Mughal and Hindu forms. His 1912 design for the Shin sect's life insurance company in Kyoto has similarly eclectic features. The dome and the leaded, arched windows show references to Indian architecture—features that would later define the modern Shin temple.

Itō's largest religious commission was the Tsukiji Honganji in Tokyo, built in 1934 to replace a traditional wooden temple destroyed in the Kanto earthquake. Itō's design called for reinforced concrete with arched, leaded windows similar to those at the Shin Life Insurance building. Its symmetrical design is a mix of forms that suggest the influence of the Buddhist architecture at Ajanta in India; other features seem to be Southeast Asian or even Hindu in character. The interior, by contrast, is similar to Kanda Myōjin, the state Shinto shrine that Itō designed around the same time, with a painted coffered ceiling and concrete walls cast to look like the inside of a building constructed of timber. The concrete, however, allowed Itō to treat the building surfaces as a plastic medium, and the interior iconography is completely divorced from the formal themes of the exterior. The temple also incorporated such Christian influences as stained glass, fluted columns, and a large pipe organ to the rear of a large congregation hall furnished with wooden pews.

Why would the Shin sect be interested in Indian and Southeast Asian references in its architecture? One reason was its emphasis on lay Buddhism, which historically included proselytizing and missionary activities, as well as involvement in political and social affairs; unlike most Buddhist sects it represented a complete social structure and territorial domain. In the modern period the sect stressed that its doctrine was based on the teachings of seven patriarchs: two from India, three from China, and two from Japan. Shin saw itself as the last developmental stage of Buddhism, which eliminated the distinction between monastic and lay life and gave Buddhist organizations a greater role in worldly affairs. By the Meiji period the Shin sect described its Buddhism as a universal religion with no particular Japanese character, but simply Buddhism that had culminated in Japan; it was construed as a religion applicable and adaptable to any cultural or national context. The sect took a leading role in the late Meiji pan-Buddhist movement.[1] Many Shin bishops during the Taishō period thought of themselves as modernist and progressive; many were pacifists concerned with creating an autonomous, international Buddhist tradition accommodating both local character and universal validity. The design of Tsukiji was a product of this thinking, a signal that this was simultaneously the most advanced and the most ancient of sects.

A darker side of Shin theology, however, was resurrected for the modern Japanese war effort. Shin had been heavily involved in missionary activities on the continent since the Sino-Japanese War, ministering to soldiers in the battlefield and burying the dead. The sect maintained a relationship with the army and the colonies through this important funerary function. After the Manchurian incident of 1931, there was a flood of propaganda from Buddhist presses, most notably a Shin pamphlet which stated that founder Shinran had never forbidden a "just war" and that Buddhists should always rise to arms when necessary. Such propaganda reflected a controversial history of local violence justified through doctrinal belief in martyrdom and the redemptive possibilities of evil licensed in service to Amida. Some Japanese scholars have gone so far as to suggest implications for fascism in Shin beliefs about death, obedience, and discipline. Through its connection with the military and the war dead in the field, Shin provided the nation's soldiers with the eschatology for wartime martyrdom in a way state Shinto could not.

By the time Tsukiji Honganji was built in 1934, it housed the closest thing to state Buddhism in the modern period. Emperor tablets stood beside portraits of the founder Shinran on the altar. The large front court and interior hall served as public rallying spaces that were all too rare in Tokyo. The Indian-inflected design of Tsukiji Honganji not only set Shin off from other sects, but it provided a clear counteridentity to state Shinto shrines in the minds of the public. The Honganji symbolized the appropriation of Asian culture as culminating in Japan; equally it served as a visual and institutional Japanization of Asian sites through the death and ritual burial of Japanese soldiers. As the war progressed, the pan-Asian iconography of the Honganji in Tokyo paralleled the geography of the Japanese war dead.

In the colonial territories of China, Korea, and the Sakhalin Islands, a number of concrete Shin temples were built in the 1930s. The nationalist power of these temples persists in contemporary Japan through the presence of grave sites at these temples. As evidence, special permission to visit the Sakhalin graves is supported by right-wing activists claiming territorial rights.[2]

Architectural historians have described Itō as an unwitting participant in any political activity, a hapless character preoccupied with arcane historical concerns. An argument for his innocence has been found in the endearing cartoonlike animal subjects that populate his facades and roof lines and which are said to reflect his love of the animated facades of Hindu architecture and the imaginary creatures of Asian mythology.[3] Itō's isolation from worldly political concerns is more problematic in light of his association with another patron, Okura Kihachiro, the arms dealer and industrialist who made an early alliance with the military and built his fortune through trade with the colonies. In this case, Itō's pan-Asian architectural aesthetic is the direct result of his contact with colonial military patronage. An active collector of Chinese art, Okura commissioned Itō to rebuild his private museum after its destruction in the 1923 earthquake, in a style appropriate to the collection. The museum was thus completed in 1926 in the form of a southern Chinese mansion (the reinforced concrete structure has a traditional tile roof), reflecting Okura's links with China. After this project Itō called for the use of Chinese architecture as a model for Japanese public monuments in the Imperial Crown style.

Alongside Itō's pan-Asian aesthetic, another cultural paradigm of identity in architecture in the 1930s seems to represent a reaction to the cosmopolitan influences of the age. The discussion of a native Japanese aesthetic, along with the marketing of "Japanese" taste in consumer goods, architecture, and interiors, was a long-standing modern phenomenon. The notion of purity, however, came to the fore in the early 1930s. The idea of "the purely Japanese thing" was played out most compellingly in the private realm, particularly in home design.

Conventionally, the years from the late 1930s through the end of the war are thought to be a hiatus in Japanese architectural history, with limits on the size of houses that could be built and a ban on the use of steel or concrete for anything unrelated to the wartime effort. During this period many prominent architects went without commissions for years. But in fact there is a significant architectural legacy in buildings constructed after the Chinese conflict in 1937. After public monument construction had halted, the building of a small corpus of important houses continued through the war years. This small body of work in the private sector helps us broaden our understanding of the Japanese self-conception in design in the late 1930s and 1940s.

The great architect Yoshida Isoya continued to work during the war years, defining his own style of architecture. By the end of the late 1930s, Yoshida had traveled throughout the countryside buying abandoned farmhouses and other architectural components left by families that had emigrated to the colonies. Small houses thus built in his "new *sukiya*" style featured a mannered simplicity intended for a series of wealthy clients. For practical and aesthetic reasons, his houses were based totally on Japanese materials, synthesizing modern and traditional forms. They provide a meaningful counterpoint to the outward-looking iconography at Honganji.

Yoshida's first important house was for a woman writer, Yoshiya Nobuko. With this project his discourse on the feminine nature of the Japanese home begins. Yoshida's houses are presented with a heightened sense of location *in* Japan, and he underscores his characterization of the home as an intimate site of pure Japanese qualities by describing his designs in terms of the female body. In an article titled "Waso no Nanahimo" [Seven threads of Japanese dress], he likens his simplification of traditional architecture to the simplification of the traditional kimono with its multiple undergarments; eliminating unnecessary undergarments in favor of a simple overgarment greatly improves the appearance of the woman's body.[4]

One of Yoshida's contributions to house design was the liberation of spatial expression and interior design from the conventionally exposed frame of timber structures. By enclosing pillars and beams inside smoothly stuccoed planes and increasing spans with hidden structural steel, Yoshida made possible a freer plan and a more plastic interior articulation that denied the "honest expression" of structure and materials favored by his peers. Yoshida explained this by saying his interior designs were a return to the sensuous qualities of *gei* in Edo—a theatricality appropriate to the traditional Japanese aesthetic sensibilities of his clients. He again drew a parallel between his architecture and the Japanese woman, to whose use of artifice in fashion and makeup the architect called attention.

Yoshida also stated that "a house that evokes an atmosphere unique to Japan is the best kind of house for a Japanese to live in," and "architecture in Japan . . . is not something which can be positively achieved by a person who is not truly Japanese and who is not directly descended from a Japanese blood-line. We should therefore be prepared to counter the best the West has to offer with a truly indigenous style of architecture." He hoped that, as a result, the day would come when Japanese architecture would "influence the West."[5]

Sited in walled compounds away from the center city, Yoshida's houses of the war years constituted private, upper-class worlds in a time of political turmoil, a space of pure Japanese quality in a time of colonial expansion and of cultural and racial mixing. Yoshida's new *sukiya* houses of the 1940s were created as safe havens, places for his elite clients to retreat into nostalgia and fantasy in time of war. Although Yoshida often spoke of his designs in terms of racial and cultural purity, he cherished his position as an aesthete beyond politics. He spoke of the long days spent within the walled compound of the house he built for himself in 1941, reading *The Tale of Genji* or *Das Kapital* to pass the time.

Yoshida's concern with Japanese purity and uniqueness certainly belongs to a long tradition of nativist thought. But his particularly racial and feminine construct of the home and his emphasis on the purity of his Japanese designs must also be read in the context of its appearance in the late 1930s, the historical moment when Nazi eugenics theory began to reach Japan. Alfred Rosenberg's treatises both warned of the racial and cultural dangers of sexual intercourse with Jews and Chinese and named women as the special protectors of racial purity.

If the question of the architects' culpability or collaboration with the empire is not, without further evidence, a question we can decide here, we are bound to note that these two men were among those whose creative visions were allowed realization in totalitarian times. Yoshida, notably, did some of his most important work in the nationalistic climate of the prewar and war years, and he was also widely published. Regardless of the question of deliberate complicity, his artistic program spoke to political ideals of purity and superiority.

Itō's Honganji style, unlike Shinto shrine architecture, is readable as both independent countertradition and fascist alliance. Yoshida's houses were built as safe havens for self-styled apolitical aesthetes like himself. His enclosed compounds were meant to be a realm of pure Japaneseness, a retreat above and apart from political realities.

As we have seen, the work of Itō Chūta and Yoshida Isoya of the 1930s and 1940s differs both formally and programmatically. But although neither's work was commissioned by the state (and thus their iconographic programs cannot be said to represent officially the desiderata of the military regime), in complementary ways the architecture they produced during the war years can be seen as supporting the goals of the empire. If historians have suggested that their work transcends politics by representing, even identifying, perceived spiritual and cultural attributes of Japan, one must counter that in the 1930s these were the attributes invoked to justify colonial domination and military aggression. Ironically, the political power of this architecture is in its utility as cultural armature, in its very claims to transcendence over political concerns.

Notes

1 It was the first to send priests overseas for study and to establish missions in Calcutta, China, and elsewhere. In the Taishō period it was a leading force in the growing field of modern Buddhist studies, promoting the study of Sanskrit as a means to retrieve Buddhism's continental past.

2 In the United States, similar architecture was used for temples in Hawaii and San Francisco. The number of Buddhist temples in Hawaii doubled during the 1930s, and the Shin missionaries built more than all other sects combined. The Honolulu Honganji was built by the U.S. firm Emory and Webb according to a design apparently sent from Japan, in the midst of growing fear and distrust of Japanese immigrants and U.S.-born Japanese and worsening animosity between Christians and Buddhists. Japanese American Buddhists saw the style of the Honganji as a welcome distancing from growing Buddhist militarism in Japan

and the obviously Japanese forms of Shinto. By contrast, a public statement issued by white Hawaiian Shin Buddhists maintained that "the Dharma was wholly compatible with the ideals of Western civilization" and that Buddhism alone among religions was "distinctively Aryan, having originated with the Indo-European branch of the Caucasian race." For white Buddhists, then, this architecture provided a link between the West and Asia. For a history of the Shin sect's activities in America see Louise Hunter's *Buddhism in Hawai'i: Its Impact on a Yankee Community* (Honolulu: University of Hawai'i Press, 1971).

3   Itō himself reinforces the notion of a childlike innocence by associating the first appearance of his imaginary animals with a boyhood dream of a walk with his mother.

4   Yoshida Isoya, "Waso no Nanahimo," *Shinsō*, October 1935, cited in Maeno Masaru, "Atarashii Nihon Kenchiku o motomete," *Yoshida Isoya Kenchikuten* (Tokyo: National University of Fine Arts and Music, 1993), 29.

5   Ibid., 29.

Contributors

Kim Brandt teaches history at Amherst College and is working on a book on the *mingei* movement in Japan.

Leo Ching teaches Japanese literature at Duke University. His book on Japanese colonialism in Taiwan, *Becoming Japanese*, is forthcoming.

Carol Ann Christ, a doctoral student at Washington University, is writing on the Fine Arts Exhibit at the 1904 St. Louis Louisiana Purchase Exhibition.

Christine M. E. Guth, an independent scholar, is the author of *Art, Tea, and Industry: Masuda Takushi and the Mitsui Circle* (1993).

Jordan Sand teaches in the Departments of History and East Asian Languages, Georgetown University. His dissertation is titled "House and Home in Modern Japan: Reforming Everyday Life, 1880–1920."

Gennifer Weisenfeld teaches art history at Duke University. Her book on the politics of the avant-garde in prewar Japan is forthcoming.

Cherie Wendelken teaches the history of art and architecture at Harvard University. Her dissertation is titled "Living with the Past: Architectural Preservation in Modern Japan."